T0212601

Lecture Notes in Business Information Processing

More information about this series at http://www.springer.com/series/7911

Harri Oinas-Kukkonen · Netta Iivari
Kari Kuutti · Anssi Öörni
Mikko Rajanen (Eds.)

Nordic Contributions in IS Research

6th Scandinavian Conference
on Information Systems, SCIS 2015
Oulu, Finland, August 9–12, 2015
Proceedings

 Springer

Editors
Harri Oinas-Kukkonen
University of Oulu
Oulu
Finland

Netta Iivari
University of Oulu
Oulu
Finland

Kari Kuutti
University of Oulu
Oulu
Finland

Anssi Öörni
University of Oulu
Oulu
Finland

Mikko Rajanen
University of Oulu
Oulu
Finland

ISSN 1865-1348   ISSN 1865-1356   (electronic)
Lecture Notes in Business Information Processing
ISBN 978-3-319-21782-6   ISBN 978-3-319-21783-3   (eBook)
DOI 10.1007/978-3-319-21783-3

Library of Congress Control Number: 2015943844

Springer Cham Heidelberg New York Dordrecht London

Printed on acid-free paper

Springer International Publishing AG Switzerland is part of Springer Science+Business Media
(www.springer.com)

Preface

The 6th Scandinavian Conference on Information Systems, SCIS 2015, hosted in Oulu, Finland, was jointly organized by the OASIS and INTERACT groups of Faculty of Information Technology and Electrical Engineering, University of Oulu, Finland.

SCIS 2015 highlighted the Scandinavian tradition of studying information systems, namely, with emphasis on the user: Designing for the user, with the user, and by the user.[1] Such a theme has characterized information systems research for decades, and it is still a vibrant topic, especially so within the Scandinavian tradition. The research themes of the conference and hence this volume nicely capture both user- and history-related aspects of the topic. The studies address design for, with, and by users, including design for disadvantaged users, design for preservation and usability, and means for creative design and development as well as studies addressing emerging information systems history research.

A total of 44 paper manuscripts were submitted for the conference. The evaluation was a careful doubleblind review process that included an average of 3.1 reviewers for any given paper. Finally, 16 papers were accepted for presentation at the conference and in these proceedings with the acceptance rate of 36 %. The event brought together researchers not only from Scandinavia and elsewhere in Europe, but also from other corners of the world, such as South Africa, Japan, Canada, and the USA.

SCIS 2015 had three outstanding keynote speakers: Yvonne Dittrich from IT University Copenhagen (Denmark), Jaana Porra from the University of Houston (USA), and Sampsa Hyysalo from Aalto University (Finland). These conference proceedings also contain contributions from the keynote speakers.

As in previous years, the SCIS conference was arranged in conjunction with the Information Systems Research Conference in Scandinavia, known as the IRIS conference, which began in 1978 and which with its 38th annual gathering is the oldest consecutive information systems conference in the world. IRIS is today organized as a working seminar between established researchers and doctoral students. The young researchers and their interest in information systems boded well for shaping the future of the field.

We would like to thank the supporters and sponsors of this conference. We are grateful to all those people who contributed to this conference, whether as organizers, Program Committee members, reviewers, scientific contributors, or otherwise. Finally,

---

[1] We wish to thank for inspiration: Briefs, U., Ciborra, C. U., & Schneider, L. (Eds.). (1983). Systems Design For, With, and by the Users: Proceedings of the IFIP WG 9.1 Working Conference on Systems Design For, With, and by the Users, Riva Del Sole, Italy, 20–24 September 1982. North Holland.

we would like to extend our warmest thanks to all those volunteers who contributed in so many ways to making this conference a successful and memorable event.

May 2015

Harri Oinas-Kukkonen
Netta Iivari
Kari Kuutti
Anssi Öörni
Mikko Rajanen

Organization

General Co-chairs

Iivari Netta	University of Oulu, Finland
Kuutti Kari	University of Oulu, Finland

Program Chair

Oinas-Kukkonen Harri	University of Oulu, Finland

Local Organizing Chair

Molin-Juustila Tonja	University of Oulu, Finland

Proceedings Chair

Rajanen Mikko	University of Oulu, Finland

Program Committee

Aaen Ivan	Aalborg University, Denmark
Baghaei Nilufar	Unitec Institute of Technology, New Zealand
Bratteteig Tone	University of Oslo, Norway
Chatterjee Samir	Claremont Graduate University, USA
Cheung Christy	Hong Kong Baptist University, Hong Kong, SAR China
Chevalier Max	IRIT, France
Eslambolchilar Parisa	Swansea University, UK
Finken Sisse	Linnaeus University, Sweden
Gholami Roya	Aston University, UK
Gretzel Ulrike	University of Queensland, Australia
Henfridsson Ola	University of Warwick, UK
Iyengar Sriram	University of Texas Houston, USA
Kinnula Marianne	University of Oulu, Finland
Krogstie John	Norwegian University of Science and Technology, Norway
Lanamäki Arto	University of Oulu, Finland
Molin-Juustila Tonja	University of Oulu, Finland
Molka-Danielsen Judith	Molde University College, Norway
Mäntymäki Matti	University of Turku, Finland

Mörtberg Christina	Linnaeus University, Sweden
Oinas-Kukkonen Henry	University of Oulu, Finland
Pekkola Samuli	Tampere University of Technology, Finland
Penttinen Esko	Aalto University, Finland
Päivärinta Tero	Luleå University of Technology, Sweden
Riedl Rene	University of Linz, Austria
Rossi Gustavo	University of La Plata, Argentina
Rossi Matti	Aalto University, Finland
Scupola Ada	Roskilde University, Denmark
Simonsen Jesper	Roskilde University, Denmark
Smolander Kari	Lappeenranta Institute of Technology, Finland
Sørensen Carsten	London School of Economics, UK
Sudzina Frantisek	Aalborg University, Denmark
Suomi Reima	University of Turku, Finland
Tikka Piiastiina	University of Oulu, Finland
Tørning Kristian	Danish School of Media and Journalism, Denmark
Tuunainen Virpi	Aalto University, Finland
Tuunanen Tuure	University of Jyväskylä, Finland
van der Heijden Hans	University of London, UK
Verner June	University of New South Wales, Australia
Väyrynen Karin	University of Oulu, Finland
Wiafe Isaac	Ghana Institute of Management and Public Administration, Ghana
Wilson Vance	Worcester Polytechnic Institute, USA
Win Khin	University of Wollongong, Australia
Yetim Fahri	FOM University of Applied Science, Germany
Zhao Li	University of Oulu, Finland

Keynotes
Extended Abstracts

Software Product Eco-Systems: Why Participatory Design Should Care

Yvonne Dittrich

IT University of Copenhagen, Rued Langgaards Vej 7,
2300 Copenhagen, Denmark, & Indian Institute of Technology Mandi,
Kamand- 175005 (H. P.), India
ydi@itu.dk

Abstract. Software is increasingly developed, adopted and deployed in the form of customizable and configurable products. This has repercussions for the design, development and implementation of a configured or customized piece of software in the end-user organization. The design decisions done at the product provider influence the local ICT infrastructure. On the one hand, methods for local participatory design need to take the ripple effects in the local infrastructure into account, as it might effect not only the local implementation but also future possibilities for participatory design and end user development. On the other hand, software providers need feedback and design input. Participation can be expected to change character from preparing implementation here and now to a sustained co-development of the common tool. The keynote is based on a series of research projects with software product providers and around evolution of organizational infrastructures and outlines a number of challenges for Participatory Design.

Keywords: Software products · Software eco-systems · Infrastructuring · Participatory design

Redrawing the Landscape of Designing for, with and by Users

Sampsa Hyysalo

Aalto University, Department of Design
sampsa.hyysalo@aalto.fi

Human-centred design, UX, codesign, and open development have been proliferating rapidly during the last two decades. However, the landscape of designing for, with and by users remains rather confusing for many practitioners and researchers alike. This is because the terrain is covered by a jungle of over 1000 methods, techniques and approaches. If there ever was a method availability problem, it has certainly by now given away to method selection problem: sorting out which approach might suit the particular project and company in question. Using the wrong method is a waste of money and resources. Our 15 year research program on how design for, with and by users is done in real life settings indicates that practitioners use approaches they happen to be acquainted with, and neglect obvious possibilities which those they are less familiar to them. Whilst this makes sense in terms of the competences that companies and public organizations have with respect to conducting design for, with and by users, it is far from optimal.

We academics appear to have been at least as much part of the method selection problem as we may have been part of the solution. This talk reviews some of the well known taxonomies on designing for, with and by users. It illustrates how most of the method selection literature operates in a rather narrow area such as with in HCD or within UX and does not address the fundamentals of approach selection: when would for instance HCD type engagement with users work best and when would collaborative or user developer community do a better job? Some taxonomies do address this wider landscape level, but typically with serious category problems, due to portraying the alternatives from a singular disciplinary point of view, be this HCI, marketing, user innovation or codesign and this typically results in inadequate portrayals of other areas where designing for, with or by users has been investigated.

To alleviate, or at least to spark discussion, the methods jungle can organized through three classifications that are less problematic. The first one is based on recourse to what is involved in theory, methodology, method, technique and "operational work" interrelations available both in information systems as well as in HCI. The second one is based on historical origins of approaches for designing for with and by users, yet because of much give and take between different disciplines over the years it is less helpful than it may first appear. The third way of sense making is thus based on prototypical mode of engagement with users in sets of design methods common today. Here we propose that a sensible classification could be built regarding how much responsibility, control and share in design activities users and designers hold. At one extreme would reside ways of working where designers carry most responsibility and control and users are mere inspiration for design. At the other extreme would reside designs by users: independent user innovation communities, hybrid user innovation communities and various platform based peer creation forms such as open APIs, crowdsourcing and user innovation toolkits. In between these two extremes reside the various approaches to human centred design and user experience (closer to designer end) and the range of approaches to collaborative design and co-creative design (closer to user end). The talk concludes by elaborating the key differences for designers in these prototypical modes of engagement and connects the dots between the three ways of classifying designing for, with and by users.

Contents

Creative Design and Development

Design with and by Users

Keynote Paper

The Power of a Good Story or the Great Potential of Information Systems History or Some Lessons from a Heroic Journey

Jaana Porra[✉]

C.T. Bauer College of Business, Department of Decision and Information Sciences,
Management Information Systems, University of Houston, Houston, TX 77204, USA
jaana@uh.edu

Abstract. This paper is an essay about my journey as an information systems (IS) historian. In the paper, I briefly outline the past and the current situation with the environmental circumstances of history writing in the IS research field. I also highlight some lessons I have learned studying and applying the historical method over the past decade and a half. I do this in the context of a four-tiered research framework. I conclude that there continues to be a great need for written IS history and urge IS researchers to take upon themselves this important quest that will benefit future generations.

Keywords: Information systems history · Information systems research field · Four-tiered research framework · The historical method

1 About the Journey

In some sense, we are all historians [1]. Life cannot be lived without the consciousness of a personal past. We draw on our experience and the experience of those who went before us. These affirm our identity and illuminate our potential. Our memories serve as a huge information repository that helps us digest and make sense of new internal and external experiences.

This is a history of sort. It is an essay about my journey that began with loving stories as a child. I used to write stories that came to my mind. They were in some form or fashion founded on my world and my experiences but I had no need to understand how. I also had no awareness that there are methods to aid story writing. Growing up, my story writing was intuitive. Today I still write about my world but my world is much broader and deeper than a child's world. My writing is still grounded on my experiences but I am keenly aware that my experiences are founded on other people's experiences and that I experience their lives through my own being.

My stories are now constructed from evidence about the past events that has often been written down by people who lived those times. These events are colored by the being of the authors and mine. For example, in writing this paper I have relied on the

H. Oinas-Kukkonen et al. (Eds.): SCIS 2015, LNBIP 223, pp. 3–10, 2015.
DOI: 10.1007/978-3-319-21783-3_1

experiences and wisdom of a long list of people from the academia and outside. I have also relied on my cultural wisdom and what my people have taught me about how to see things. But at the end of the day, my stories are as unique as I am. Like every other human being, I have traveled a solitary path through life. I see things through my two eyes.

During my travels in this world through time, I have learned just how powerful stories can be measured by their consequences. I have also learned that stories are constructed methodically and that the authors of the stories make decision on whose story they tell, to what aim and how the record is constructed. Over the years I have come to believe that the historical method is the most powerful method available for researchers today. I call it "the mother of all methods". By this I mean that the historical method is a metamethod - a method that contains all other methods. Therein lies the power of the story and thus the power of history (herstory or theirstory).

I found history quite by accident as a doctoral student and fell in love with the process and product. Over the past decade and a half, I have written information systems (IS) history [2, 3]; about IS history [4]; about the historical method in IS research [5]; and about pioneers of the IS research field [6–8]. One history project led to another and I eagerly followed the path.

As much as I have always loved writing stories, becoming an IS historian was not a realistic career option. Writing IS history was not a good idea if I wanted to be a professor in the IS field. Over the past few years there have been two special issues on IS history in top ranking IS journals. The first one was published by the *Journal of the Association for Information Systems* in 2012 and the second one appeared in the *Journal of Information Technology* as a double-issue in March and June of 2013. While these events were celebrated as a small victory amongst the handful of IS historians in the world, there are no IS journals that could boast of a proven record of publishing IS history or an organized way of attracting historical papers. Nonexistent publishing outlets is one of the reasons why combining a successful academic career and IS history writing is still founded on heroic acts of individuals who risk their careers to follow their passion.

Those few who courageously embark on the mission impossible will face many more obstacles on their journeys. Compared to any other type of research, learning the history writing craft takes the longest time. The historical method is cross disciplinary. To be able do history well today, one needs to train in a variety of different philosophies, research approaches, methods and techniques. For reasons like these the method is also the most demanding of the research methods to apply.

Like in heroics tales, however, heroes prevail. They overcome every obstacle and complete their inhumanely challenging journeys to achieve their destinies to live happily ever after. The reward of the persevering historians is that they will be forever changed from within. The rest of the research and methods will never seem satisfactory again. These heroes will be able to see the world through many lenses and vantage points and comprehend the power of the story from within. Like a martial arts master, they will be enlightened through continuous practicing of their craft. On their future travels they will learn again and again that humanity's destiny hinges on a good story.

2   About the Environment

Maria Montessori, the creator of the Montessori Method of educating children, under-stood the power of a well-designed environment in supporting the development of a child to their full potential as members of humanity [9, 21].

> *"When we say the child's freedom must be complete, that this independence and normal func-tioning must be guaranteed by society...Only through freedom and environmental experience is it practically possible for human development to occur." (p. 89–90).*

Montessori discovered that children have an innate need to learn provided that they have a safe and thoughtfully crafted, age appropriate environment where they can explore life and apply themselves. Montessori challenged the conventional wisdom that there needs to be an adult in control of the learning processes or what becomes of the child. Given an opportunity to grow up in a Montessori environment, children thrive and become successful adults seemingly on their own. They learn how to learn and how to solve problems for results. They develop a strong and positive sense of who they are in relation to the world.

According to Montessori principles, children should be in control of designing their own environment and in charge of their own their destinies in it. Maria Montessori's environment was a classroom. In this context, environmental design meant providing a variety of furniture, house hold items and toys for children to choose from. The purpose of the environment is to help children grow up to be a mentally independent adult. As they grow up the environment expands from a carefully designed classroom outwards until the whole world is the classroom.

Maria Montessori revolutionized children's education. Her method is used in Montessori schools today in 27 countries [10]. Today these schools provide an envi-ronment for children from pre-kindergarten through high school. Maria Montessori's vision, however, was much farther reaching. She saw that her way or relating to learning and knowledge would change the world.

> *"...the child absorbs his environment, takes everything from it, and incarnates it in himself. With his unlimited possibilities, he can well be the transformer of humanity just as he is its creator. The child brings us great hope and a new vision."* [9, p. 66].

We can see the academia as one of the world's classrooms. If we would follow Maria Montessori's footsteps, academic disciplines would designed to support students, professors and researchers to reach their full potential in advancing knowledge. Academic environments would be designed from this goal in mind. Montessori princi-ples would direct our attitudes towards research careers, areas, topics, methods, publishing outlets and our understanding for what constitutes knowledge.

In today's academia, Maria Montessori's ideas sound like utopia. The current academic environments are a far cry from celebrating independent minds in pursuit of knowledge from their own perspectives. Also the IS research field is set in its ways of carefully controlling what constitutes IS knowledge in terms of research topics and methods. The primary tools for environmental control are the top journals of the disci-pline. The result of this control is that large numbers of papers are published about very few topics. As the paths of preferred contributions to knowledge solidify they channel academics and their works into ever fewer areas of research and methods.

In the IS research field, an example of this phenomenon is Technology Acceptance Model (TAM) and related research [11, 12]. This research area has expanded to reserve a disproportionately large share of top academic journal pages. For example, between 1989 and 2007 there were over 345 papers published in IT adoption and diffusion in 19 peer reviewed journals [12, 19, 20]. Over the same time period, I could find a total of 5 papers of IS history published in all IS journals [2, 3, 13–15]. I don't believe that generating knowledge about TAM is 69 times more important than writing IS history and I do believe that today, it probably is 69 times easier to publish a TAM paper than an IS history.[1] Because of the environmental politics, IS researchers congregate around few topics that will get them tenured most effectively. As a result, humanity will know more and more about less and less. By the same token, those academics who choose roads less traveled, will face obstacles and marginalization.

In today's academia, it takes the strength and determination of a hero to pursue IS history. I never meant to be a hero but in retrospect I see my own experience as a heroic story. There was no classroom for learning the craft. There was no supportive environment for practicing IS history. To publish one IS history took risking my tenure as a professor. The process of producing just one history is simply too long for tenure track, which requires constant publishing in top journals for six consequent years. Moreover, no publishing outlets existed for IS history that would count toward tenure in my college. The annual post-tenure performance evaluations posed similar obstacles. I risked further promotions and performance based raises because these are based on numbers of top journal articles and writing IS history just simply cannot be a numbers game. Until this environment changes, IS history will likely remain nonexistent.

If academia would follow Maria Montessori's footsteps we would create an environment where all research areas, also IS history, are encouraged and supported. We would design reward systems and publishing avenues that would match the diversity of researchers, topics and methods. The common goal of the academia would be *"to transform humanity"* [9, p. 66]. Different ways of understanding what knowledge is and how it can be acquired would be allowed to flourish distributively without a need to control or reconcile. Heroism would stop being a necessary characteristic of an IS historian. For me, Montessori's kind of academia would mean returning to my childhood environment. I thought then that all over the world academia is like a Montessori classroom.

3   About the Rewards

In mythical stories, heroes' journeys are spiritual and their rewards are ample. Applied to history writing, the prize of overcoming the obstacles is a new level of understanding of

---

[1] I am using TAM as an example for no other reason that I happened to have easy access to the numbers of published papers in that area that were useful for making a point. I could have just as well chosen several other similarly popular IS research topics that are over represented in academic journals.

knowledge generation. The historical method is much broader and deeper than any other method [5]. It calls for four distinct levels of understanding. These levels include philosophies, approaches, methods and techniques. At each level historians have many more choices available to them than is common in either qualitative or quantitative research. Another way of saying this is that writing a story is a more complex undertaking than research in general. I found this out by accident as I contacted several proper historians to find out a list of seminal works to study. I wanted to learn the historical method as I had learned many other methods – by reading a few articles or books. The historians I contacted scratched their heads – figuratively speaking. Two of them said to me that my question was "silly" [5, p. 5]. Over the next decade I grew to understand why no such list existed.

The more I studied the roots and directions of the historical method, the more the method seemed to expand to all directions. There was no consensus about the method in the world. Historians of varied backgrounds had their own views about where the history writing craft is coming from and where it should be going in the future. Historians had an ongoing debate on various disciplines' capabilities as producers of historical "knowledge" rooted in a multitude of ideas about what constitutes the ways of the craft.

As I explored, I learned that the historical method had created a political environment around itself that was very similar to what I had witnessed in IS research. An important difference was that the historical method debate took place within the methodological boundaries whereas the IS research methodological discourse occupied a place between quantitative and qualitative research method camps. To my surprise, the historical method discourse easily contained the entire methodological discourse of the IS research field –quantitative and qualitative. This is where I truly comprehended just how powerful stories can be.

Another revelation was that from the perspective of the four-tiered research network, all research methods are like the historical method. All qualitative and quantitative methods call for conscious decisions by researchers at all four levels of analysis [5]. At the highest level, the researchers should be aware of their philosophical foundations and be able to articulate them in their papers. Today in IS research, quantitative researchers rarely state their philosophy because it is assumed to be commonly shared. Another reason for the missing discussion of researcher's philosophical assumptions in quantitative research is the general lack of philosophical training amongst IS researchers. Qualitative IS researchers are much more open and capable of articulating their philosophical assumptions in their articles. One reason for this practice is that publishing qualitative research still requires more justification. Perhaps this is also why many quantitative IS researchers are philosophically savvy today.

Interestingly enough, proper historians are often more like quantitative researchers in that they too are often silent about their philosophical premises [16]. Historians have many reasons for their reticence to talk about philosophical foundations but one important reason is that traditional historians do not necessarily know philosophy. As qualitative researchers in a variety of disciplines turn into historians, however, this is changing to a situation similar to the one with qualitative IS researchers of the IS discipline.

From a Montessori perspective on academic research, the historical method and the four-tiered research framework could act as great equalizers of all methods. From this perspective, philosophies, approaches, methods or techniques are not ranked. There is no philosophical stance that is superior over any other for producing knowledge. No approach, method or technique is "better" than another. At all four levels researchers should make choices guided by what they are attempting to find out. If academia would accept this simple truth, a bulk of research environmental politics would simply go away. Researchers across disciplines would benefit from being aware of what their underlying belief system is and how this impacts knowledge creation. Learning to articulate these would open up the research assumptions for examination by others. This in turn would open new avenues for advancing knowledge currently shut down by the design of the various disciplines.

4　About Environmental Consequences

My journey has opened my eyes to see the consequences of the prevailing academic environment not supportive of IS history writing. For example, I understand now why my students and business people do not know what an "information system" is. Most understand "Web pages", "software" and "the Internet". They know the features of their latest pads, pods and phones. But the idea of an information system is foreign to them. That there is an academic discipline that has studied IS since the 1960's worldwide and accumulated knowledge about information systems is news to most people. Similarly the experiences of IS professionals that begun in the 1950's in organizations large and small are not written down anywhere and so the new generations cannot inherit their wisdom. My fear is that IS students become professionals doomed to repeat the mistakes of their predecessors. Without historical knowledge of their professional field, they will likely continue to see all IS situations as new and unique.

Over sixty years ago, Bloch [17] made the observation that histories had been written about most everything in this world. He listed histories of games, mail-order houses, delusions, transportation and highways in addition to more common political, economic and social histories. We can add to the list military histories, business histories, art histories, histories of science, populations, families and diplomacy to name a few [18]. Compared to how much history there seems to be in written form most everything in this world, it is astonishing how little the general public knows about IS history. Moreover, the time we have left to write down IS history is getting shorter. The first generations of IS professionals and researchers are aging and many of them have already passed away taking their IS knowledge with them. Without written history, the past disappears. The empty space is filled by histories written by others and from other perspectives whether individuals, professions, or academic disciplines. The difficult environmental conditions for academic IS history writing have created a vacuum Today, nearly 70 years into IS, there is no IS history to speak of. There is no story to share or perpetuate. There is not much to pass on to future generations of academics or professionals. There is no wisdom to build on. There are no people to remember. There are just a few scattered pieces produced as a labor of love by a handful of heroes where abundant IS history should flourish by now.

Written history is comparable to accumulating wealth. Stories are a form of affluence. They work like all investments in the infrastructure. They build and fortify identities.

They foster belonging. They teach compassion and understanding. They convey wisdom. They teach about those who came before paving the way. Because of our histories we are more. By the same token, having no written history means having no leg to stand on. It is comparable with being a poor drifter at the mercy of the surroundings. Studying history helped me see why we must write IS history. I began to see clearly the significant consequences of the missing IS story on humanity.

5 Some Concluding Remarks

The purpose of this paper has been to illuminate one story of an aspiring IS historian in order to raise awareness of the long term consequences of not having an academic environment supportive of IS history writing on knowledge. All research in all academic disciplines is political no matter what philosophies, approaches methods or techniques are being used and to what aim. This is true when researchers acknowledge their premises and when they don't. It is true whether researchers are aware of their foundations and when they can't tell what their assumptions about the world are. It is an inherent characteristic of human beings that when they engage in research, producing knowledge becomes politically motivated. For the same reasons, academic environments are also inherently political. Being political poses no problem as long as the politics of research and research environments is brought out into the open for everyone to examine and as long the aim of the politics is not to elevate or suppress any particular discipline, research stream, topic or method.

The historical method has taught me to see all research philosophies, approaches, methods and techniques as part of a broad quest of humanity to become wiser. This quest should be supported distributively. Like any other discipline and profession, the IS field is entitled to a written history. There have been some signs of change for a better environment for IS history writers since my adventures. The two history special issues in top IS journals are a start. I am also happy to report that my heroic journey ended well. I was tenured at my college and my work in IS history has been recognized as a significant contribution to knowledge.

So times are changing perhaps but rather slowly and unpredictably. One important point of my story is that we should not wait for times and environments to change. Looking back at my travels so far, I regret that I was not even more courageous and daring in choosing my academic path. In retrospect I wasted some considerable time doing things that I know consider as academic "busy work" in my early career. To my defense I try remember that during such times I felt a pressing need to save my career. If I wish anything, it is that I would have been even more courageous in my choices, spent more time writing IS history for future generations and less time fighting the environment.

References

1. Tosh, J.: The Pursuit of History, 3rd edn. Pearson Education Ltd., Essex (2000)
2. Porra, J., Hirschheim, R., Parks, M.S.: The history of Texaco's corporate IT function—a general systems theoretical interpretation. MIS Q. **29**(4), 721–746 (2005)

3. Porra, J., Hirschheim, R., Parks, M.S.: Forty years of corporate information technology function at Texaco Inc.—a history. Inf. Organ. **16**(1), 82–107 (2006)
4. Bryant, A., Black, A., Land, F., Porra, J.: What is history? What is IS history? What IS history? ... and why even bother with history? J. Inf. Technol. **28**(1), 1–17 (2013)
5. Porra, J., Hirschheim, R., Parks, M.S.: The historical research method and IS research. J. Assoc. IS **15**(9), 536–576 (2014)
6. Porra, J.: A dialogue with C. West Churchman. Inf. Syst. Front. **3**(1), 19–27 (2001)
7. Porra, J., Hirschheim,R.: Enid Mumford's contribution to IS theory and theoretical thinking – introduction to the special issue. J. Assoc. IS **8**(9), 463–466 (2007a)
8. Porra, J., Hirschheim, R.: A lifetime of ethical use of computers – a dialogue with Enid Mumford. J. Assoc. IS **8**(9), 467–479 (2007b)
9. Montessori, M.: The Absorbent Mind. (Translated from the Italian by Claude A. Claremont). Holt, Rinehart and Winston, New York (1967)
10. Montessori: Montessori – The International Montessori Index. http://www.montessori.edu/index.html (2015)
11. Davis, F.D.: Perceived usefulness, perceived ease of use, and user acceptance of information technology. MIS Q. **13**(3), 319–340 (1989)
12. Bagozzi, R.P.: The legacy of the technology acceptance model and a proposal for a paradigm shift. J. Assoc. IS **8**(4), 244–254 (2007)
13. Mason, R.O., McKenney, J.L., Copeland, D.G.: Developing an historical tradition in MIS research. MIS Q. **21**(3), 257–278 (1997)
14. Mason, R.O., McKenney, J.L., Copeland, D.G.: An historical method for MIS research: steps and assumptions. MIS Q. **21**(3), 307–320 (1997)
15. McKenney, J.L., Mason, R.O., Copeland, D.G.: Bank of America: the crest and trough of technological leadership. MIS Q. **21**(3), 321–353 (1997)
16. Marwick, A.: The Nature of History. MacMillan, London (1970)
17. Bloch, M.: The Historian's Craft. Vintage Books, New York (1953)
18. Cannadine, D. (ed.): What is History Now?. Palgrave Macmillan, New York (2002)
19. Bagozzi, R.P., Davis, F.D., Warshaw, P.R.: Development and test of a theory of technological learning and usage. Hum. Relat. **45**(7), 660–686 (1992)
20. Williams, M.D., Dwivedi, Y.K., Lal, B., Schwartz, A.: Contemporary trends and issues in IT adoption and diffusion research. J. Inf. Technol. **24**, 1–10 (2007)
21. Montessori, M.: The Secret of Childhood. Ballantine, New York (1982)

Design for and with Disadvantaged Users

Assembling Fragments into Continuous Design: On Participatory Design with Old People

Suhas Govind Joshi[✉] and Tone Bratteteig

Department of Informatics, University of Oslo, Oslo, Norway
{joshi,tone}@ifi.uio.no

Abstract. The paper takes a close look at a participatory design (PD) process with old users. We discuss how we organized and carried out the PD process so that they could participate in the mutual learning and co-construction activities on their own terms. We use the design of a radio to illustrate how the old users participated in the co-construction. We discuss some important topics to consider when organizing PD with old users: recruiting, timing, continuity, representativity and immediacy.

Keywords: Participatory design · Old users · Mutual learning · Co-construction

1 Introduction

The origin of Participatory Design (PD) is the democratic ideal that those who will be using an artifact should be given the right to decide on its design: its functioning as well as its form, and through this gain more control over the use situation and achieve a larger space for action [1–4]. The most important consequence of this view is that users are seen as experts on their work [5–8]. Hence their expertise is needed in the design in order to build such "participatory artifacts". Design in PD becomes a collaborative process where both use expertise and technical expertise are necessary ingredients. This in turn affects how the design process is organized and carried out, making processes of mutual learning and co-construction essential [9].

This paper discusses how PD can be tailored to users who have limited capacities for participation as user representatives in organized participatory design activities due to their physical or socio-cultural conditions like illness, age, cognitive skills, education etc. We report from a PD project in which we succeeded in involving old people in active design: both mutual learning and co-construction. We discuss how the participation was organized and carried out in order to achieve a good result. Our story demonstrates how mutual learning combines analysis and design, and how design ideas co-constructed in PD collaboration include elements originating from both designers and users.

The paper is structured as follows: Sect. 2 presents the main characteristics of mutual learning and co-construction in PD and in Sect. 3 we give an overview of related work. Section 4 describes our empirical basis: a large PD project with old people, and Sect. 5 reports from one of the smaller PD sub-projects. In Sect. 6 we present our analysis of how PD with old users unfolds in practice. Based on this Sect. 7 ends the paper with a

© Springer International Publishing Switzerland 2015
H. Oinas-Kukkonen et al. (Eds.): SCIS 2015, LNBIP 223, pp. 13–29, 2015.
DOI: 10.1007/978-3-319-21783-3_2

discussion about how we managed to have our user group participate in designing artifacts that enhanced their space of action.

2   Mutual Learning

Seeing the design process as collaboration between two expert groups with little knowledge about each other's expertise suggests that they need to learn from each other. The first phase of PD is therefore "mutual learning" [9, 10]: designers need to learn about the use context and the users' activities, users need to learn about technology and technical possibilities. They both should learn enough to recognize the logic of the other expert group, so that they can recognize their professional reasoning about a design idea. The use expertise is demonstrated in their use practices; hence observation and interview of users in situ are necessary for understanding the use logic [10].

A successful mutual learning enables both groups to widen their imaginative capacity and to build on each other's ideas, hence designing really new artifacts. It is therefore important that the two groups spend time together as their knowledge about the other profession (as well as of their own) grows during the process [9, 10]. A description and analysis of the use context and users' activities can therefore not replace involving real users over time: both their imagination about design possibilities and their needs and wishes for artifact support will change [9, 10]. The users should have a voice as well as a say in the design process [11].

Mutual learning includes both analysis and design [9], and mixes the two: understanding more of a problem area gives a better basis for imagining possible solutions. A prototyping workshop could be used as a method for inquiry, while a study tour to see a similar artifact in use in its use setting could be used for evaluation. PD spends time on establishing a common problem definition based on input from both use and technology.

This view is based on Schön's conceptual framework on design [12, 13]. More specifically we see that users and designers collaborate on what Schön [13] calls sequences of "see – move – see": seeing the design possibilities, choosing one of them to try out, and then seeing /evaluating the result – continuing forward if the move is considered productive with respect to the design process goal, moving back and trying another move if not [4, 12, 13]. In co-construction processes both users and designers participate in creating choices or design ideas to choose from, they work together on making the move by means of various design and prototyping techniques, and they evaluate the result together. The co-construction process can be intertwined with mutual learning activities: trying to concretize a design idea can spur a discussion not only about the problem solution but also about its definition [4, 13, 14].

PD of new design ideas requires an open and trusting collaboration, acknowledging differences but treating them with respect and interest rather than as problems [4, 9, 10, 14]. PD trusts the users to act as co-designers of their own activities – the concretizing of the design (its form and function) should not be left to the designers alone. This also means that the artifact is seen just as an element of the final design: its habitual use in everyday activities is the objective and hence the unit of analysis and evaluation. Thus, PD is organized with more time spent on mutual learning activities (learning both ways), more activities that involve both users and designers so that they share experiences and knowledge over time, more negotiations and building on each other's ideas, and including more contextual evaluations in all phases. The organization of PD puts a lot of claims on both designers and users, and in practice one has to make compromises as to how the collaboration can be facilitated.

A standard model of the PD process emphasizes that the development of a problem definition and solution goes hand in hand, and evolves together over time. Defining the problem typically involves fieldwork (interviews, observations on-site) and analysis of needs and their rationale and priority, while solving the problem typically involves various concretizing activities (design workshops, experiments, tests). Each move opens up for new ways of looking at both problems and solutions, hence the iterations can be very small [4, 9]. The full cycle typically involves a field study, needs identification, requirements specification, concretizing, experimental testing, and evaluation-in-use – sometimes collapsed into the same activity.

3   Related Work

Over last decade, the PD community has discussed ways to better organize PD processes with vulnerable users, among them elderly people. The selection of user participants when working with elderly people has been discussed [15–17]. The diversity of health conditions, contextual factors and daily activities of elderly people complicates the facilitation of PD. Grönvall and Kyng [18] explain how moving the PD process into a home environment affects the organization, participation and recruitment, especially when working with ill and fragile participants. Anderberg and Berglund [19] paint a very realistic picture of the everyday lives of elderly persons in their description of thoughts and perspectives of inhabitants receiving care in nurse homes. The contextual factors they emphasize have also been addressed by others. Scandurra and Sjölinder [20] argue for the importance of bringing contextual considerations when co-designing with elderly. Similarly, Ballegaard et al. [21] discuss the design of the development process and how contextual considerations such as daily activities must be integrated as a part of the whole approach in order for the technology to sustain.

Ekdahl et al. [22] discuss elderly patients' needs and preferences when making decisions about care and medical treatment, discussing the limitations involved when engaging elderly participants. Aarhus et al. [15] point at a variety of challenges and roles of participation in their study of old people suffering from vertigo, and argue for involving users despite their limited capacity to participate: their users contributed significantly to the end result. Uzor et al. [17] involved elderly users with limited opportunity to participate in the early stages of PD to achieve better results. Hendriks et al. [23] contribute to this discussion by demonstrating the value of bringing in trust-worthy companions such as family members. They also stress the importance of being selective since many participants only participate "as a favor" rather than the desire to contribute to the design process. This is also seen in the case of [18] where half-day participation tired the participant totally and affected her for days. Grönvall and Kyng discuss how providing the participants with a meaningful engagement would help in recruiting: they argue that elderly people with chronic illness needs a purpose in order to spend their few "good days" participating in a project. The danger of "overselling" the outcome of PD activities to such participants is also stressed. Lindsay et al. [24] argue for the importance of empathy when engaging elderly in order to provide meaningful engagements, and Yamauchi [25] share a similar view towards using empathic relations to better understand the participants.

The research literature also includes discussions on how we involve various stakeholders such as proxy-users in order to strengthen the design process. Clemensen et al. [26] use interdisciplinary teams as an approach to overcome practical challenges of involving elderly people related to medical issues, and Huldtgren et al. [27] present a concept for community-based co-creation where the goal is to facilitate long-term collaboration with various stakeholders in a community-based environment. One of the PD concepts they emphasize is mutual learning. Their discussion on commitment and how to engage participants is relevant for some of the topics experienced in our empirical context.

Finally, a part of the discussion about the organization of PD concerns the diversity of senior citizens. The danger of seeing them as a homogeneous group can result in a group with too diverse participants, which may not result in optimal group dynamics. Aarhus et al. [15, 18] exemplify how similar-aged elderly have different attitudes and perspectives towards technology, and Vines et al. [28] choose to use the term eighty-something to describe the age group rather than old or oldest old. Huldtgren et al. [27] discuss how age is not bound to our biological age, but rather to the individual perception of age. Malmborg et al. [29] discuss difficulties finding characteristics for elderly participants that are not grounded in age and at the same time avoid stigmatizing their self-image. Their studies suggest different approaches, e.g., the concept of "situated elderliness" as a way of addressing the elderly participants and simultaneously acknowledging context-specific challenges [30].

4   Collaboration with Old People: The Case

As part of a long-term collaboration with Oslo Municipality, one of the studies in the A3 project[1] was carried out in a residence for elderly people named Kampen care+. The building contains 92 apartments for elderly people – at the moment housing 104 persons with the average age 84 years (ranging from 74 to 101). The building includes a reception desk with 24/7 staffing (three people every day, one person during night), a café where the residents can buy dinner, a gym, an activity centre open to public etc. The building also has installed "welfare technology" mainly for increased safety: automatic energy regulation (light, heating), electrical sockets with timers, stove guard, motion sensors in all rooms (e.g., for night light), video calling and door lock (RFID). In addition, they have a tablet with an Internet connection for communication and information exchange (e.g., telephone, calendar and bulletin board). This public installation of welfare

---

[1] A3: "Autonomy and Automation in an information society for all", see: http://a3.ifi.uio.no.

technology is the largest in Europe, hence enabling a good basis for studying use practices on a larger scale. One apartment has been reserved for our project: it is equipped with the standard welfare technology solution and is used for experimenting with alternative designs and enhancing the existing solution.

The aim of the collaboration with Kampen care+ was to evaluate the practical application of the welfare technology solution, and suggest improvements and alternative solutions [31, 32]. The collaboration has involved approx. 70 people from Kampen care+: employees (4) and residents (52), as well as relatives, friends and volunteer workers. In addition, three faculty and three PhD students as well as 10–15 graduate students and 16 undergraduate student projects has spent time in Kampen care+ over the last two years. The project therefore was organized as a collection of separate but not independent smaller projects on top of a set of regular weekly activities (IT workshop every Thursday evening, IT course every Monday at noon, regular visits involving workshops or interviews and observations).

The Kampen care+ has a large common area beside the reception desk, which acts as a meeting point for the residents. Coffee is served there every day at 5 PM, and also during the day groups of residents sit there and talk and watch what happens (or the employees sit down and talk for a while). The area enables an overview of the entrance, the café, and the library meeting room where many of our workshops and interviews were carried out. When returning to the common area people always talked about what they had participated in. All the people from our department have been very well received – even often invited in for a coffee. The attention from researchers and students and from media (reporting on welfare technology) has over time "cultivated" a group of positive and enthusiastic – almost professional – users as well as a need to be realistic about what is hype and what is reality of welfare technology.

4.1 Ageing Bodies in PD

Ageing changes the body in many and non-linear ways, and vary enormously [33]. Normal characteristics of the ageing body, like declining sensing (eye sight, hearing, taste), loss of strength and balance, and changes in skin texture, fine motor skills and tremors make many computer appliances difficult to use. Also decline of memory and the ability to understand abstractions (like maps) make many standard interaction mechanisms and symbolic representations difficult or impossible to use. Designing for ageing bodies therefore needs to pay attention to what the design presupposes that the user is able to do and adjust these to the skills that are present [8]. However, we also claim that one of the features of PD is that even if the loss of abilities tends to dominate the practical design challenges, the actual design process is based on the existing abilities, focusing on what the can do rather than what they cannot [33].

The PD process we carried out can be described as a combination of several iterations of smaller projects, where the old users participated in some parts of some projects over time, and that this long-term relationship enabled both us and them to develop a coherent PD process from it (see Fig. 1). The figure pictures three cycles of iterations. Each of the cycles includes several smaller activities [9]: interviews and observations (in their homes), brainstorming sessions, group discussions, workshops, and prototype evaluations. We had

different people participating in different activities depending on their abilities and interests. Below we use the participation lifecycle for five residents to illustrate how their
participation varied, and how focusing on shorter and more frequent activities allowed
participants to join even when they experienced to have limited capacity. Their health
conditions led to practical difficulties concerned with participation, and we organized the
process so that they still could participate.

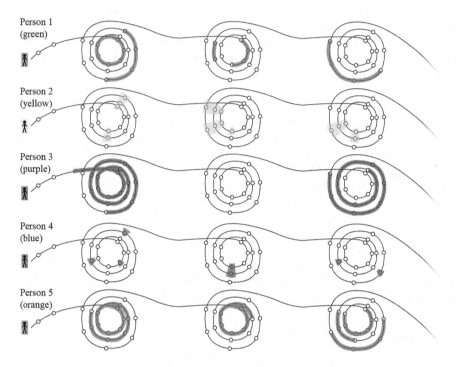

Fig. 1. The participation activity for five of the participants throughout the project (Color figure
online).

Person 1 (green in Fig. 1) was a gentleman who depended on having "a good day"
in order to participate. His health conditions prevented him from scheduling activities
beforehand: he had to wait until the very same day to determine whether he was able to
participate or not. Participation required a great effort of him in preparing as he had to
get up early, wash himself, and motivate himself to interact not only with us, but also
with other residents. This introduced some unpredictability: his participation was a direct
reflection of his daily capacity. The most important for him was not which activities he
joined, but instead that he participated for as long as he could.

The second person (yellow) was very meticulous with which activities she would
join. She did not want to participate in any activities involving "tasks" on devices such
as demonstrative interviews or testing of prototypes; she was very self-aware and aware
of her limited experience with technology and she did not feel comfortable using devices
for the first time in front of others. She was only present for those activities that

(she felt) allowed her to learn and contribute, but she participated consistently in the activities she preferred. She was a very social person and seemed motivated by the social aspect of the participation: "It is nice to hear how I am not the only one struggling with this".

The third person (purple) was a very motivated and energetic participant during the first cycle and one of our main contributors. She was present in all activities and seemed to be less affected by fatigue than the rest. However, she was hospitalized close to the end of the first cycle and stayed in the hospital during the whole second cycle; she did not return to Kampen Care + until the third cycle. Once she had fully recovered, she jumped straight back into the process and continued as before. As her attendance was very frequent when she was able to participate, she ended up having one of the highest overall attendances.

The fourth person (blue) was one of our most unpredictable participants. His participation was very sporadic and seemed to be independent of health condition. He was always invited, but only showed up once in a while. He explained his absence with "it was not a good time due to other commitments". He participated consistently throughout the three cycles. His general health condition was good, but his endurance was limited. He could never participate in more than one activity, even when it only lasted half an hour.

The fifth person (orange) was very ambitious in the beginning and participated in all activities. However, in the middle of the first cycle she suddenly became sick, and was unable to participate for a long time. As she had little prior experience with such activities, she later said she was caught by a surprise of how exhausting participation can be, even in good company. She returned for the second cycle, but only participated in half of the activities compared to previous cycle, and managed to participate without any negative effects on her health. In the final round, she chose to participate in even shorter, but multiple, periods, as this allowed her to participate more throughout the cycle than if she were to do it all in one consecutive stretch.

These five life cycles demonstrate how we attempted to adapt the design process to the limitations of the elderly participants. The process of organizing the activities was very flexible from our side in order to recruit more participants and adapt the process to their opportunities to contribute.

We also saw how the participants learned about their own capacity to participate during the design process. The co-design experience was new to most of them, and they did not know how it would affect their endurance. Some were very careful with overcommitting, and had to complete several activities before they dared to participate more. Others contributed so much that they became ill, and had to reduce their commitment when they returned. All participants adapted their participation pattern based on their experiences from the first cycle. We observed that our organization of the design process gave participants more space: it allowed for flexibility in duration and frequency of participation, and it gave several opportunities to rejoin even after longer periods of absence. Some participants only wanted to participate together, and high frequency of activities allowed them to coordinate their participation in design with their other commitments.

5   Tangible Design for Simple Interaction

In this section we describe one of the smaller PD projects in which the old users were very active in both mutual learning and co-construction. The background for the project is that the government in Norway has decided to shift from frequency modulation (FM) to digital audio broadcasting (DAB) in 2017, hence the old radios will not work anymore. A modern DAB radio is a computer, and many of them make use of new interaction mechanisms, new metaphors and new interfaces, e.g., a small screen with frequency numbers or radio station name. Aiming to meet the problems before they arise, a small PD project was initiated and carried out aimed at designing a DAB radio that included what was thought to be useful functions and was easy to operate based on the skills of the participating users.

The PiRadio (see Fig. 2) was designed a usable radio based on a new DAB-radio equipped with the newest technology but with interaction mechanism and interface based on older interfaces with traditional interaction mechanisms [34]. The radio was co-constructed with some of the Kampen Care + residents: in total 25 of the residents participated in the mutual learning and co-construction of the radio.

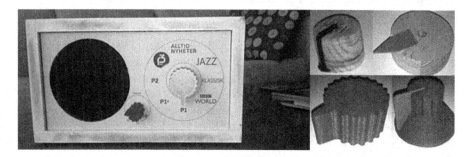

Fig. 2. The PiRadio (left) and the prototypes for the knob (right).

The co-construction aimed at using rotary controls for operating the radio. In this way the interaction could make use of familiar gestures building on their habitual bodily skills [34, 35], the idea being that if they could not make sense of the interface intellectually, their body would remember how to turn on the radio by recognizing the button as a device for rotary movement (the "maximum grip" [35]).

The co-construction process involved designing a series of knobs and testing them to evaluate how easy they were to turn when used by old fingers. Ageing often implies loss of strength in hands and fingers, and several of our participants struggled with getting a proper grip on some of the prototypes. A smooth plastic surface was, for example, difficult to operate, in particular for fine-tuning the radio. The knob went through several iterations of redesign – co-design – where our old user-participants tried out knobs of different shapes, sizes and materials in the search for the best grip. At the end we arrived at a knob with a knurled and coarse surface that could compensate for reduced strength of their grip as well as reduced dexterity (reduced mobility and flexibility due to rheumatism or involuntary movements due to tremors). The testing aimed at arriving at providing our old co-designers with a maximal grip (see Fig. 2). A second feature was the feedback of the knob when turned, i.e., its resistance and snap. The friction and snap into position was adjusted in cooperation with the participants in order to ensure that the feedback from the radio was familiar and immediately understood. The process made use of blindfolded testing to investigate how the touch between the hand and the knob by itself, i.e., without visual stimuli, was able to trigger the habitual understanding of the interaction based on their experiences: "I understood when I touched it". The result selected by all participants was confirmed by a one-tailed t-test used to compare the efficiency and effectiveness, and results showed that tasks were completed faster and with fewer errors when tested against two standard off-the-shelf radio models (95 % CI) [34].

As the capacity to contribute in the design process weakened and they were forced to only participate in a few activities, some activities suddenly became much more popular. In particular, the blindfold testing and the material testing were very popular. They were both tests where we discussed future technology through non-digital artifacts. The blindfold testing was a social and entertaining activity in addition to being a way of discussing the design. Due to this, it also became popular among those who talked less during the workshops, and it seemed like they enjoyed the social setting more than the actual outcome of the design process. Thus, the reduced capacity of our old participants resulted in selective participation: they chose to participate in certain activities consistently over time, rather than participating more sporadically in whatever activity was available. Selective participation was also the case for other residents who wanted to only join certain activities. One participant for example wanted to only participate in a few activities per cycle as he felt that was enough for him. Organizing short and frequent activities allowed the residents to participate without disturbing other commitments.

6   Topics for Tailoring PD

Our analysis of the PD process and how we had to adjust the PD process to facilitate participation by our old users in mutual learning and co-construction, resulted in five topics: recruiting, timing, continuity, representativity and immediacy. Collaborating with the oldest old has been – and is – a pleasure. Their view on technology and quality of life differs from ours and represents a different logic that should be recognizable in the design result.

6.1   Recruiting

Recruiting participants for a particular activity proved to be easier than recruiting for long-term commitment. In our consent form we inform the participants that we will keep the recorded data until 2016, and we have several examples that the participants refused to sign – and to participate – because *"I might not even be alive then. This is not for me!"*. Many of the residents also did not want to engage in activities that were planned long time ahead. One reason is their determination to keep their promise and being uncertain about their health condition: they were reluctant to promise something that depended on them having *"a good day"* but agreed to participate if they could give the final answer in the morning on the day of the activity. If this was not an option, they often did not want to commit to participating. Some also tried to avoid thinking too much about the future as *"I become sad when I think about how I will soon not be able to walk"*. The future is a sensitive subject, and many old people do not see themselves as old and in need – they design to help others [19].

After some time we managed to establish a group of eight committed participants, and we asked them to find other people who would be interested in participating during a week or two. This snowballing recruiting strategy proved more efficient than our direct one-to-one method. A particular side of working with old people is that they are vulnerable to illness and injuries, and two of our participants happened to get hospitalized during one of the iterations. They returned to the process when returning from the hospital. Two of our participants died – we think they appreciated the fact that they could be active to their final moment.

Most residents at Kampen Care + are women, and we wanted to recruit some men to our workshops. Therefore, we went after the weekly football game on TV, where the men were gathered in the reception area and were in a good mood. We easily recruited three men to a quick workshop in this situation. The strategy of making appointments for future activities had earlier proved to be difficult. This demonstrates a much more flexible strategy for recruiting people, spending more time with them and seizing the opportunity for recruiting people when the situation made it possible.

6.2   Timing

Linked to the previous theme is the duration of the participation. First of all, working with the users who inhabit the future use context means adjusting to that context. Working with old people in their homes means adjusting to their rhythms: their sleeping patterns (many sleep late) and regular appointments (e.g., with home care services), their everyday practical-and-social routines, like the long meal together around lunch time, and the regular coffee at 5 PM, in addition to occasional appointments with the doctor or a physiotherapist. Also the Kampen Care + organizes several activities during the week – all considered to be more important than our activities – and many of the old people had really full schedules. We had to look for open windows and opportunities for engagement in-between; hence we always needed to keep ourselves oriented about activities and happenings at Kampen Care +.

This made us change our plans from doing a few long sessions to planning for several shorter ones. This organization enabled more people to participate in more sessions as our activities became easier to fit to their schedules. An additional reason for shortening the sessions was the fact that old people get tired from long sessions. Some of our old participants could only manage a half hour, while some got a headache from looking at the screen for long.

More frequent and shorter sessions made our participants exposed to our themes more often. Most of the residents find technology to be difficult and strange, and do not meet IT much in their everyday life. Having frequent discussions with us exposed them for the topics more often, reminding them about our topics and contributed to maintaining the continuity in the project. This was particularly helpful for those whose short-term memory is weak.

6.3 Continuity

A lesson from the two years spent at Kampen Care+ is the importance of creating continuity even though consistent commitment over time is not possible for most participants. We used several strategies for supporting the experience of continuity.

After some time we moved our workshops and meetings to the library-meeting room inside of the reception area, with windows facing the reception area. As mentioned before, this is the meeting point for everyone at Kampen care+. When our workshop participants left the room they were always encouraged to tell the curious spectators what happened – what they did, what we discussed, what they got to try out. The visibility of the project activities evoked curiosity and made recruitment easier. It also helped establishing continuity between the activities. The visible activities were positive reminders of our presence and of the project topics. One of our colleagues, Rune Rosseland, has been arranging IT workshops every Thursday afternoon for those who want to join. Seeing him every week was also a reminder and has contributed to creating a feeling of continuity and confidence in our commitment. His regular presence gave him a different basis for contact than the less frequent visitors from our project.

In line with other PD projects we left things after our activities to enhance the learning and attention without our presence (similar to [25]). The active residents made use of papers, photos, prototypes etc. that we left behind. This "after learning" also worked to recruit new participants as the continuing discussion encouraged wider engagement. Above all, the discussions became less strange and not threatening.

The elderly residents took their appointments very seriously, and not keeping appointments threatened the trust we had built throughout the project. Sometimes the home care nurses were too busy and did not show up to scheduled design activities with the residents. This made us more determined to control the appointments ourselves – trust is a fragile relation that can easily be destroyed by only a few examples of breaking the contract [36].

6.4 Representativity

Old people are as different as everyone else – maybe even more. Ageing meets us in very different ways; hence the diversity is not easily represented through a few participants (see also [37]). Including employees and health care professionals in the project provides information about the variety and frequency of abilities and problems, and all the daytime employees have been part of workshops and interviews. This increases the feeling of trust and makes the participants relax because of their good personal relationships [36]. We take the participants to represent themselves rather than pre-defined groups of people.

Our strategy of recruiting ad hoc the people present in the reception area also resulted in recruiting people from the friends-of-Kampen care+ community. This has proved very useful as they are close to the residents; they know them and their problems very well. They added to the discussion with experiences from living in their own homes rather than at Kampen care+. We have also included relatives in our workshops. They often participated as observers, but sometimes commented on challenges that the residents forget to mention. They definitely contributed to a richer picture of the problem area. We also find that not distinguishing between the people in the reception area, including guests and visitors, made the project more socially acceptable and interesting. The residents did not miss out of a social possibility, and including more people made the project activity a part of the social community hence adding to the reasons for joining in.

6.5 Immediacy

Reducing the threshold and "seriousness" of participating in project activities made it easier for everyone to participate. The division of activities into smaller units as well as addressing smaller elements of the project contributed to making participation in the project more accessible. A second strategy was to demonstrate that the project aimed at addressing problems that they experienced in their everyday lives. We were interested in hearing about their technology problems, and also offer help in solving (some of) them [32]. Their problems were often not difficult to solve (e.g., in the weekly Thursday evening workshop), and the concrete offers to help acted as a door opener for the project as a whole. More people became curious about participating. The difficult part was to have them understand the mutuality of the process where they learned something and we did as well. The "aha moment" demonstrating that learning had happened, often occurred when some concrete problem was solved: just talking about a technical feature did normally not result in increased understanding [33]. Problems and solutions needed to be concretized to contribute to the mutual learning.

As a way of increasing the old residents' understanding of technology design we arranged "testing of materials". An example is the co-construction of the radio buttons: we brought buttons with very different properties: form, size, material, color etc. and had them look and feel their way to a decision about the best solution. The pedagogy principle of "show, not tell" was also useful for understanding the interaction mechanisms as well as the possibilities for design options.

7 Fragments Making a Picture

PD is first and foremost characterized by its organization of work, distributing design work to users and learning to the designers [4, 9]. Organization of PD, like all organization of work, is concerned with the division of the work into tasks suitable for the available work resources as well as the coordination of these tasks to a coherent whole. PD with old people puts particular requirements to what kind of tasks can be carried out by the participating old people, and how the task performance is organized.

7.1   Time

When collaborating with old people time is crucial: the scope of the project, the planning horizon, the stamina of the participants, the maintenance of dialogue over time, and the everyday rhythms that structure the days at home. All the topics discussed in Sect. 6: recruiting, timing, continuity, representativity and immediacy, refer to how old people experience time differently – and as less time. The commonly experienced loss of short-term memory makes the immediate concrete activity more important: abstractions and representations beyond oneself in the here-and-now-communication is not engaging or even understandable. The topics of representativity and immediacy both concern the reluctance to deal with issues outside of the context or situation. Hence, the transferability of the PD results needs to build on more general knowledge about old bodies and old people's habits, needs, and quality of life.

7.2   Assembling the Pieces

The design of small-enough work tasks for the participants' competencies and abilities resulted in a complex collection of small PD projects that each contributed with a PD result. The larger PD project aimed at designing technical support for old people to live independently longer at home emerges from these bits and pieces of that support. However, participation in the larger PD project requires more resources than the average resident-participant has got.

In order to see the bigger picture, we put together the puzzle of participants and activities (see Fig. 3). In each of the three phases we have represented how our residents participated, giving an overview of the types as well as the amount of activity. We see that many residents only participated in one kind of activity (e.g., workshops) but for several iterations and in several phases. We see that some participated in a full iteration, and we see that some occur in all phases but in different ways.

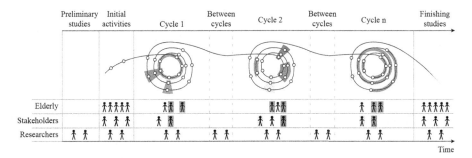

Fig. 3. A description of the actual participation over time in the overall PD process (Color figure online).

The bigger picture also shows that the continuity of the larger PD project is the use context: the everyday living at Kampen Care+, and that there is a community of resident-participants. The community as a whole has more resources and capacities than any individual participant. By utilizing the larger (use) context we can involve the community to participate in the larger PD project.

8 Tailoring PD to Old People

Our aim in this paper has been to discuss how PD can be tailored to users such as the old residents at Kampen Care + . We have argued that we needed to divide the PD work in smaller pieces that fitted the capacities of our resident-participants. Furthermore, by utilizing the use context as a frame for the larger PD project we made it possible for them to also influence the bigger picture emerging from the puzzle of the pieces. Cooperation in PD is based on mutual respect and trust, which in turn is based on knowledge about each other's perspectives and competencies. The careful timing of PD activities as well as the utilization of the use context to support the continuity in and between activities contributed to establishing the necessary common ground. Mutual learning is a fundamental characteristic of PD, and is not so easy to achieve in practice. Our resident-participants learned from small activity chunks, supported by reminders happening in regular patterns of activities (like the Thursday IT workshops) as well as from the activities that supported the continuity between activities. Our own learning happened as we discovered the practical and rather mundane problems that the old residents experienced, some very easily solved and some easily solvable with a better design [38].

PD often focuses on technology questions and hence looks for problems that can be solved by technology. This is alien to most of our old resident-participants, but characterizes most of the smaller projects organized around a problem or a solution (like most of the student projects). The most difficult part of the project was therefore to facilitate the resident-participants in getting enough time for reflection and for developing their own questions and wishes; resisting the urge to drive the process too fast and influence too much a technology focus. Coming closer to a process where their worldview decides the moves have led to different designs and priorities in design. Old peoples' lives are both more fragmented and have more continuity than the average (younger) designer's life. Assembling the pieces of PD into a larger context of mastery of technology hence resonates differently for the two groups. The patience to build a continuous account from smaller snippets of stories is the basis for critical thinking as well as alternative designs for old people.

PD emphasizes co-construction of solutions as well as of problems. Our project showed that activities that demonstrate that the knowledge of the user-participants is necessary for a successful design result are needed for co-construction of form and function to happen. The detailed co-construction of the radio button showed that a concrete design task was engaging while more abstract developments (e.g., navigation) needed to be concretized in order to facilitate participation. The many prototypes co-constructed in the project contributed to concretizing what technology can do, and acted as a basis for the resident-participants' imagination and evaluation in the design process.

PD is about participation, and working with the oldest old sets limits to the forms and level of participation in design. Getting to know the old residents over time certainly improved our abilities to facilitate their participation, but we also needed the supplement of others who sometimes represented the interests of the residents better than they could do themselves. Our experience is, that redesigning PD methods to fit the capacities of the users, enabling them to participate, can result in really novel and innovative solutions.

References

1. Simonsen, J., Robertson, T.: Routledge Handbook of Participatory Design. Routledge, New York (2012)
2. Nygaard, K.: The iron and metal project trade union participation. In: Sandberg, A. (ed.) Computers Dividing Man and Work, vol. 12, pp. 94–107. (1979)
3. Nygaard, K.: "Those were the days"? or heroic times are here again. Scand. J. Inf. Syst. **8**(2), 91–108 (1996)
4. Bratteteig, T., Wagner, I.: Disentangling Participation: Power and Decision-making in Participatory Design. Springer, Heidelberg (2014)
5. Ehn, P.: Work-Oriented Design of Computer Artifacts. Lawrence Erlbaum, Hillsdale (1989)
6. Bjerknes, G., Bratteteig, T.: User participation and democracy: a discussion of Scandinavian research on system development. Scand. J. Inf. Syst. **7**(1), 73–98 (1995)
7. Bjerknes, G., Ehn, P., Kyng, M. (eds.): Computers and Democracy - A Scandinavian Challenge. Avebury, Aldershot (1987)
8. Bratteteig, T., Verne, G.B.: Conditions for autonomy in the information society: disentangling as a public service. Scand. J. Inf. Syst. **24**(2–3), 51–78 (2012)
9. Bratteteig, T., Bødker, K., Dittrich, Y., Mogensen, P.H., Simonsen, J.: Methods: organising principles and general guidelines for participatory design projects. In: Simonsen, J., Robertson, T. (eds.) Routledge International Handbook of Participatory Design. Routledge, London (2012)
10. Bratteteig, T.: Mutual learning: enabling cooperation in systems design. In: Braa, K., Monteiro, E. (eds) Proceedings of IRIS 1920 Department of Informatics, University of Oslo (1997)
11. Kensing, F., Greenbaum, J.: Heritage: having a say. In: Simonsen, J., Robertson, T. (eds.) Routledge International Handbook of Participatory Design, pp. 21–37. Routledge, London/New York (2012)
12. Schön, D.A.: The Reflective Practitioner. Harper Collins, Pennsylvania (1983)
13. Schön, D.A., Wiggins, G.: Kinds of seeing and their function in designing. Des. Stud. **13**, 135–156 (1992)
14. Bjerknes, G., Bratteteig, T.: Florence in Wonderland: system development with nurses. In: Bjerknes, G., Ehn, P., Kyng, M. (eds.) Computers and Democracy, A Scandinavian Challenge. Avebury, Aldershot (1987)
15. Aarhus, R., Gronvall, E., Kyng, M.: Challenges in participation. In: 2010 4th International Conference Pervasive Computing Technologies for Healthcare (PervasiveHealth). IEEE
16. Lindsay, S., et al.: Engaging older people using participatory design. In: Proceedings of the 2012 ACM annual Conference on Human Factors in Computing Systems. ACM (2012)
17. Uzor, S., Baillie, L., Skelton, D.: Senior designers: empowering seniors to design enjoyable falls rehabilitation tools. In: Proceedings of the SIGCHI Conference on Human Factors in Computing Systems. ACM (2012)
18. Grönvall, E., Kyng, M.: On participatory design of home-based healthcare. Cogn. Technol. Work **15**(4), 389–401 (2013)

19. Anderberg, P., Berglund, A.L.: Elderly persons' experiences of striving to receive care on their own terms in nursing homes. Int. J. Nurs. Pract. **16**(1), 64–68 (2010)
20. Scandurra, I., Sjölinder, M.: Participatory design with seniors: design of future services and iterative refinements of interactive eHealth services for old citizens. Medicine 2.0 **2**(2), e12 (2013)
21. Ballegaard, S.A., Hansen, T.R., Kyng, M.: Healthcare in everyday life: designing healthcare services for daily life. In: Proceedings of the SIGCHI Conference on Human Factors in Computing Systems. ACM (2008)
22. Ekdahl, A.W., Andersson, L., Friedrichsen, M.: "They do what they think is the best for me." Frail elderly patients' preferences for participation in their care during hospitalization. Patient Educ. Couns. **80**(2), 233–240 (2010)
23. Hendriks, N., et al.: Challenges in doing participatory design with people with dementia. In: Proceedings of the 13th Participatory Design Conference: Short Papers, Industry Cases, Workshop Descriptions, Doctoral Consortium papers, and Keynote abstracts, vol. 2. ACM (2014)
24. Lindsay, S., et al.: Empathy, participatory design and people with dementia. In: Proceedings of the SIGCHI Conference on Human Factors in Computing Systems. ACM (2012)
25. Yamauchi, Y.: Power of peripheral designers: how users learn to design. In: Proceedings of the 4th International Conference on Design Science Research in Information Systems and Technology. ACM (2009)
26. Clemensen, J., et al.: Participatory design in health sciences: using cooperative experimental methods in developing health services and computer technology. Qual. Health Res. **17**(1), 122–130 (2007)
27. Huldtgren, A., Detweiler, C., Alers, H., Fitrianie, S., Guldemond, N.A.: Towards community-based co-creation. In: Holzinger, A., Ziefle, M., Hitz, M., Debevc, M. (eds.) SouthCHI 2013. LNCS, vol. 7946, pp. 585–592. Springer, Heidelberg (2013)
28. Vines, J., et al.: Questionable concepts: critique as resource for designing with eighty somethings. In: Proceedings of the SIGCHI Conference on Human Factors in Computing Systems. ACM (2012)
29. Malmborg, L., Binder, T., Brandt, E.: Co-designing senior interaction: inspiration stories for participatory design with health and social care institutions. In: Workshop, PDC 2010 (2010)
30. Brandt, E., et al.: Communities of everyday practice and situated elderliness as an approach to co-design for senior interaction. In: Proceedings of the 22nd Conference of the Computer-Human Interaction Special Interest Group of Australia on Computer-Human Interaction. ACM (2010)
31. Bratteteig, T., et al.: Welfare Technology in Practice: Evaluation from Studies at Kampen Care+. Department of informatics, University of Oslo, Oslo (2015)
32. Joshi, S.G.: When simple technologies makes life difficult. In: Eighth International Conference on Advances in Computer-Human Interactions (ACHI 2015). IARIA (2015)
33. Newell, A.F., Arnott, J., Carmichael, A., Morgan, M.: Methodologies for involving older adults in the design process. In: Stephanidis, C. (ed.) HCI 2007. LNCS, vol. 4554, pp. 982–989. Springer, Heidelberg (2007)
34. Johnsson, E., Ofstad, M., Subaschandran, S.: Care+: Can we Make the Interface of the Radio Easier for Elderly Users in the Digital Age?. Department of informatics, University of Oslo, Oslo (2015)
35. Merleau-Ponty, M.: Phenomenology of Perception. Routledge & Kegan Paul, London (1962)
36. Joshi, S.G.: Emerging ethical considerations from the perspectives of the elderly. In: Ninth International Conference on Culture, Technology, and Communication 2014, Culture Technology Communication, (2014). ISBN 978-82-999770-0-5

37. Fuglerud, K.S.: Universal design in ICT, diversity in users, devices and usage, Ph.D. dissertation, University of Oslo (2014)
38. Sustar, H.: Facilitating and measuring older people's creative engagement in a user centred design process. In: Proceedings BCS-HCI 2008, Proceedings of the 22nd British HCI Group Annual Conference on People and Computers: Culture, Creativity, Interaction, vol. 2, pp. 253–254 (2008)

Children and Web 2.0: What They Do, What We Fear, and What Is Done to Make Them Safe

Heidi Hartikainen[✉], Netta Iivari, and Marianne Kinnula

Department of Information Processing Science,
University of Oulu, Oulu, Finland
{heidi.hartikainen,netta.iivari,marianne.kinnula}@oulu.fi

Abstract. Children nowadays start using Internet earlier and earlier. This has gained attention of scholars in various disciplines such as psychology, sociology, and media. Concerns about children's online safety have increased but Information Systems (IS) research on this area is still scarce despite of the fact that information security is an established research field within IS research. In this paper we review the existing research on children's online activities and related threats and risks, as well as initiatives to achieve online safety. We identify gaps in current research, such as lack of qualitative studies and research related to young children, and lack of research addressing the effectiveness of educational initiatives. We also argue that IS research should contribute to this research field for example by studying children's information security and privacy related behavior, as good information security skills lay the groundwork for privacy, the cornerstone for online safety.

Keywords: Online safety · Information security · Web 2.0 · Social media · Media skills · Children

1 Introduction

The term Web 2.0 is used to describe a new generation of web development that facilitates collaboration, interactivity, end user contributions, and information sharing [43]. Social media is a group of Internet-based applications that build on the ideological and technological foundations of Web 2.0, allowing (co-)creation and sharing, discussing, and modifying of user generated content [20, 21]. The core of social media is in "one-to-few" or "one-to-many" communication [23]. This often contains sharing of private information like gender, age, address, phone number, photographs etc., despite concerns related to privacy issues [32].

Examples of social media include *blogs or microblogs* like Tumblr or Twitter, *social networking services* like Facebook and Google + , *virtual gaming worlds* where one interacts with others like World of Warcraft, *virtual social worlds* like Second Life, *content communities* like YouTube and Flickr, and *collaborative projects* like Wikipedia [20]. With the widespread adoption of smart phones and tablet computers also social media is turning mobile, and this turn brings in a plethora of mobile apps that concentrate on instant messaging, chatting or networking like Kik Messenger and Snapchat [35].

© Springer International Publishing Switzerland 2015
H. Oinas-Kukkonen et al. (Eds.): SCIS 2015, LNBIP 223, pp. 30–43, 2015.
DOI: 10.1007/978-3-319-21783-3_3

The users of web 2.0 and different social media services are getting ever younger [27]. Children grow up in an increasingly digital world and their communication, socialization, creation, and learning processes are strongly affected by technology [37]. Children are increasingly surfing the web [31] and social networking sites, playing online games and using video sharing sites, and gadgets like iPods and mobile phones are well-established fixtures of youth culture [19]. The term "digital native" was coined to describe children that have grown up "surrounded by and using computers, video games, digital music players, video cams, cell phones and all of the other toys of the digital age" [36]. As the Internet and social media have truly entered the lives of today's children, concerns about children's online safety are also growing.

In addition to parental concerns, online safety of children is an area that has raised much academic interest within a variety disciplines, such as media and communication studies, psychology, pedagogy and sociology. While information security is an established field of research within Information Systems (IS) research, children and their information security and online safety concerns, however, have not received much attention in IS research. Information security within IS research is usually interpreted as securing confidentiality, integrity, and availability of information [11] and the IS community has studied social media and different privacy and safety issues involved, mainly focusing on adults [8], organizational aspects [14] or technological developments [28]. However, information security and online safety of children are valid concerns also for IS researchers and this study will map the field for the IS researchers to enter into. This mapping is quite complicated as these topics have been studied within various disciplines due to which it is necessary to review a multidisciplinary body of research. The review is further complicated by the fact that online safety is a diverse and relatively new research field without widely accepted theoretical frameworks or standard methodologies, and where definitional, measurement, and interpretative challenges still prevail [27].

In this paper we aim to produce an understanding of the state-of-the-art of research on children's online safety. This will be accomplished by first reviewing research on children's online activities, showing the relevance of social media in their lives, then moving on to research reporting threats and risks associated with children's online activities, and ending up with reviewing research on the different initiatives taken to secure children online. A special focus will be paid on studies carried out in Finland, the context in which the empirical part of this study will be later carried out. Finland has been categorised as a 'high use' country in terms of its young people's Internet habits, similar to the case of other Nordic countries [9]. However, literature on the topic will be included also from other countries and the results should be utilizable by researchers interested in the topic in general.

The paper proceeds as follows: Next, the methodology for the literature review is presented. Section three reviews literature on children's online activities, section four on the threats that children might face online, and section five on the efforts that have been introduced to ensure their online safety. The last sections feature discussion of our results and conclusions.

2   Methodology

Three strategies were employed to collect the literature used in this review. First Google Scholar services were used to search with keywords and phrases such as social media, children, online safety and information security as well as different variations of those. Second, databases such as Scopus, ProQuest and Web of Science were used to perform searches with same terms. An example search carried out in the Scopus database is as follows: (TITLE-ABS-KEY ("social media" OR Facebook OR Instagram OR Twitter OR "social network" OR sns OR internet OR www) AND TITLE-ABS-KEY ("information security" OR privacy OR trust OR "cyber security" OR "internet security" OR "online safety") AND TITLE-ABS-KEY (child* OR youth OR young OR kids OR adolescent* OR "digital native*")). Finally, additional literature was obtained by going through the reference lists of the articles.

The search was performed in articles written in English and Finnish, but it was not limited to specific journals, conferences, databases, or fields of research as the aim was to gain as rich picture as possible of the ongoing research. Inclusion/exclusion criteria were based on the researcher's insight and judgment of the relevance of the examined studies (c.f. [2, 12]). Publication years of the articles were not limited. A paper trail was established to keep track of what was done to avoid repeating the same search tasks during the process. The collected material was organized into a RefWorks database.

During three months, a total of 318 articles or book chapters were collected. When analyzing the material we found that literature discussing children online and their safety could be categorized under three broader themes: *what they do*, i.e. children's online activities, *what we fear* will threaten children online, and *what we do* to make them safe. When coding the material under these themes we discovered further subcategories under each theme. These categories and their subcategories will be further discussed in the following chapters, and illustrated later in Fig. 1.

As most papers could be categorized into more than one category (i.e. papers that discussed what threatens children online also most likely discussed their online activities to some extent), a quantitative analysis on how many papers fall under each category and subcategory was not meaningful. Instead, we prepared a narrative synthesis of the literature review, using some of the collected papers to exemplify the themes, in order to provide the reader an easy to read background for understanding the current knowledge in the area and highlighting the significance of new knowledge [5].

3   What Do Children Do Online?

The Internet and mobile technologies have opened up a world of possibilities for children, expanding their horizons and providing opportunities to learn, create identities, and participate in society [7, 27]. The number of online activities young people engage in increases with age and years of Internet use [27]. This section reviews literature concerning those activities.

The most popular online activities among children are use of Internet for schoolwork and playing games on their own. Watching video clips is also popular as well as instant messaging, sending and receiving emails, and visiting social networking sites. The more active Internet users also engage in playing games against others, downloading music or films, posting photos, using webcams, or posting messages on websites. Visiting chat rooms, spending time in virtual worlds, or writing a blog or a diary are practiced by a smaller percentage [13].

Finnish children have a lower number of online activities than children in Europe on average, even though their daily use of the Internet is much higher than European average. The most popular Internet activities among Finnish children are playing games alone, watching video clips, receiving and sending email, using the Internet for school-work, and visiting social networking sites [9].

Online activities of children have been divided into three genres of participation that describe young people's engagement with new media: *Hanging out* refers to friendship driven participation corresponding to typical practices of children as they go about their daily life and interact with others [18], for example, browsing social network profiles, instant messaging, and phone and video conversations [17]. *Geeking out* refers to interest driven participation centering upon specific activities, interests, or niche, and marginalized identities [18]. It involves intense commitment with media or technology, often with one particular media property, genre or a type of technology [17], e.g. intense gaming or media production, long term video and music file sharing or engaging in interest groups [17]. Finally, *messing around* describes media engagement in which kids are tinkering, learning, and getting serious about something, often supported by the social networks developed in their friendship- or interest-driven groups [18]. It is also a transition zone between geeking out and hanging out and between interest-driven and friendship-driven participation [18], including e.g. use of search words to find information about interesting issues and experimenting with media for example by using photo and video editing tools [17].

No matter whether hanging out, geeking out, or messing around, presence in social media is getting more and more important among children: for instance in Finland the use of social media was mentioned to be the most important use of the Internet for girls aged as young as 10–12; for the boys of same age it was trumped only by watching video clips and gaming [39]. Favorite social media of Finnish teens and preteens include Facebook, YouTube, Instagram, Ask FM, and Pinterest; gaming platforms like Habbo and World of Warcraft are also familiar to them [31]. Wikipedia is used in schoolwork [31] and a new favorite is mobile online messaging app WhatsApp [31]. In 2010, 67 % of Finnish children who used the Internet had their own social networking profile, including 46 % of 9–12 year olds, despite the fact that most use Facebook, where the minimum age is 13 [9]. In a national media barometer conducted a few of years later, it was found out that 82 % of Finnish children aged 10–12 had a social networking profile [39].

It is a notable development that even if absorption in online communication, i.e. social networking and use of smart phones and video sharing sites, has been seen as typical for teenagers [19], it is becoming characteristic for ever younger children [27]. Current research reveals that there has been an increase in Internet usage by children under nine years old [16, 42]. 19 % of Finnish children aged 0–3 use the Internet in some way, and between the ages 4–6 the percentage increases to 58 % [10]. In addition to

watching videos, gaming, and doing homework these young Internet users are social-
izing in virtual worlds meant for children or, as underage participants, in social media
meant for teenagers and adults [16]. This is a problem as it has not been established that
young children have the capacity to engage in the Internet in a safe manner, especially
when it comes to social media [16]. The presence of young children in social media can
be risky especially concerning contact requests, the publicity of friend network, and the
visibility of personal information [22].

4   What Do We Fear When Children Are Online?

Societal and parental fears over children are not new but Internet and different technologies have brought additional things to worry about. Some are unique to the Internet,
but many can be seen as reformulations or extensions to offline threats [4].

Next, existing research on the threats associated with children's Internet activities is
reviewed. In addition to the traditional online threats to information security, children
can also encounter threats to their personal safety online. A threat is something that can
(intentionally or accidentally) exploit some vulnerability and cause some harm in the
process, while risk is a calculation based on probability and the likely consequences of
harm, when exposed to a threat [27]. Harm is a distinct and negative outcome, whether
measured objectively or, more usually, through subjective self-report [27]. For example,
there is a risk that when positioned as a recipient of some inappropriate content [27],
children might experience psychological harm [4], or when a child participates in certain
online interactions [27], they might experience physical harm [4]. Personal safety is
defined as an individual's ability to go about their everyday life free from threats or fear
of psychological, emotional or physical harm [44]. Online threats to personal safety can
include for example cyberbullying, online predators, and exposure to offensive content.

The threats usually associated with the use of mobile technology and Internet have
been subdivided into content threats and contact threats [4], but also conduct threats [4]
and computer/Internet threats [29] can be included in the categorization. *Content threats*
include inappropriate content for children, such as commercial spam, targeted emails/
ads, and unwanted pop-ups, treating children as active consumers, as well as adult/
abusive content such as pornography, violence, pro-anorexia, and drug related content
[29]. *Contact threats* include grooming (adult forming an emotional bond with a child
for the purpose of sexual abuse), sexting (sending sexually explicit messages via text or
chat), cyberbullying and cyberstalking (using technology to harass someone), and
privacy loss [29]. *Conduct threats* include a child being engaged in activities such as
illegal file sharing or bullying others [4]. Finally, *Computer/Internet threats* include
information security threats like malware (software used to damage a system, to gain
access to computers, to gather sensitive information), phishing (trying to get the user to
reveal private information by impersonating a trustworthy entity), data theft/loss, password stealing or cracking, and Internet addiction [29].

The most common risk among Finnish 9–16 year olds is communicating online with
persons they have never met offline. Most of these online acquaintances might be friends
of friends or friends of family, but children did acknowledge that strangers are a risk.

When asked if they had had contact with these persons, previously unknown to them, also offline, 6 % of the Finnish children answered they had. "Stranger danger" is one of the most talked about concerns today, even if the danger of actual harm seems to be relatively low, most likely because the possible harm would be so severe. It should be noted, however, that contact with strangers is an integral part of many Internet activities, like gaming, social media, and publishing online. Children are creating a relationship towards the Internet audience and they are using the Internet to maintain and expand their social contacts [22].

Children are usually considered to be passively involved in most online threats (for example nobody specifically invites suspicious emails or wants to get bullied or stalked), however, they do actively participate in the leakage of their own personal information online [29], for example when using social media. If children are not aware of the risks associated with the inappropriate use of their personal and sensitive data, they are vulnerable not only to privacy loss and other contact threats, but also to content and information security related threats [29]. If they share their email address freely, they are easier to approach by online predators, but can also start receiving spam email, links containing viruses and so on. Just over half of the European 11–12-year-olds, rising to over three-quarters of the 15–16-year-olds, know how to change the privacy settings on their profile [13]. Younger children are more likely to have a public profile; however, they are slightly less likely to disclose their address, telephone number or the name of their school on their profile [13]. Most Finnish children have their profile set to private or partially private so that most things they post is only visible to their friends, but 28 % still have a public profile [9].

On the other hand, it is also important to remember that just because there is a risk that something bad might happen it does not mean it actually will: most European 9–16 year old children have not been bothered by something experienced on the Internet. Seeing sexual images and receiving sexual messages online is relatively common but generally not experienced as very harmful. By contrast, being bullied online is relatively uncommon but is more likely to upset children. It should also be remembered that more use facilitates more digital literacy and safety skills and European pre-teens and teens are generally not unskilled when it comes to online safety: most 11–16 -year olds said that they can block messages from people they do not want to contact and that they can find safety advice online. Around half of them said that they are able to change the privacy settings of their social media, block websites, and judge the quality of a website. The younger children, however, tend to lack skills and confidence [25].

5   What Has Been Done to Keep Children Safe?

The fast adoption of the Internet and different online technologies presents policy makers, governments, and the industry the tasks of identifying the threats and risks of Internet use and developing strategies and tools to make sure that harm linked with them is minimized [34]. In a more grass-root level, parents, schools, and even other children are involved in a more practical way in seeking to maximize online opportunities while minimizing the possibility of harm [13]. Next, a variety of mechanisms aiming at protecting children's online information security and personal safety are identified from the existing literature.

5.1 Industry Mediation

Most social media are intended for teenagers and adults. Age limit to use for example Facebook, Tumblr, Instagram, ask.fm, YouTube, and Google + is 13 years. Some social media such as Momio, Club penguin and Habbo are, nonetheless, clearly targeted for children. Service providers rely on users' self-professed age, however [3]. Although they try to limit their services for appropriate users only, in the Internet no-one knows if you're are as young or old as you say you are. Moreover, the services have different privacy policies and settings available for their users but the settings have been criticized for having too weak defaults for their younger users [16] and the privacy policies for being generally vague or non-transparent [1].

Additionally, the industry applies different mechanisms to screen off offensive content, using e.g. keyword blacklists or offering users possibility to report offensive content. However, most social media use a simple lexicon-based automatic filtering approach that is not very accurate and might generate many false positive alerts [40]. In addition, when these systems depend on users and administrators to detect and report offensive content, they might fail to take quick actions. For children who often lack cognitive awareness of risks these approaches are not effective either [40].

5.2 Technical Mediation

In addition to protecting the computer itself from e.g. viruses, other solutions for technical mediation are also available, such as software for filtering and restricting unwanted use. Three quarters of parents adopt technical mediation through the use of parental control or some other means of blocking and filtering websites [13].

Criticism against these kind of software include, e.g., that they are not very good in blocking non-English language content and that there is a tradeoff between under-blocking (permitting sites that should be blocked) and overblocking (blocking sites that should be permitted). There are also some ethical considerations: although law might give the parents grounds to monitor their children online to keep them safe it should still be asked if full-scale monitoring of children is ethically acceptable [29].

5.3 Social Mediation

Today, children's use of Internet and mobile technology is becoming more private and inaccessible to parental oversight [24], thus making monitoring of children's online activities harder. Parents are often caught in the middle, wanting their children to fit in and to widen their social circles, but at the same time knowing that most social media were not designed for children [26]. Making sure that children are safe is a combination of protecting children and giving them tools to cope with the potentially harmful things they encounter, but also making sure that they are not making wrong decisions that might have severe consequences [47]. Parents are encouraged to take measures to protect their children from risks and proactively engaged parents are seen as 'good' parents [4].

Different kinds of strategies can be employed for reducing the risks that children face online, e.g. active mediation of children's Internet use (talking to them and offering help), restricting the use, or monitoring it (checking the computer, profiles on a social networking site, or messages etc.). Nine out of ten European 9–16-year-olds tell that their *parents* advise them about Internet use and Internet safety, and they have restrictive rules at home, whereas monitoring is only experienced by half of the children. Parents are the main mediators about safety. However, the role of *teachers* is also important especially for children from lower income homes. This should lead to larger amount of public information campaigns targeted at teachers. Teachers mostly practice restrictive mediation: over 60 % of European children say that their teachers set rules for using Internet at school. Only one-quarter say their teachers have helped when something bothered them on the Internet and one in five reports that their teachers have not engaged with them at all regarding Internet use. However, this can reflect the fact that relatively few incidents bother children. On the other hand, *peers* play a major role when children are seeking social support: children turn to them first, whatever the problem. Three-quarters of children say their peers have helped or supported their Internet use in practical matters but not as often when they are bothered by something but, again, this may reflect the fact that few are bothered [13]. Children do want to talk to someone about their experiences online, however [33].

5.4 Policies and Educational Efforts

There are diverse efforts underway in many countries to promote digital learning technologies in schools, e-governance initiatives, digital participation, and digital literacy [34]. These include initiatives on European Union (EU) level, such as "The Safer Internet Programme" and "European Strategy for a Better Internet for Children". The associated "Safer Social Networking principles for the EU" have been signed by most of the industry providers in Europe. The aim is to give children the skills and tools they need to safely benefit from being online. To do this, the European Commission is seeking to identify how national education systems approach online safety issues and what children learn about online safety in school [7].

In Finland, topics related to online safety are included at schools in subjects related to the development of media and communication skills [7, 41]. Educational efforts are also made by national actors such as the Mannerheim League for Child Welfare, National Audiovisual Institute, Save the Children Finland, and Finland's national public service broadcasting company. There are also countless educational efforts made by researchers and other interested parties, for example different guidebooks for children [30, 46] or parents [6, 45], and a prototype of an educational information security board game [38]. However, educating children can be problematic, especially if children feel they are more competent technology users than their instructors [38]. This likely will not be a problem in Finland as Finnish children have acknowledged that their parents are more competent media users than they are [31]. Moreover, we often erroneously presume a gap between educators and students. If such a gap does exist, it is definitely possible to close it by acquiring skills and experience [15].

In addition to viewing children's online safety as something that depends on others' actions, it can also be seen as an action by children themselves, enabled by their growing independence and as a developmental process [47]. Their skills related to online behavior also develop differently [41] and their developing moral judgment skills affect their behavior [47].

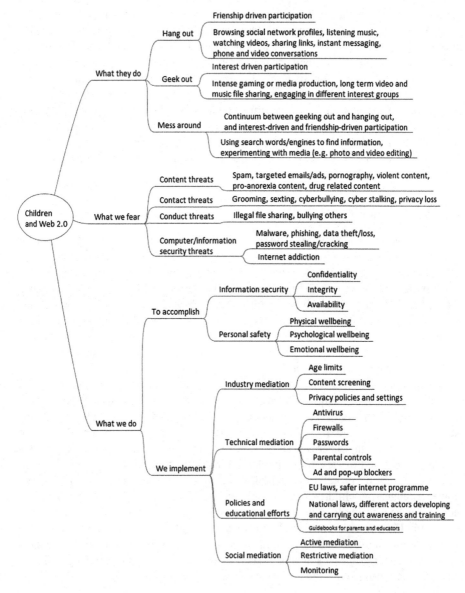

Fig. 1. Children online: what they do, what we fear, what is done to make them safe

6   Research Contributions and Gaps

This study aimed to produce an understanding of the state-of-the-art of multidisciplinary research on children's online safety for the IS researchers to enter into. This was quite a complicated task as research on the topic forms a diverse and relatively new field with definitional, measurement, and interpretative challenges, lacking widely accepted theoretical frameworks or standard methodologies [27]. Figure 1 summarizes the main findings of our literature review.

Children engage online in a variety of activities, characterized as *hanging out*, *geeking out* and *messing around*. Their presence in social media is getting more and more important. There has been a substantial increase in Internet usage by very young children, whose presence in social media can be risky in many respects.

The threats associated with Internet use have been divided into *content threats*, *contact threats*, *conduct threats*, and *computer/Internet threats*. Most European teens and preteens are quite skilled in online safety; however, younger children more likely lack skills and confidence.

Luckily, however, there are many actors and efforts involved in trying to make children safe online. To accomplish *information security* and *personal safety* of children *industry mediation* offers privacy policies and settings in services and enforces age limits, as well as applies mechanisms to screen off offensive content, while they are not very accurate and might generate many false positive alerts. *Technical mediation* can be employed, while criticism against software for filtering and restricting has also been expressed. Moreover, there are ethical considerations related to this. Different *policies and educational efforts*, on the other hand, include diverse efforts to promote digital learning in schools, different e-governance initiatives, digital participation, and digital literacy and online safety. As regards *social mediation*, different kinds of strategies can be employed e.g. active mediation of child's Internet use, restricting the use or monitoring it. Parents are the main agents; however, the role of teachers and peers also appears as important.

A number of research gaps were also identified during the literature review, related to which also IS researchers could contribute. Those are listed in Fig. 2.

While personal safety is a much-researched topic for example by psychologists, sociologists and pedagogy professionals, there seems to be room for information security related research concerning children and their online activities, as seen in Fig. 2. Information security threats were the least discussed threat category in the literature. Also while for example the social mediation of online threats gained much discussion, the effectiveness of industry mediation, technical mediation solutions and educational efforts received less attention. These topics should not be avoided by IS researchers: instead of assessing the risk of harm to firewalls or corporate assets, the focus here is in the risk of harm to a much more precious entity – the child. Possibilities for IS research in the area of children's online safety could include, for example, researching different mediation tactics employed by the industry, the effectiveness of current technical mediation or educational solutions, or children's privacy and information security related online behavior as well as developing new age-appropriate training and awareness solutions for them. While research on online risky behavior and possible harm to children is perhaps best left to someone better equipped to assess psychological factors, IS research could also clearly contribute to this new, extremely important and highly fascinating topic of study either as part of multidisciplinary research teams or as nerdy superheroes flying solo, saving children from information security threats one kid at a time.

Studies on young children and online safety

- Majority of research concentrates on older children and teenagers [42], thus more research related to younger children is needed [34], [42] as it may be that younger children do not have the capacity to act on the Internet in a safe manner [16].
- This could also help to inform the development of future educational strategies for schools, parents and young people [47].

Qualitative studies

- A trend in the existing research is quantitative research: e.g. the EUKids online network has had a sample size of over 25 000 children from 25 countries [25]. More qualitative research is warranted to get a richer understanding of the experiences of children [34] as well as of their parents and teachers.

Effectiveness of the existing online safety solutions

- Initiatives by industry providers and different international and national actors to develop technological and educational solutions for children's online safety exist, but there is a lack of research on which solutions work and which do not [34]. A lot of material has been produced but left to live its own life.

Role of parents and teachers in social mediation

- Further research on the role of parents and teachers in ensuring children's online safety, along with other forms of safety mediation, is needed [34].

Involvement of children in developing their online safety education

- Educating children can be difficult, if children feel they are more competent technology users than their instructors [38]. Their involvement in the development of the education may alleviate this problem.

IS studies on information security and privacy related behavior of children

- IS research specifically could contribute for example by studying the information security and privacy related behavior of children – what they are sharing online, with whom, do they know what they should and should not share, as well as the current training offered at schools.

Fig. 2. Research gaps and their explanations

7   Conclusions

This study aimed to produce an understanding of the state-of-the-art of multidisciplinary research on children's online safety for the IS researchers to enter into. This was accomplished by reviewing the current body of knowledge concerning children's online activities and related threats and risks, as well as initiatives to achieve online safety. Personal safety of children online, regarding the risks they take and the threats they face, seems to interest scholars the most. Large amount of research originates from disciplines such as psychology, sociology, and media studies. Although there is much research in the IS field on the Internet and related information security, it tends to focus on adults and organizational or technical aspects. A worthy goal for the IS community, in addition to securing corporate reputation and assets, would be to help securing the future – the children. At this moment research originating from the IS community concerning this topic is scarce. However, good information security lays the groundwork for privacy, which in turn is the cornerstone for children's online safety.

References

1. Anthonysamy, P., Greenwood, P., Rashid, A.: Social networking privacy: understanding the disconnect from policy to controls. Computer **46**, 60–67 (2013)
2. Boell, S.K., Cecez-Kecmanovic, D.: On being 'systematic' in literature reviews in IS. J. Inf. Technol. **30**, 161–173 (2015). www.palgrave-journals.com/jit/journal/v30/n2/full/jit201426a.html
3. Boyd, D., Hargittai, E.: Facebook privacy settings: who cares? First Monday **15**(8), 1–17 (2010)
4. Boyd, D., Hargittai, E.: Connected and concerned: variation in parents' online safety concerns. Policy Internet **5**, 245–269 (2013)
5. Cronin, P., Ryan, F., Coughlan, M.: Undertaking a literature review: a step-by-step approach. Br. J. Nurs. **17**, 38–43 (2008)
6. Edgington, S.M.: The Parent's Guide to Texting, Facebook, and Social Media: Understanding the Benefits and Dangers of Parenting in a Digital World. Brown Books Publishing Group, Dallas (2011)
7. Eurydice network: Summary Report: Education on Online Safety in Schools in Europe, p. 20 (2010)
8. Gross, R., Acquisti, A.: Information revelation and privacy in online social networks, pp. 71–80 (2005)
9. Haddon, L., Livingstone, S.: EU Kids Online: National Perspectives, p. 74. LSE, London (2012)
10. Happo, H.: Lapsiperheiden mediakysely 2012: 0–12 vuotiaiden lasten internetin käyttö ja mediakasvatus kotiympäristössä. In: Kupiainen, R., Kotilainen, S., Nikunen, K., et al. (eds.) Lapset netissä: Puheenvuoroja lasten ja nuorten netin käytöstä ja riskeistä, pp. 25–36. Mediakasvatusseura, Helsinki (2013)
11. Harris, S.: Cissp certification exam guide. Osborne/McGraw-Hill, New York (2002)
12. Hart, C.: Doing a Literature Review: Releasing the Social Science Research Imagination. SAGE Publications Ltd., London (1999)

13. Hasebrink, U., Görzig, A., Haddon, L., et al.: Patterns of Risk and Safety Online: In-Depth Analyses from the EU Kids Online Survey of 9- to 16-Year-Olds and their Parents in 25 European Countries, p. 87. LSE, London (2011)
14. Hekkala, R., Väyrynen, K., Wiander, T.: Information security challenges of social media for companies. In: ECIS 2012 Proceedings (2012)
15. Helsper, E.J., Eynon, R.: Digital natives: where is the evidence? Br. Educ. Res. J. **36**, 503–520 (2010)
16. Holloway, D., Green, L., Livingstone, S.: Zero to Eight: Young Children and their Internet Use, p. 36. LSE, London (2013)
17. Horst, H.A., Herr-Stephenson, R., Robinson, L.: Media ecologies. In: Ito, M. (ed.) Hanging out, Messing around and Geeking out: Kids living and learning with new media, pp. 29–78. MIT Press, Cambridge (2010)
18. Horst, H.A., Herr-Stephenson, R., Robinson, L.: Media Ecologies, Genres of Participation (2008). www.spotlight.macfound.org/blog/entry/horst-herr-robinson-media-ecologies/
19. Ito, M., Horst, H.A., Antin, J., et al.: Hanging Out, Messing Around, and Geeking Out: Kids Living and Learning with New Media. MIT Press, Cambridge (2010)
20. Kaplan, A.M., Haenlein, M.: Users of the world, unite! the challenges and opportunities of social media. Bus. Horiz. **53**, 59–68 (2010)
21. Kietzmann, J.H., Hermkens, K., McCarthy, I.P., et al.: Social media? get serious! understanding the functional building blocks of social media. Bus. Horiz. **54**, 241–251 (2011)
22. Kupiainen, R.: EU Kids Online: Suomalaislasten netin käyttö, riskit ja mahdollisuudet. In: Kupiainen, R., Kotilainen, S., Nikunen, K., et al. (eds.) Lapset netissä: Puheenvuoroja lasten ja nuorten netin käytöstä ja riskeistä, pp. 6–15. Mediakasvatusseura, Helsinki (2013)
23. Lietsala, K., Sirkkunen, E.: Social Media: Introduction to the Tools and Processes of Participatory Economy. Hypermedia Laboratory Net Series, 17th edn. University of Tampere, Tampere (2008)
24. Livingstone, S.: Children and the Internet. Polity Press, Cambridge (2009)
25. Livingstone, S., Haddon, L., Görzig, A., et al.: Risks and Safety on the Internet: The Perspective of European Children. Full Findings. LSE, London (2011)
26. Livingstone, S., Ólafsson, K., Staksrud, E.: Risky social networking practices among 'underage' users: lessons for evidence-based policy. J Comput Mediat Commun **18**, 303–320 (2013)
27. Livingstone, S., Smith, P.K.: Annual research review: harms experienced by child users of online and mobile technologies: the nature, prevalence and management of sexual and aggressive risks in the digital age. J. Child Psychol. Psychiatry **55**, 635–654 (2014)
28. Lucas, M.M., Borisov, N.: FlyByNight: mitigating the privacy risks of social networking. In: WPES 2008, p. 1 (2008)
29. Magkos, E., Kleisiari, E., Chanias, P., et al.: Parental control and children's internet safety: the good, the bad and the ugly. In: ICIL, p. 18 (2014)
30. Minton, E.: Social Networking and Social Media Safety: Stay Safe Online. Powerkids Press, New York (2014)
31. Noppari, E.: Mobiilimuksut. lasten ja nuorten mediaympäristön muutos, osa 3. Tampereen Yliopisto, Tampere (2014)
32. Nosko, A., Wood, E., Molema, S.: All about me: disclosure in online social networking profiles: the case of FACEBOOK. Comput. Hum. Behav. **26**, 406–418 (2010)
33. Oinas-Kukkonen, H., Kurki, H.: Internet through the Eyes of 11-year old children: first-hand experiences from the technological environment the children live. Human Technol. **5**, 146–162 (2009)

34. Ólafsson, K., Livingstone, S., Haddon, L.: Children's use of online technologies in Europe: a review of the European evidence base. LSE, London (2013)
35. Pönkä, H.: Sosiaalisen median käsikirja. Docendo, Jyväskylä (2014)
36. Prensky, M.: Digital natives, digital immigrants Part 1. Horizon **9**, 1–6 (2001)
37. Prensky, M.: Digital natives, digital immigrants Part II: do they really think differently? Horizon **9**, 1–6 (2001)
38. Reid, R., Van Niekerk, J.: Snakes and Ladders for digital natives: information security education for the youth. Inf. Manage. Comput. Secur. **22**, 179–190 (2014)
39. Suoninen, A.: Lasten mediabarometri 2012: 10–12 vuotiaiden tyttöjen ja poikien mediankäyttö. Verkkojulkaisuja, vol. 62. Nuorisotutkimusverkosto, Helsinki (2013)
40. Tomer, P., Lade, S., Kumar, M.S., et al.: On line social network content and image filtering classifications. IJERST **2**, 16 (2013)
41. Tuominen, S.: Toiminnallisuutta nettikasvatukseen. In: Kupiainen, R., Kotilainen, S., Nikunen, K., et al. (eds.) Lapset netissä - Puheenvuoroja lasten ja nuorten netin käytöstä ja riskeistä, pp. 92–100. Mediakasvatusseura, Helsinki (2013)
42. Walamies, T.: Poimintoja 0-8-vuotiaiden mediasuhteita koskevasta tutkimuksesta. In: Kotilainen, S. (ed.) Mediabarometri 2010: 0-8 vuotiaiden lasten mediankäyttö Suomessa, pp. 9–14. Mediakasvatusseura, Helsinki (2011)
43. Wallace, P.: Information Systems in Organizations. Prentice Hall, New Jersey (2013)
44. Waters, J., Neale, R., Hutson, S., et al.: Personal safety on university campuses - defining personal safety using the delphi method. In: 20th Annual ARCOM Conference, vol. 1, pp. 411–418 (2004)
45. Whitby, P.: Is your child safe online? a parent's guide to the internet, facebook, mobile phones and other new media. White Ladder Press, London (2011)
46. Willard, N.E.: Cyber savvy: Embracing Digital Safety and Civility. Corwin, Thousand Oaks (2011)
47. Wisniewski, P.J., Xu, H., Rosson, M.B., et al.: Adolescent online safety: the "Moral" of the story. In: 17th ACM Conference on Computer Supported Cooperative Work and Social Computing, pp. 1258–1271 (2014)

Leveraging the Usage of Sensors and the Social Web: Towards Systems for Socially Challenging Situations

Salman Qayyum Mian[✉], Harri Oinas-Kukkonen, and Jukka Riekki

University of Oulu, Linnanmaa, 90570 Oulu, Finland
{Salman.Mian,Harri.Oinas-kukkonen,Jukka.Riekki}@oulu.fi

Abstract. This paper studies the design of information systems that leverage the use of both sensors and the social web, while addressing solutions for children in socially challenging situations. Socially challenging situations are defined as situations in which one experiences negative social pressure and, therefore, requires immediate help from trusted people. The authors first provide a glimpse into the rapid development in sensors and the rise in the importance of the social web. The paper then sheds light on the theme of socially challenging situations, which is elaborated through two workshops, and defines the core areas of focus. Further, a low-fidelity prototype for the safety of children is created and evaluated in a small-scale user experiment. The state of the current technology is then reviewed in order to visualize the possible practical realization of solutions. The outcomes of these steps provide interesting insights for possible future work.

Keywords: Social web · Sensor · Socially challenging situation · Interaction design · Health · Wellness · Monitoring · Safety of children · Bullying

1   Introduction

We live in a technology-mediated society, in which interactions take place through the social web and practically every individual has an online presence. The emergence of the social web has introduced new ways to create and share information, while the advent of technological gadgets has led to its easy access. In their book, *Humanizing the Web*, Oinas-kukkonen and Oinas-kukkonen [43] describe how the web has transformed from a one-way information delivery channel to a platform socially rich in communication, which continues to transform society and human life. On a different note, the ever-increasing computing power, the device portability and the ubiquitous presence of mobile devices in our daily lives point towards a technology-driven future. There is a penetration of millions of everyday devices, which make use of modern sensors to detect and measure physical quantities such as touch screen devices, motion detection systems, and heart rate monitoring systems. With the advent of the Internet, all of these sensor-based devices have the ability to be online and to send/receive information from the web.

One of the prominent areas for healthcare improvement in modern societies concerns the role of the web in fostering healthier lifestyles [30]. It is widely known that the adoption of a particular lifestyle affects the ways in which individuals maintain their

© Springer International Publishing Switzerland 2015
H. Oinas-Kukkonen et al. (Eds.): SCIS 2015, LNBIP 223, pp. 44–60, 2015.
DOI: 10.1007/978-3-319-21783-3_4

health. Since the social web is an entity that has become significantly influential in the modern era, it presents its own way of life, which involves interaction with devices. Thus, the social web is readily available for lifestyle-changing interventions. Moreover, the social web, along with sensor-based devices, can provide breakthroughs on a global level, which can be scalable and may increase productivity and effectiveness. The lives of social web users have become increasingly connected with the popularity of mobile devices, which supports all kinds of social networks and, more importantly, the transfer of social web data. The introduction of sensors has given an extra edge to the kinds of information that can be transferred to the social web, thereby improving the chances for encouraging long-term positive changes in individuals through competitive healthcare solutions.

In the following sections, the authors highlight the rapid development of sensors and their emerging role in the social web. The paper then elaborates on the theme of socially challenging situations. After that, the focus shifts to the results of a user experiment based on a low-fidelity prototype. The authors further review the state of the current technology to visualize the possible practical realization of emerging solutions for children. Further, they provide a snapshot of what others have done in relation to the theme presented in this paper. Finally, all of the above lead to an interesting conclusion regarding possible future work.

2 Sensors and the Social Web

2.1 Sensors

Sensors are detectors that measure various kinds of physical quantities. Most modern sensors are core aspects of electronic devices, and they have communication abilities for the purposes of measuring and recording. Sensors are categorized based on the physical quantities they measure: motion, lightness, pressure, temperature, vibration. etc. One of the most common sensor types is the touch screen sensor, which can be found in modern smartphones and tablets. Different sensors collect different sets of data based on changes in an environment or an object, making them useful tools that are applicable to numerous environments [55].

Sensors act as boundaries that measure physical environments and transform the measured information into digital form, thereby bridging the physical world with the virtual one. Many health and fitness experts base their solutions on physiological sensor readings, such as motion or electrocardiograms (ECGs). Another example of a general health application involves sensors being used to measure the cortisol in saliva as a proxy for stress. Irrespective of industry, sensors have contributed significantly to modern solutions to various problems. Moreover, they can be easily used together with smartphones (and other hardware platforms) to access the social web. In sum, sensors form the core of the embedded intelligence aspect of modern technologies [16].

2.2 Emerging Role of Sensors in the Social Web

The web has become an important factor in how we conduct business. In modern society, the web is a key driver for media consumption, rapid communication, and social engagement. This revolution has been driven by the Internet becoming a platform for applications, as well as by the provision of rich user experiences on a more profound psychological level. Ultimately, it is the social aspect of content generation that characterizes the concept of 'connectedness,' or when the data we generate through various devices is linked to a multitude of other data [43]. Other applications further harness the relationships in these data, thereby enhancing the broader social context. Thus, the web becomes more interactive, and engages the user deeply through the use of video, audio, and text through several processes: pushing information out, bringing it back in, storing it and presenting it, all in real time. Increased interactivity has also been made possible via the multiple ways in which the web can be accessed and its mobility, which has made it possible to conduct activities at the point of interest rather than from a fixed location. It has also led to the creation of more content, since events can be captured at any time as they un-fold.

In parallel, the rapid advancement and the ubiquitous use of devices has led to a greater opportunity and need for humans to interact with portable technological products [35]. An integral part of people's daily activities is the social web which manifests through sensors in physical products and objects, especially a smartphone in a user's hand. Sensors can also be mobile devices that perform specific actions, such as calculating the distance covered by a person during a run and sharing this information on the person's social network page without the need for intervention. The concept of the "Internet of things" (IoT) is not new, and it tends to remind us that, in the future, even more physical devices will contribute data to the Internet without human intervention. Most of the objects in the concept of IoT embed sensors as key components in order to be discovered or located [23]. In particular, Rosalind Picard, the author of the seminal book on 'affective wearables', *Affective Computing*, highlighted the need for the development of robust sensing equipment [45].

In relation to children and young adults, Project Salus [47] demonstrated how computer mediation could help tackle bullying at school. The results showed improved social interaction among pupils and indicated an opportunity to utilize new forms of technology such as sensors. Aggarwal and Abdelzaher [4] discussed the motivations behind integrating sensors with the social web, focusing mainly on social networks. One of the key incentives for users is a real-time awareness of one another's updates; specifically, in an unprecedented way, sensors allow the global behaviour of users as a whole to become visible. On the other hand, sensors allow the measurement of the users' environments, making context awareness possible. For example, City Sense is a social networking application that provides information on the locations of people in a city, and it is used to plan human activities. City Sense extracts information from sensors and GPS-enabled phones to obtain people's locations, and then provides this information to subscribed clients [54]. Consider a situation in which, as you stroll through a city enter, your sensor device informs you that some of your friends are sitting in a nearby cafeteria and that you should go and say "Hi." This interaction completely changes the role of sensors in the social web.

Along with all of its positive effects, technology also has negative effects on society. The usage of sensors for monitoring introduces significant privacy and trust issues. Abbas et al. [1] investigated how applications like mobile covert surveillance within a community can change the nature of personal relationships in terms of privacy, trust, and control. Morozov [38] provided a detailed and interesting view of the "nonsense" created along with the advent of the Internet, the rise of the social web, and the smart gadgets that are making humans less intelligent. Further, as critical theorist David Berry's interesting read, *Critical Theory and the Digital* [10], discusses how conceptualizing the digital media world has implications across a range of societal norms.

3   Socially Challenging Situations

3.1   Nature of the Theme

Definition. The theme of socially challenging situations was chosen as the domain of our research because it covers a multitude of aspects related to children's technology use, particularly those aspects in which the development of technology-specific sensors, in collaboration with the social web, may provide highly effective solutions. There is relatively little previous literature on such concepts in the fields of information systems and human-computer interaction. The ideal target audience for such a theme includes, not only children (up to the age of 12), but also young adults (from age 12 to age 16). The need for a focus on safety in the context of young children, compared to that of young adults, is clear because of the age factor. However, studies have shown that, although physical bullying declines with age, verbal, social, and cyber bullying tend to increase between the ages of 11 and 15 [5]. Thus, the theme explored in our paper includes such issues as bullying at school, the safety of children, and autism etc. The theme can be described as:

> *"Situations in which one experiences negative social pressure and, therefore, requires immediate help from trusted people."*

Conceptualization. To further the agenda of this theme, two workshops were organized by the authors, with the objective to brainstorm, define, and conceptualize an abstract-level solution to socially challenging situations. These workshops involved 17 Information Technology (IT) experts, some with the background knowledge in the 'Safety of Children' domain. Most of the experts had prior experience in multi-disciplinary projects targeted towards children and/or had been involved in psychological sciences, social work, education, etc. The theme was thoroughly discussed from the perspective of how sensors and the social web can fill in gaps to facilitate effective solutions. The workshops resulted in the identification of five sub-concepts, which are considered to form the core of any solution seeking to provide support in socially challenging situations by making use of sensors and the social web. In the following sub-sections, these sub-concepts are discussed further and critically analyzed from the perspective of possible limitations.

Personal Safety Network (PSN). A PSN represents the networks of people a user wants to connect with in the case of a challenging situation. A PSN can be defined as a logical group based on, for example, friends, family, teachers, or the severity of a situation. The need for different types of contacts is evident, since, in real life, we contact our friends and close relatives to discuss a range of problems. For instance, for young children who are still in school, teachers should be the immediate contacts, while, at home, this role should be taken over by parents. Thus, the context must be understood in contact selection (e.g., a situation of a child breaking an arm at school would require first the school nurse and then the parents). The list of contacts in the PSN should be dynamic, changing to accommodate changes in relationships or personal preferences. Moreover, a PSN for emergencies and life-threatening situations is not the same as one for daily challenging situations. For solutions targeted towards young children, a PSN must be created and managed with the consent of the parents. Further, groupings could be made either dynamic (e.g., based on geographical location), which is highly useful, or static (e.g., parents on the first level and grandparents on the second level).

Emergency Notification. A notification is considered as an act of informing a target person of critical information. Notifications can be user- or sensor-initiated, and they can be either predefined or created on the spot. For example, a dangerous level of air pollution can trigger a notification and inform a user automatically based on a sensor reading. In the case of a child having respiratory problems, sensors can trigger predefined notifications and inform both the closest contact and the parents. Sensor-triggered notifications should include self-notifications, especially for situations in which notifying the user him- or herself could help to control the issue. Thus, it is essential to know the differences among individuals, since a stressful situation may be severe for one person, but controllable (i.e., capable of being resolved through a self-notification, without the need for external help) for another. For example, if there is a trend over time in a user and the system recognizes that stress is building up, it can notify the user to pay more attention to his or her environment.

A one-click notification can be considered the quickest step to take. In such a notification, a single click of any button can be used to inform an immediate contact about a challenging situation. Users should be able to predefine emergency notifications for their PSNs, as well as possibly also add custom messages for other situations. Sensor-initiated notifications are mainly designed to notify either users themselves or trusted contacts about a user's condition. Further, notifications can also be classified as 'reactive' and 'proactive.' Consider a situation in which a pupil at school invites friends to join him during a lunch break to avoid meeting bullies. This is a case in which the pupil is not currently experiencing a challenging situation, but foresees one, and proactive measures are required. In contrast, a reactive notification may occur while the user is experiencing the challenging situation. In this model, there are certain issues to address, such as how to deal with false alarms.

Challenging Situation. It represents the narrative of how an actual situation is experienced by a user. The key question to consider: Who decides what constitutes a challenging situation? Let us take the simple perspective first: In most cases, the user is the one who foresees or realizes a situation to be problematic and/or a challenge. However, a challenging situation could also be defined purely based upon sensor measurements and context. An abnormal heartbeat or an increase in stress can trigger the realization of a challenging situation, irrespective of whether a self-notification is triggered as a result or whether the PSN is notified. In any case, the user would realize the challenge and either address it on his or her own or further initiate a notification to a PSN contact. The determination of a challenging situation highly uses the context and sensor data for support.

Context and Sensor Data. The purpose of context and sensor data mainly revolves around monitoring the user and his or her environment. The term "context" has specifically been used to prevent us from being limited to sensor measurements; as we must also include how to make sense of these measurements. For example, a heartrate sensor can measure a heart's beats per minute (bpm); however, the bpm may vary according to the physical needs of the individual. A heart rate measurement of 90 bpm is considered to be sensor measurement; however, in the case of an individual whose average heart rate is 76 bpm, 90 bpm indicates cause for alarm. Further still, if that individual goes for a run, a heart rate of 90 bpm should not evoke alarm because heart rates increase during physical activity. Therefore, it is necessary to know the context in which a sensor measurement will be used.

A person can carry a variety of sensors, ranging from multiple body sensors to sensors measuring externals factors, such as wind speed and geographic location [33]. There may be a few situations in which sensor data are not be required and only user input can form the basis for a challenging situation; however, given the ability of modern sensors to measure different aspects of users and their environment, ubiquitous use of sensor input is imminent. For example, a system notification to a user regarding an abnormal heartbeat would require the sensor to take an actual reading of the heartbeat, as well as collect other helpful sensory data, such as the temperature of the body or the air.

Communication Channel. The communication channel exists on a different level of conceptualization. Communication can take place in many different ways, and not all networked people communicate in the same way. Thus, this entity should support a variety of communication mechanisms, such as voice, text, video, etc., which should be chosen based on the situation and the severity of a notification. Obviously, users should be able to filter and interpret notifications according to their needs. One of the communication channels should be a portal through which friends and relatives should be able to see the "status" (i.e., the timeline or a snapshot) of what a person has been doing. An important aspect to consider in designing communication channels is power consumption monitoring, since it is important to avoid situations in which a person is "missing" (e.g., due to not charging the sensor device). Apart from the importance of how a notification is delivered through various communication channels, it is also essential to consider how notifications are presented to the user. For example, the user interface might vary based on the complexity of the contextual data. In sum, the communication channel ensures the transmission of notifications from and to members of PSNs. Senders can be both users and sensors, while receivers can be members of PSNs and users themselves (in the case of self-notifications).

3.2   Concept Validation

Low-Fidelity Prototype. For the purpose of concept validation and to understand the interaction with the user, a low-fidelity prototype was created as paper mockups. The mockups were developed using a typical iPhone 4 s user interface. The theme of the mockups was chosen to be the safety of children. The complete interaction flow of the scenario was created on paper in terms of user interfaces. The aim was to gain a quick overview of the validity of the concept and to collect usability feedback on a possible prototype design in terms of determining the level of detail.

Paper mockups, such as those presented in Fig. 1, were used. In designing the paper mockups, emphasis was given to replicating the sub-concepts discussed and presented earlier. Some of the mockups were elaborated as follows.

Fig. 1. Low-fidelity prototype (paper).

The left section of Fig. 2 shows an example in which a user is manually creating a PSN. The user has made two groups—one for parents and the other for friends—and has the option to add more. The right section of Fig. 2 visualizes the one-click notification as a single click of the 'Help' button that can be used to notify an immediate contact with the message, 'Please help!' The paper mockup is designed based on the example of a child becoming lost; however, it takes a different approach by depicting a dynamic PSN based on geographic location. The notification is sent, based on priority level, to those people who are within a 1 km radius of the child.

The Fig. 3 represents a user-initiated notification illustrating a challenging situation of a child becoming separated from his family and getting lost. The mother is notified of the situation through a message that includes the current location of the child and a possible route to reach him using a map.

For message recipients, the geographical location, along with additional sensor data, such as the child's stress level or heartbeat, can elaborate the magnitude of the challenge. The Fig. 4 represents a sensor-initiated notification where the sensor measuring the geographic location triggers a notification to the mother that the child has left school and should reach home by certain time. In this particular case, the child plays no part in

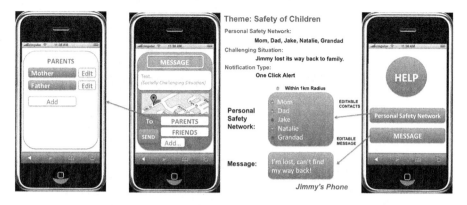

Fig. 2. Personal safety network (left) and one-click notification (right).

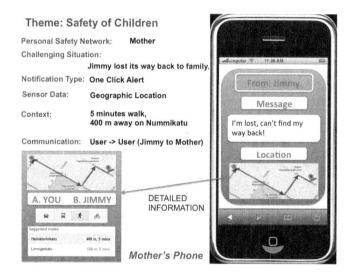

Fig. 3. User-initiated notification.

the form of an input, and the example portrays a proactive notification step in ensuring the safety of children.

User Experiment and Results. The low-fidelity paper prototype was used in a user experiment involving five participants from the field of IT and were not related to this research in any way. In addition, we used a storyboard technique (depicted in Fig. 5) to collaboratively draw user interfaces with the participants to facilitate a better understanding of the requirements. The focus of the experiment was on the participants as the users of the mockups, their context of use, and the flow of events for the chosen scenario. The findings from the experiment ensured the validity of the concept and suggested refinements for the paper mockups.

Fig. 4. Sensor-initiated notification.

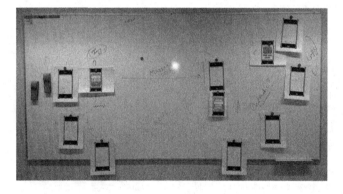

Fig. 5. The storyboard technique.

The feedback was translated to the following guidelines to aid in the design of a high-fidelity prototype:

Instant Communication. In certain challenging situations, the reaction time available to a user can be very short; therefore, a system should have quick options, such as one-click notifications or instant status snapshot. Communications initiated based on sounds or vibrating alerts could also be helpful in difficult challenging situations, during which the user may not be able to concentrate on the user interface. It would be necessary for the system to be able to provide phone-based directions for both the user and the trusted contact while they are in communication, which should focus on allowing the parties to meet in the quickest and safest way.

Interactive Feedback. Short status updates to both the user and the PSN are of significant importance. The provision of automatic messages, status updates, pop-up alerts and real-time notifications may help the user in the challenging situation, while also updating the PSN contacts. Such pop-ups would ideally provide timely updates about changes in certain conditions (e.g., how far away the user is or how many minutes are required for a PSN contact to reach the user's location). At the same time, it is important to ensure that the communication channel is always on. For example, when the battery of a cellphone reaches a predefined level, then a specific notification should be generated and sent to both the user and his or her immediate contacts (particularly for young children).

Magnitude of Challenge. Since the theme of the scenario revolves around ensuring safety against any kind of physical danger or challenging situation, the provision of sufficient information is always the key. To understand the severity or the magnitude of a challenging situation, context is important. To better understand this context, it is critical for the system to employ various content techniques, such as live video feeds and/or maximum sensory information.

User's Control. Most of the primary users in the concerned scenario will be children or young adults; therefore, the system behavior should be clear and simple. On the other hand, though children should have maximum control of the system in order to contact a trusted person easily, though certain aspects of the application should be controlled by the PSN contacts. For example, a parent should be able to monitor a child's geographical location, even without the child initiating a call for help. Naturally, in the case of young adults, parents should attempt to agree with their children on the level of access.

Privacy and Trust. These two terms go hand in hand, such that the utilization of the user's context and personal information requires strict privacy rules. With young children, this may not be a significant constraint; however, with young adults, access may require some approval from the user, since user information should be shared only with people that the user trusts. The same is true for the creation of a PSN, if the target audience is young adults.

These guidelines provide interesting insights; however, the authors do understand that sensors can be noisy, and machine-learning algorithms are not always accurate. The proposed prototype might feel too technology-centric and the expectation of parents to submit their children to extensive physiological monitoring might be unsuccessful. Further, the use of the new system might constitute a new source of stress in itself as pointed out by Riedl [51]. Therefore, many current assumptions might not hold true in challenging situations in the real world. Thus, it is necessary to further the prototype design by creating a high-fidelity version, which should be evaluated to gain educational insights and address accountability.

4   State of the Art for Supporting Socially Challenging Situations

There are numerous emerging solutions, both commercial and in research, that make use of sensors and the social web to resolve two main issues [4]. First, the publishing of user data increases real-time awareness of different users to others, as well as about the global behavior of users in the social web. Second, these data facilitate the measuring and analyzing of current trends and environments where users are located. Jabeur et al. [28] provides an excellent classification of online social applications intended for mobile users into location-aware, proximity-aware, and server-based groups, while diving into architecture, business domain, user groups, and other issues.

One of the first solutions, the CenceMe application [36], uses off-the-shelf components to infer the presence of users, recognize their activity, and then publish this information on popular social networks. Curmi et al. [19] studied how publishing biometric data (heart rates) in social networks affects a user's wellbeing and physiological performance in a project called HeartLink. Pavel et al. [44] propose an integrated lifestyle management system, which records various social web activities and physical sensor data to "support people in better understanding of what happened and why it happened." The system focuses on understanding the influence of users' daily activities on their health by mapping these sensor data with the users' daily events/activities. Social Telescope [53] combines users' location data with user interaction data (extracted from social networks) in order to create a better location-based search engine. Another system, developed in [21], fuses social networking with real-world sensing by combining location tracking, conversation monitoring and interactions with physical objects into a sensor-driven social sharing application for the working environment of a research institution.

To gain a better understanding of the state-of-the-art, it is imperative to analyze the technologies that have already penetrated the society and detect challenging situations by analyzing, not only biological data, but also contextual data. Therefore, the authors conducted two studies: The first explores the technologies for stress measurement, and the second limits its focus to mobile technologies targeting safety of children.

4.1   Study 1: Technologies Empowering Society for Stress Measurement

It is understood that a user's stress level is a core indicator of the existence of a challenging situation. Therefore, various solutions that measure (either directly or indirectly) users' stress levels were explored, as were technologies that specify the context for a situation. Table 1 presents a list of the technologies analyzed by the authors, and the following section discusses the results of this study. The Scopus Database and Google Scholar were used as the primary search tools during the preparation of this study. To collect the requisite data, the authors used the keywords "sensors," "sensing technologies," and "stress" and then manually browsed through the results.

Table 1. Technologies empowering society for stress measurement and personal fitness.

Measuring stress and wellbeing through biological data	
AutoSense [7]	Cardio-respiratory sensor [48]
DroidJacket [15]	Electronic stress assistant [61]
Stress check app[a] [60]	Stress sensing device [6]
Q Sensor[a] [2]	Wearable sensor system [9]
StressWatch prototype [57]	
Measuring stress and wellbeing through contextual data to identify a situation	
Remote sensing app[a] [3]	MSF framework [12]
Google glass [24, 25]	UbiFit garden [18]
UbiqLog [49]	Aware framework [8]

[a]*indicates commercial availability*

Wearable computing facilitates the measurement of human stress levels by processing information acquired by biological or physiological sensors, which usually include: ECGs (electrocardiograms), GSR (galvanic skin responses), EMG (electro-myograms), RESP (respiration), and cortisol hormone levels in saliva. Cortisol is the hormone released by the body during a stressed or agitated state, and it has been used frequently used as a biomarker of psychological stress [27]. A recent state-of-the-art survey on wearable computing and artificial intelligence for medicine, which was published in [13], presents a categorization and an overview of various projects, devices, and technologies for monitoring and measuring the different medical characteristics of humans. René Riedl along with others [50–52] has performed an extensive research on neuro information systems especially focusing on the concept of technostress. Though the use and ubiquity of technology has greatly benefited human race, it can also be a source of stress. The importance of using psychometric methods along with the phys-iological data to understand technostress from a biological perspective has also been echoed in [58].

Lane et al. [32] published an excellent survey on how mobile phones can be used to collect measurements (i.e., context information) for different purposes. The authors discussed the technical abilities of mobile phones, analyzed application domains (e.g. wellbeing, environmental monitoring, social networking, transportation, etc.), and clas-sified existing solutions according to their sensing scale (i.e., individual, group, community) and sensing paradigm. Lifelogging is an emerging concept involving the continuous recording of users' physiological data. For this matter, multiple new smart-phone apps are used by lifeloggers to assist in their efforts of tracking for example, their movements throughout the day. Several commercial applications, devices, and personal fitness solutions are characterized by their exclusive focus on fitness, sports activities, and wellbeing. Athletes are always looking for new information systems that can not only record and analyze data, but can also facilitate the detection of over-training symptoms and the identification of injury risks, among other things [59]. Popular magazines focus on the reporting precision of measurement and mobile applications, such as Endomondo [22], and web communities developed by manufacturers of personal fitness tracking devices (e.g., Polar Personal Trainer [46], Nike+ [41]), which can be considered as social networks for sport enthusiasts.

4.2   Study 2: Geofencing and Child Safety

The second study focused on solutions for children based on geo-fencing and child safety. The Scopus Database and Google Scholar were used as the primary search tools for this study. The authors used the keywords "mobile child protection," "child protection application," "mobile child safety," "geo fence application,"and "child tracking application" and then manually browsed for relevant material.

A geofence is a virtual perimeter for a real-world geographic area, and such systems allow users to draw zones around places of interest based on either dynamic or predefined sets. Geofence systems utilize a device with a location-based service (LBS), which generates a notification when the device enters or exits a geofence through continuous monitoring. According to Kupper et al. [31], GPS is currently the only method that delivers the accuracy required for geofencing solutions. Geofencing is useful for parental control of children and is extensively used for asset tracking in applications for security and logistics; however, its potential use for personal safety (e.g., caretaking services for children, the elderly, and domestic pets) is substantial. For example, Saranya and Selvakumar [53] suggested a hybrid software-hardware solution for tracking the movements of children outdoors and detecting abnormal behavior, which would be reported to the children's parents (e.g., such a system may detect a child crying using voice recognition). Geofencing can also take the form of a proximity detection service, such as MoBiLoCo [37], which offers users the ability to locate their friends and family members using their phones. Two other commercial applications, Cloak [14] and GottaSplit [26], however, serve an opposite purpose: that is, avoiding others. These applications scan various LBS applications to identify the locations of people a user wants to avoid. Geofencing is a promising tool in relation to the physical safety of children as it continuously monitors a person's location.

The authors define a child safety solution as a set of functionalities designed to ensure family stability and to protect children and young teens from physically dangerous situations. Czeskis et al. [20] developed new methods, approaches, and technical solutions related to child safety while analyzing how safety goals come into conflict with such human values as perceptions of safety, trust, human development, and the privileged relationships between parents and children. Another application, MyMobileWitness [39], utilizes suspicious activity reporting (SAR) technology. The SAR reports act as a safety net between children and security authorities, who investigate suspicious activities reported. Further, My Location Monitor (MyLO) is a suite supporting automated threat recognition and child safety [17]. MyLO is a combination of a geofence and a child safety solution, which comprises a mobile application and web-based software. The application provides a panic alarm, real-time active GPS monitoring (tracking) of family members, and tools for assisting persons in challenging situations. The FreeFamilyWatch application [40] monitors the environment and notifies family members in real-time of weather, allergy warnings, or a family member going into an unsafe neighborhood. Another recent application Alert-360 [63] enables users to crowd-source their location to other nearby Alert-360 users and alert family members in case of emergency.

5   Limitations and Ethical Concerns

Integrating sensors and the social web is currently an active research topic, with studies exploring various effects related to user privacy, usability, user acceptance issues, etc. On the other hand, effects related to the technical side—for example, system architectures, data fusion, energy efficiency issues, etc.—are also present. Jedrzejczyk et al. [29] proposed the real-time feedback mechanism as a means for visibility, awareness, and accountability in location-sharing applications. Bristow [11] discussed issues regarding the balance between safety and parental control, as well as the use of personal location services for commercial use.

The major challenges for geofencing services are related to the protection of privacy and the preservation of battery life on smartphone-based applications. According to a survey by the Pew Internet Research Center, poor privacy was the major reason for 11- to 17-year-old teens deciding to switch off all location-tracking services on their devices [62]. Czeskis et al. [20] detailed that most high-level ethical challenges faced by child protection applications are related to location sharing. Secondly, technical challenges involved in energy-preserving solutions were related to battery usage, the security of private data, and the dissemination of these data in case of emergency. Finally, an apparent challenge that is faced by the research community is the accuracy of detecting a user's environment and its related context.

6   Conclusion and Future Work

According to UNICEF, the most promising mobile application areas for child protection are related to data collection, awareness raising and violence reporting, family tracing and reunification, and birth registration [34]. Technologies that focus on detecting users' wellbeing rely on either explicit or implicit sensing methods (or both). Explicit methods assume that the information about a user's wellbeing can be read directly from the user's body using attached sensors. Implicit methods detect a user's wellbeing by reasoning and analyzing the situation and the environment where the user is located (i.e., the user's context) [4].

This research provides key insights into the fertile space of social and ubiquitous computing. The authors found the multi-disciplinary domain to be highly exciting; however, collaboration with subject-matter experts is critical to shape the design of such systems and evaluate them. Further, an evaluation of a high-fidelity prototype based on the paper mockups discussed earlier might reveal much more realistic insights. Although technologies are improving quickly, the social effect of technologies needs to be studied in detail. There are, of course, prominent issues, such as privacy, trust, security, and user experience, which must still be addressed. On the other hand, exploiting user information is critical to success in encouraging proactivity, self-tuning, and behavioral change. Systems for socially challenging situations can be advanced by 1) combining both implicit and explicit sensor methods; 2) more deeply integrating the social web and sensors, observing behavior through sensors, and sharing to the social web; and 3) using persuasive technology in designing applications for long-term effects [42].

Acknowledgements. This work was carried out as part of the SEWEB research project on Sensors and the Social Web (40027/13, 40028/13). It was funded by TEKES, the Finnish Funding Agency for Technology and Innovation. The research was part of the OASIS research group of the Martti Ahtisaari Institute, University of Oulu.

References

1. Abbas, R., Michael, K., Michael, M.G., Aloudat, A.: Emerging forms of covert surveillance using GPS enabled devices. JCIT **13**(2), 19–33 (2011)
2. Affectiva Q-Sensor. http://www.affdex.com
3. AIRS-Record your life app. http://play.google.com
4. Aggarwal, C., Abdelzaher, T.: Integrating sensors and social networks. In: Aggarwal, C.C. (ed.) Social Network Data Analytics, pp. 379–412. Springer, Heidelberg (2011)
5. Archer, J., Cote, S.: Sex differences in aggressive behavior. In: Tremblay, R.E., Hartup, W.W., Archer, J. (eds.) Developmental Origins of Agg, pp. 425–443. Guilford, New York (2005)
6. Arizona State University. http://azte.technologypublisher.com/technology/9999
7. AutoSense Project. https://sites.google.com/site/autosenseproject/
8. AWARE. Android Mobile Context Instr. Framework. http://www.awareframework.com
9. Bakker, J., Pechenizkiy, M., Sidorova, N.: What's your current stress level? detection of stress patterns from GSR sensor data. In: 11th ICDMW (2001)
10. Berry, D.M.: Critical Theory and the Digital. Bloomsbury Publishing, New York (2014)
11. Bristow, J.: Mobile Phones and Child Protection: How Far Should We Go? Report Spiked! Online (2006)
12. Cardone, G., Cirri, A., Corradi, A., Foschini, L., Maio, D.: MSF: an efficient mobile phone sensing framework, IJDSN (2013)
13. Chan, M., Estève, D., Fourniols, J.Y., Escriba, C., Campo, E.: Smart wearable systems: current status and future challenges. AI Med. **56**(3), 137–156 (2012)
14. Cloak – Social Sense app. http://itunes.apple.com
15. Colunas, M.F.M., Fernandes, J.M.A., Oliveira, I.C., Cunha, J.P.S.: Droid jacket: using an android based smartphone for team monitoring. In: IWCMC (2011)
16. Conner, M.: Sensors empower "the Internet of things", Technical Editor EDN Networks, 27 May 2010
17. Conover, J.: MYLO: Active Threat Recognition System. HoopBoom Inc., Asbury city (2012). http://www.hoopboom.com
18. Consolvo, S., McDonald, D.W., Toscos, T., Chen, M.Y., Froehlich, J., Harrison, B., Klasnja, P., LaMarca, A., LeGrand, L., Libby, R., Smith, I., Landay, J.A.: Activity sensing in the wild: a field trial of ubifit garden. In: CHI. ACM (2008)
19. Curmi, F., Ferrario, M.A., Southern, J., Whittle, J.: HeartLink: open broadcast of live biometric data to social networks. In: CHI. ACM (2013)

20. Czeskis, A., Dermendjieva, I., Yapit, H., Borning, A., Friedman, B., Gill, B., Kohno, T.: Parenting from the pocket: value tensions and technical directions for secure and private parent teen mobile safety. In: 6th SOUPS (2010)
21. Efstratiou, C., Leontiadis, I., Picone, M., Rachuri, K.K., Mascolo, C., Crowcroft, J.: Sense and Sensibility in a pervasive world. In: 10th ICPC, pp. 406–424 (2012)
22. Endomondo. http://www.endomondo.com/
23. Fairgrieve, S., Falke, S.: Sensor web standards and the Internet of things. COM.Geo. ACM (2011)
24. Google Glass. http://www.google.com/glass/start/
25. Google, Project Glass – One day. http://www.youtube.com/watch?v=9c6W4CCU9M4
26. GottaSplit Application. http://gottasplit.com
27. Hellhammer, D., Wust, S., Kudielka, B.: Salivary cortisol as a biomarker in stress research. Psychoneuroendocrinology **34**(2), 163–171 (2009)
28. Mobile social networking applications: Jabeur, N., Zeadally, S., B. Sayed, B. Comm. ACM **56**, 71–79 (2013)
29. Jedrzejczyk, L., Price, B. A, Bandara, A.K., Nuseibeh, B.: On The impact of realtime feedback on users' behaviour. In: Mobile Location Sharing Applications. SOUPS (2010)
30. Kraft, P., Drozd, F., Olsen, E.: ePsychology: designing theory-based health promotion interventions. Comm. AIS **24**, 24 (2009)
31. Küpper, A., Bareth, U., Freese, B.: Geofencing and Background tracking – the next features in LBSs. In: INFORMATIK (2011)
32. Lane, N. D., Miluzzo, E., Lu, H., Peebles, D., Choudhury, T., Campbell, A. T.: A survey of mobile phone sensing. Comm Mag 48, 9 (Sep), 140–150 (2010)
33. Lo, B., Thiemjarus, S., King, R., Yang, G.Z.: Body sensor network - a wireless sensor platform for pervasive healthcare monitoring. In: 3rd IICPC (2005)
34. Mattila, M.: Mobile technologies for child protection: a briefing note. In: UNICEF WCARO (2011)
35. Mian, S.Q., Teixeira, J., Koskivaara, E.: Open-source software implications in the competitive mobile platforms market. In: Skersys, T., Butleris, R., Nemuraite, L., Suomi, R. (eds.) Building the e-World Ecosystem. IFIP AICT, vol. 353, pp. 110–128. Springer, Heidelberg (2011)
36. Miluzzo, E., Lane, N.D., Fodor, K., Peterson, R., Lu, H., Musolesi, M., Eisenman, S.B., Zheng, X., Campbell, A.T.: Sensing Meets Mobile Social Networks: The Design, Implementation and Evaluation of the CenceMe application, SenSys.ACM (2008)
37. Mobiloco Application. http://www.mobiloco.de
38. Morozov E.: To save everything, click here: technology, solutionism, and the urge to fix problems that don't exist. Penguin, UK (2013)
39. My Mobile Witness. http://mymobilewitness.com
40. NaVee, FreeFamilyWatch. http://pdroms.de/android/freefamilywatch-android-application
41. Nike Plus. http://www.nike.com/us/en_us/c/nikeplusfuelband
42. Oinas-Kukkonen, H.: A foundation for the study of behavior change support systems. Pers. Ubiquit. Comput. **17**(6), 1223–1235 (2013)
43. Oinas-Kukkonen, H., Oinas-Kukkonen, H.: Humanizing the Web, Change and Social Innovation. Palgrave Macmillan, Basingstoke (2013)
44. Pavel, D., Callaghan, V., Dey, A.K.: Supporting wellbeing through improving interactions and understanding in self-monitoring systems. In: AI and SE, vol. 11, pp. 408–433 (2012)
45. Picard, R.: Affective Computing. MIT Press, Cambridge (1997)
46. Polar Personal Trainer. http://www.polarpersonaltrainer.com

47. Project Salus: Research shows how computers can help combat bullying in schools. University of Kent (2012)

48. PSI Lab, Stress Measurement. http://psi.cse.tamu.edu/portfolio_item/stress-measurement/

49. Rawassizadeh, R., Tomitsch, M., Wac, K., Tjoa, A.M.: UbiqLog: a generic mobile phonebased lifelog framework. Per. Ubi. Comp. 17(4), 621–637 (2013)

50. Riedl, R., Kindermann, H., Auinger, A., Javor, A.: Technostress from a neurobiological perspective - system breakdown increases the stress hormone cortisol in computer users. BISE 4(2), 61–69 (2012)

51. Riedl, R.: On the biology of technostress: literature review and research agenda. SIGMIS Database 44(1), 18–55 (2013)

52. Riedl, R., Davis, F.D., Hevner, A.R.: Towards a NeuroIS research methodology: intensifying the discussion on methods, tools, and measurement. JAIS 15(10), 4 (2014)

53. Saranya, J., Selvakumar, J.: Implementation of children tracking system on android mobile terminals. In: ICCSP, pp. 961–965 (2013)

54. Sensor Networks. http://www.citysense.com

55. Sensors. http://what-is-a-sensor.com/

56. Shankar, P., Huang, Y.W., Castro, P., Nath, B., Iftode, L.: Crowds replace experts: building better LBS using mobile social network interactions, Perv. Comp, 20–29 (2012)

57. Stress Watch. http://www.stresswatch.com

58. Tams, S., Hill, K., Ortiz de Guinea, A., Thatcher, J., Grover, V.: NeuroIS—alternative or complement to existing methods? Illustrating the holistic effects of neuroscience and self-reported data in the context of technostress research. JAIS 15(10), 1 (2014)

59. Teixeira, J., Mian S.Q.: Open-source mobile software for sports: a new disruptive phenomenon in an Era of innovative devices. In: IADIS (2011)

60. The Stress Check. http://www.azumio.com

61. Wearable Comp. http://www.ethlife.ethz.ch/archive_articles/100308_stress_assistent_per/

62. Zickuhr, K. Survey of LBS. http://pewinternet.org/Reports/2013/Location.asp

63. 360-Alert, Life Safety Technology. http://www.alert360.com

Co-Design for Development: Lessons Learnt from an Information Systems Project in Underserved Communities

R. De la Harpe[1(✉)], M. Korpela[1,2], and I. Van Zyl[1]

[1] Faculty Informatics and Design, Cape Peninsula University of Technology,
Cape Town, South Africa
delaharper@cput.ac.za
[2] Computing, University of Eastern Finland, Kuopio, Finland

Abstract. This paper is a reflection on the lessons learnt during an information systems development for development (ISD4D) project in underserved community contexts. The level of participation of health intermediaries and community members is considered for the design of an mHealth application to facilitate access to relevant health information. The paper highlights two key aspects to be incorporated in the co-design of IS interventions, namely the importance of contextual factors and the dynamic nature of intermediaries' work and life practices. Lessons learnt are organised according to the following components of an IS for societal development: people, information, technology, practice and purpose, context, and ethics. The key lesson derived is that IS design and development has to consider *practices for a purpose*. These are influenced by the context of development, the manner in which a community functions, the capabilities of community members, their literacy levels and cultural practices.

Keywords: Co-design · User participation · IS for development · Design for development · Underserved communities · Participatory action research

1 Introduction

The theme of the 6th Scandinavian Conference on Information Systems is 'System design for, with and by users'. This paper addresses the theme from the viewpoint of communities in resource-restricted contexts in Southern Africa. How can such information systems be designed that are explicitly intended to benefit such communities? How can the communities become active co-designers?

Introducing ICT solutions in an underserved community context is adding to an already complex environment. Typically, underserved communities are affected by complex socio-economic factors that influence the characteristics of the design and development process as well as the final information system (IS). The aim of this paper is to consider the aspects relevant to the design and development of an IS in underserved community contexts. We specifically focus on the people, information, technology, practices and context(s) that could be part of the proposed IS. In addition, we examine

© Springer International Publishing Switzerland 2015
H. Oinas-Kukkonen et al. (Eds.): SCIS 2015, LNBIP 223, pp. 61–74, 2015.
DOI: 10.1007/978-3-319-21783-3_5

the *level of participation* of the social actors (people) in the design and development process. In the IS field, there is still a paucity of literature on the real-life challenges of doing participatory design in underserved communities, exploring which methods and tools are suitable to that end [1]. The research question that we consider for this paper is:

What are the factors that influence the level of participation during the design and development of an IS in an underserved community?

The paper is organised as follows: we firstly provide a brief literature review, followed by a background of the INDEHELA-ISD4D project. We then reflect on our experiences during the empirical part of the project to propose the considerations for designing and developing an IS with the active involvement of all the social actors in an underserved community.

The context relevant to this paper is the consideration of an IS to facilitate better health and wellbeing services in underserved communities. mHealth is found to be suitable for information recording, processing and reporting by stakeholders operating in these underserved contexts. The role of intermediaries in providing health and wellbeing services at the point of care and extending these services to the homes of patients, is recognised as an important component of community services. Intermediaries and community members do not have easy access to the vast amount of health and wellbeing information [2–6]. It was also found that these intermediaries can work better if appropriate technologies are designed with their involvement [2–5]. The intermediaries that we involved in our project are the health and wellbeing service providers located in a peri-urban and semi-agricultural community in the Western Cape, including local non-government organisations, nurses, caregivers and health promoters.

2   Information Systems and Societal Development

In this section, we first discuss the components of 'real-life information systems', followed by a discussion specific to the creation and use of IS in an underserved community. The INDEHELA-ISD4D project, from which we draw our lessons, is then described.

2.1   Information System Design

Within an information systems approach, an information system is not always a systemic entity but rather composed of "bits and pieces" of processes and technology incorporated in a systemic work activity [7]. We also agree with Alter [8] that the notion of the 'artefact' may not best describe the different components of the IS as proposed by Lee et al., for example [9]. Instead of trying to define the different components of our IS, we would rather regard information systems as consisting of **people**, **information** and **technology** (both electronic and non-electronic) that are linked together by a **practice** directed towards a **purpose**. This holistic approach to IS recognises both static and dynamic components that are "always embedded in some time, place, discourse and community emerging from ongoing social and economic practices" [8, 10]. In our study, the context of the underserved community requires us to consider the constraints typically associated with such an environment to understand the time, place and discourses that will influence the proposed IS.

Although our aim is to consider an information system, we also recognise that a new information technology (IT) artefact will need to be designed and developed to eventually become part of the proposed IS. In our case, this artefact was envisioned as a mobile application to enable access to health information and educational services. In this case, it may be useful to conceptualise the IT artefact in terms of Design Science Research (DSR). Design science research has recently been considered as a suitable approach to design IT artefacts while considering the prescriptive knowledge created during the design process and the characteristics of the design outcome as an artefact, method, instantiation or model [11–13]. DSR has been considered as an alternative to behavioural studies based on Simon's well-known concept of the artificial world [14]. Whereas a behavioural approach considers human behaviour in interaction with artefacts, design science is concerned with the creation of the artefact for a specific purpose that has a utility value. The IT artefact, when implemented, becomes part of the social world, and human behaviour in interaction with it can then be studied. DSR provides the methodology to consider the aspects relevant to the design and development *process* and the *behaviour* of the designer/developer as they interact with the users of the proposed IT artefact as well as with the design and development tools, methods and constructs. This approach provides a valuable contribution to IS research considering the IT artefact [11–13, 15, 16].

The IT artefact, although it can have different components, is still a "thing" and by focusing only on that does not provide for the other components of an information system.

2.2 IS for Human and Societal Development

The introduction of information systems in underserved communities needs to be carefully considered to establish whether it is desirable and feasible for the potential beneficiaries [17–19]. Underserved communities refer to those groups on the peripheries of society – that are marginalised, and without opportunities or capabilities to empower themselves or improve their position. According to Lorini et al. [20], there is a "worrisome trend of exclusion" in the IS for human and societal development literature. The authors, supported by Diaz Andrade and Urquhart [21], go on to state that grassroots beneficiaries of IS interventions/solutions are often not formally involved in the development process, be it in conceptualisation or implementation. In the Southern African context, particularly, information and digital exclusion is recognised as a significant obstacle in addressing issues of social, economic and cultural equality [20].

When introducing information systems in complex environments, it is important to consider who will benefit and who loses out – an IS solution should not lead to exclusion of some. Information systems do have the potential to stimulate economic growth and ultimately contribute to human development. The practice and notion of human development is here highly complex; we therefore regard it as a holistic and dialogical enterprise in which participants (including researchers, designers and developers) *nego-tiate* the intended outcomes to avoid failure.

Indeed, the field of information and communication technology for development (ICT4D) has a long history of project failure. Da Silva and Fernandez [22] argue that to achieve sustainability, projects should be regarded as nuanced social-technical processes that intend to maximise both technological and social outcomes. To achieve this, they suggest that sustainable IS use must be a priority throughout the IS development life cycle.

In participatory design, it is assumed that every participant is an expert in their work and life practices, and that design ideas are jointly created by all so that persons who are affected by a decision or event should have an opportunity to influence it. Hussain et al. [1] identify the barriers to the level of participation in design inter-ventions as human, social, cultural and religious, financial, and organisational. In overcoming these barriers, participatory design should not only seek different levels of participation, but also foster capacity development for future projects, i.e. to empower local community members [1, 23].

3   Methodology

This paper is a meta-level reflection on the experiences of implementing an information systems development project in Southern African communities (see Sect. 3.1). In what follows, we will reflect on the design and development activity of the project, as well as on respective design methods, probes and outcomes. From this reflection, we derive several 'lessons learnt'. We establish some considerations based on these lessons for designing an IS in underserved communities with the active participation of community members and service providers.

3.1   INDEHELA-ISD4D: A Holistic Information Systems Development Approach for Community Development

INDEHELA (Informatics Development for Health in Africa) is a long-term initiative to strengthen the capacity of participating African higher education institutions to contribute to socio-economic and human development in their countries, particularly in the scientific field of Health Informatics and the practice of e-health. The network involves universities from Finland, Mozambique, Nigeria and South Africa. Previous research projects within the initiative have focused on the methods [24] and contextual issues [25] of information systems development.

The current flagship project of INDEHELA is named ISD4D (2011–2015), and aims at creating a holistic information systems development approach that is geared towards community development in disadvantaged contexts, unlike mainstream textbook meth-odologies and approaches that usually focus on business development in well-to-do contexts. The project draws from previous experience in the INDEHELA initiative and methodological literature from other sources. Methods consolidated from these sources are experimented with in real-life information systems analysis and design settings in South Africa and Mozambique, mostly in the area of maternal and home care services for local communities. The results are reported in two forms – firstly, academic papers, and secondly, in practicable guidelines intended for use by system analyst-designers, development project managers and community leaders as well as in university education.

The ISD4D project adopts a collaborative, participatory action approach to design an IS that will result in the improvement of the current health landscape in Southern African communities. Through this activity, the project aims to understand the contexts, needs and work practices of social actors in community health settings. Stakeholders include community members, healthcare professionals and -workers, researchers, designers and developers. Since the inception of ISD4D, the majority of these stakeholders actively participated in the design of the IS, in the form of co-design sessions, facilitated by various researchers from the project.

4   Lessons Learnt from the ISD4D Project

In this section, we reflect on the lessons learnt so far based on our experiences and observations. We first examine the lessons according to our view of information systems as consisting of people, information and technology that are linked together by a practice directed towards a purpose. Subsequently, we identify some crosscutting issues.

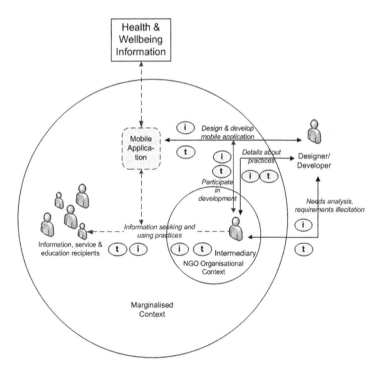

Fig. 1. Design and development of a mobile application to enable access to relevant health and wellbeing information with the active participation of intermediaries in the context of an underserved community.

We propose a diagram (Fig. 1) to depict the different components of a proposed mobile health application in the ISD4D project to enable access to health and wellbeing information. Three areas of participation are depicted; in each case, active participation is important. The t (technology) and i (information) are depicted as those components of the IS where they can influence the level of participation. The selection of these components are important to ensure that the proposed IS is designed and developed *with* the participation of the intermediaries on behalf of the community members instead of developing an IS *for* or *by* them.

4.1 People

The parties and people involved in providing healthcare services in underserved communities are mostly non-governmental organisations (NGOs) and *intermediaries*: lay workers that "translate and adapt health-related information for local use, thus acting as conduits or dependable information sources" [3]. There are a limited number of health professionals in the region, and NGOs mostly have to rely on these lay workers with only basic training [6]. The NGOs are also in most cases responsible for the training of intermediaries.

We found that intermediaries are much more than local service providers. Since they are mostly from the communities in which they provide services, they are regarded as important spokespersons and gatekeepers. Community members rely on them as information sources. We found that the level of participation of community members is particularly influenced by the involvement of intermediaries. Community members will only participate in co-design sessions if approached by the intermediary and "instructed" to participate.

Many communities suffer from research exhaustion and are sceptical of 'promises' since their expectations are often not met. It is therefore important to form a trustworthy relationship with community representatives and to continue to actively manage the relationship. In our case, intermediaries already carry a heavy workload (there are often not enough resources) and any research or co-design sessions take them away from providing their healthcare services.

It is also difficult to observe health intermediaries' actual work practices since they work with patients. This raises an ethical question of engaging vulnerable groups in research and design activities. It is therefore important to rely on inputs from the personal reflections of intermediaries, and to use methods that could simulate their existing practices.

Literacy Levels (Including Digital Literacy). Literacy is no longer only about the ability to read or write but other types of literacy may now also need to be considered such as such informational, technological and digital literacy. Researchers, designers or developers also need to consider inter-cultural communication and multi-cultural literacy during the research and/or IS design and development process. When researchers are novices, the research literacy level also needs to be taken into account. One can therefore consider the literacy level of participants to determine how they will interact. It may even be possible to refer to the design or development literacy to reflect the experience of the IS development team. The literacy level will influence the level of participation and therefore also an important consideration.

Health literacy entails the knowledge, motivation and competence of individuals to use relevant information for decision-making to maintain or improve the quality of their lives [26]. Furthermore, in an increasingly hyperconnected world with vast quantities of information, it is essential that individuals know how to seek, find, understand and appraise health and wellbeing information to address a health problem or to improve their wellbeing – this is defined as eHealth literacy [27]. The complexity around eHealth literacy is even more problematic in underserved community contexts where there may already be low literacy levels.

4.2 Technology

In underserved communities, most of the available 'information systems' are still paper-based. In the ISD4D project, the following aspects will inform the proposed IS in addition to current paper-based practices.

(Mobile) Application Design and Development Tools/Methods. The (mobile) technology components in our study include those that are related to the IS itself, as well as those technologies and information used as tools to develop the IS. Examples of mHealth technologies can include mobile phones, patient monitoring devices, personal digital assistants (PDAs), and other wireless devices. From this, a key lesson is derived, namely that the technology components used in IS development itself influences the IS and that in an underserved context, these may be severely constrained. The design concepts and technology components may not form part of the final IS but are important building blocks towards the eventual IS. Examples include the design models and constructs that are used to understand the needs of users and their perceived views of the potential IS. Other examples include the architecture, interfaces, and code.

Technology Infrastructure. In an underserved community context, the availability of technology components is an important consideration since the infrastructures in these contexts are usually severely constrained. Examples of technologies that form part of the community's technology infrastructure are: connectivity (usually limited and has a cost implication); access to electricity; availability of handheld devices (usually previous generation devices).

Technology Components. Examples of the technologies that are part of the final IS may include: code; servers; protocols; modems; devices used to interface the back-end system; database; and user interfaces. All these components must be built and selected according to contextual dynamics and constraints.

4.3 Information and Information Needs

Our results so far indicated that intermediaries have diverse information needs that are: locally defined information about treatments, prevention and health promotion;

information that supports the services provided including information about health facilities, resources, services, partners and training opportunities; and information about guidelines, policies, international best practices and laws [3]. Community members often rely on intermediaries to inform them about aspects relevant to them, e.g., safe sex, nutrition, child care, and the like. As health intermediaries and community members become more information and technologically literate, they may want to access global information as alternative information sources. Information is an important component of intermediaries' work practices since their efforts are both in processing patient information and using health information for health promotion and disease prevention.

4.4   Practice and Purpose

Thus far, we found that the social aspect is a significant consideration that influences the design and development process, involvement of IS stakeholders, and proposed IS. This confirms the view that drivers for mHealth applications are socio-economic and even cultural, rather than purely technical [28, 29]. In underserved contexts, furthermore, people generally have limited to no access to information or information and communication technologies, and they do not have the means and resources to effectively participate as digital citizens [30]. The following themes were derived from our research that we now consider as considerations for the practices of community members as they interact with technology and information for a specific purpose.

People Interacting with Technology and Information. Many studies consider the interaction between humans and computers from a computer science perspective (human computer interaction (HCI)), a design perspective (interaction design), and the like. There are also considerations for interaction in underserved communities, for example, HCI4D [31]. The interactional aspect was identified as an important consideration for the ISD4D project and we refer to this as the interaction *moment*, i.e. the moment that/ when humans interact with technology. We also recognise that this moment is temporary for the duration of the interaction. Outside these moments, the technology artefacts are static and have at most the potential for performitivity [32]. We are interested in the interaction moments since these become the user interfaces of the IS. It is therefore important to design for the interaction moments by considering what happens during these moments. For example, when a caregiver provides a care service to a patient, how will the introduction of a mobile application and/or electronic information influence their care activities? A caregiver cannot simultaneously work with the patient and use a mobile phone. Humans also do not interact with technology and information artefacts in isolation. These interactions are influenced by the context of use and the purpose that necessitates the linking of people, technology and information as part of the interaction moment.

Information Seeking and Using Behaviour. This aspect deals with how information is obtained, recorded, shared, exchanged, used and reported and is influenced by how the information is interpreted, i.e. making sense of how it is used for a specific purpose.

It is therefore much more than the passing of information between the sender and receiver. If we consider the information seeking purposes of individuals and collectives (e.g. communities of practice), as proposed by Diaz Andrade and Urquhart [33], adapted from Dervin [34], we can investigate different purposes for information of both intermediaries and community members. In addition, we consider what information is needed to satisfy its purpose; the sources; media used; and relevancy. We can therefore regard the information seeking practice as the interaction between the human and the information, and possibly mediated by the technology. The information object or architecture can be regarded as static information while the information seeking and using behaviour can be regarded as the practice for a purpose (dynamic). It is important, furthermore, to consider communicative aspects in conjunction with information seeking and using behaviour [35].

4.5   The Context for Development (Static and Dynamic)

The context of underserved communities is complex and has different layers. We found that it is necessary to identify these layers and to consider both static and dynamic contexts [3, 25]. The static aspect of the context could be regarded as the extant technologies and information. The moment these components are used for a purpose then this interaction or relationship between the humans and the technology and/or information is regarded as the dynamic context of the social artefact. An example would be a mobile phone (technology) that is used to access health information (information) where the interaction between these components, namely the information seeking and using behaviour, is regarded as the dynamic aspect of the IS (linking people with the technology and/or information for a purpose). When there is no autonomous interaction between the mobile phone (technology) and health information, these components are static.

The (Indigenous) Rhythms of Communities. Communities tend to exhibit dynamic and fluid rhythms that influence their practices, activities and social interactions. In our project, we found that community members will not participate in any co-design sessions on Fridays when those who are employed are paid their wages. Members often use their wages to buy essential foodstuffs but also generally for alcohol. This means that a Monday is also not a good day for co-design sessions since many people still recover from the weekend binge, and often do not show up for work. Other community-based interventions such as support groups and training sessions need to be considered when planning co-design activities. Any co-design session must therefore be planned carefully in terms of which days are feasible, what time to start the sessions, and how long the sessions should be. Even when a day and time are agreed upon, it is highly possible that community members arrive late or in some cases may not even arrive. Therefore, participation in research or co-design sessions has to be sensitively negotiated and adapted to the local context [22]. It is therefore important to have a good understanding of respective daily practices and to communicate with health intermediaries who could advise researchers, designers, and developers on the means of interaction.

Lost in Translation. In our research context, there are many local languages and researchers, designers, developers and users often have to communicate in their second or third language. This adds a layer of complexity to the co-design activity. We found, for example, that there are not direct translations for some concepts in the indigenous language. These need to be described using other means rather than translated. Furthermore, we observed 'abstracted interactions' between interpreters/translators and community members, in which the interpreter offers a summary of the discussion rather than a direct translation. Interpreters also often interpret what the community members have said instead of translating [23].

We also found that, since the researchers in the ISD4D project are local postgraduate students – often emanating from underserved communities – they are mostly novice researchers. Consequently, the research process is new to them and it is possible that they will miss important aspects due to their inexperience. There is therefore a need for the more experienced researchers of the project, who are often also the supervisors of the students, to be more involved than is normally the case.

The designers and developers of the proposed IS are also mostly inexperienced since they are generally postgraduate students. They may also be unfamiliar with the design and development methods and tools. The activity of translating needs into requirements, designs and code, may therefore be challenging and result in translation errors. This will influence their level of participation. Although this aspect could be seen as specific to the project, we found that community members do not have access to sophisticated design and development resources, methods, tools and technologies. They often have to rely on novices to design and develop an IS.

4.6 Matters of Ethics

Introducing technology to promote desirable social outcomes raises ethical issues [36]. There is limited advice on the quantity, quality and detail of engagement for considering IS interventions in underserved communities and these should be investigated and debated.

The general ethical aspects such as voluntarily participation, informed consent, and permission for data collection may be differently interpreted in different contexts. For example, to collect data in one particular community, a rural village, we needed to obtain permission from the chief. Once permission is granted the chief then calls a meeting and instructs all community members to attend – participation is therefore not voluntarily. This is similar to the recent experiences of Sabiescu et al. [37] in conducting co-design sessions with remote-rural communities in Romania and Mozambique.

In our case, co-design session often took the form of a communal meeting, which is opened by one of the elders. Questionnaires are completed in groups since not all are able to read or write. Anonymity is therefore not possible. Poverty, limited healthcare services, illiteracy, cultural and linguistic differences, and limited understanding of the nature of scientific research by community participants could increase the risk of exploitation.

Community-based participatory research requires involvement and relationship building to establish trust and to ensure that the fieldwork is socio-politically, logistically, or ethically feasible [38]. Woodsong and Karim [39] propose a conceptual model of the informed consent process with the participation of community members. Co-design in underserved communities can involve vulnerable groups and it is possible that their very participation can result in stigma (e.g. in our case, caregivers treating HIV/AIDS). Care should also be taken to collect, store, protect, retain and destroy research data according to sound ethical principles. These principles also apply to the process of requirement-elicitation to inform the IS design. In the context of healthcare, the research often involves sensitive data, e.g. patient health records; reporting of conditions with an associated stigma; and the like. Care should thus be taken in identifying the participants and deciding which methods and tools to use during the design and the development of the IS.

5   Conclusion

From the research conducted thus far in the ISD4D project, we derived a number of key lessons that were detailed in the previous section. What we have learnt, ultimately, is that IS design and development has to consider *practices for a purpose*. These are influenced by the context of development, the manner in which a community functions, the capabilities of community members, their literacy levels and cultural practices. These aspects also influence the level of participation of intermediaries and recipients of health services in the design and development process. Furthermore, information and technologies also form part of the design and development process; the manner in which they are used during this process will also influence the level of participation of the end-users of the proposed IS. The technologies and information used during development are to establish the needs of the users; to elicit their requirements and to develop the IS. The level of participation will be influenced by the choice of information and technologies during the development phases of the IS – from needs analysis to implementation.

The context of both the development and use of the IS needs to be considered specifically for IS-development-for-development. Regardless of literacy level and cultural practices, end-users (should) have the capability to participate in the design and development process. The level of participation can be increased if the right technologies and information are used to encourage active participation. It is also important to use methods with relevant technologies and information to "translate" the practices of the users of the proposed IS into IS processes. It is important to specifically consider the purposes of these practices and contextual factors influencing them to obtain a good understanding of what the IS should achieve. Again, methods with appropriate technologies and information should be used to involve the users of the IS.

During the design and development of the new IS knowledge is created about the characteristics of the technology components (designed and those used to design new ones). Focusing on the utility of the technology components during the design and development should be aligned to the purpose of the associated practise. It is then possible to create prescriptive knowledge during the three areas of participation illustrated in Fig. 1 around the characteristics of the designs of the technology components, as well as the process of designing these components.

The level of participation of community members will be influenced by contextual factors, and by the extent to which appropriate information and technologies are used to "bridge" the gap of what is *known* to what is *possible*. It is important to focus on the dynamic aspects of IS development by making an effort to understand community members' life and work practices in real-life situations.

We posed the following research question at the beginning of the paper: *What are the factors that influence the level of participation during the design and development of an IS in an underserved community?* Based on the lessons learnt the factors that influence the level of participation during the proposed three areas of participation are grouped around the following components: people (the role of the intermediaries); technology (the use of relevant tools/methods; consideration of infrastructural constraints); information (relevant to the practices of the users); contextual factors (both static and dynamic); and ethics considerations. It is important that the intermediaries, important representatives of the end-user in the case of underserved communities, participates actively in all areas of IS design and development. In all cases the linking of the people, technology and information around practices for a purpose needs to be considered. It is also important to consider the role of the IS for development of the underserved communities that should aim for a positive impact.

In this paper, we shift our focus from solely people, information and technology components toward dynamic practices for a purpose. This provided us with a holistic lens to consider the components of an IS in an underserved community context. We were able to draw from our experiences to indicate that social, cultural, economic, and ethical factors are highly significant in a context where the ultimate goal is to develop the capabilities of people. IS designers and researchers are responsible to facilitate appropriate, context-sensitive information systems in cases where information can directly affect the health status and wellbeing of people from underserved communities. Further research is required to understand how people make sense of available health information, to know what is relevant to their needs. The complex interactions between the different IS components – especially during the practices when these components link – remains unclear at this stage. This aspect needs to be further unpacked to understand the complexities of the design and development of the IS as well as its use in practice.

We have thus far sought to provide only a preliminary set of considerations for IS design and development in an underserved community context. These are by no means definitive and further research is required to fully understand the different considerations that influence the participation of all in the design and development process.

References

1. Hussain, S., Sanders, E.B., Steinert, M.: Participatory design with marginalized people in developing countries: challenges and opportunities experienced in a field study in Cambodia. Int. J. Des. **6**(2), 91–109 (2012)
2. Van Zyl, I., De la Harpe, R.: AT-HOME 2.0 – an educational framework for home-based healthcare. J. Univ. Comput. Sci. **18**(3), 429–453 (2012)

3. De la Harpe, R., Van Zyl, I.: Mobile application design for health intermediaries: considerations for information access and use. In: Proceedings of the 7th International Conference of Health Informatics: HealthInf2014, Angers, France, 3–6 Mar 2014
4. De la Harpe, R.: The level of participation during the development of a mobile application for home-based healthcare data in a developing context: an actor-network theory perspective. S. Afr. Comput. J. **54**, 20–33 (2014)
5. De la Harpe, R.: Interactions of participants during mobile development of a healthcare application. In: 8th Multi Conference on Computer Science and Information Systems 2014: Interfaces and Human Computer Interaction IHCI2014, Lisbon, Portugal, 15–17 Jul 2014
6. Van Zyl, I.: Mutual isolation and the fight for care: an ethnography of South African homebased healthcare contexts. J. Health Inf. Dev. Ctries. **5**(1), 15–37 (2011)
7. Luukkonen, I., Toivanen, M., Mursu, A., Saranto, K., Korpela, M.: Researching an activity-driven approach to information systems development. In: Cruz-Cunha, M.M., Miranda, I.M., Gonçalves, P. (eds.) Handbook of Research on ICTs and Management Systems for Improving Efficiency in Healthcare and Social Care, vol. 1, pp. 431–450. IGI Global, Hershey (2013)
8. Alter, S.: The concept of 'IT artifact' has outlived its usefulness and should be retired now. Inf. Syst. J. **25**, 47–60 (2015)
9. Lee, A.S., Thomas, M., Baskerville, R.L.: Going back to basics in design science: from the information technology artifact to the information systems artifact. Inf. Syst. J. **25**, 5–21 (2015)
10. Orlikowski, W.J., Iacono, C.S.: Research commentary: desperately seeking the "IT" in IT research—a call to theorizing the IT artifact. Inf. Syst. Res. **12**(2), 121–134 (2001)
11. Hevner, A., March, S., Park, J., Ram, S.: Design science in information systems research. MIS Q. **28**(1), 75–105 (2004)
12. March, S., Smith, G.: Design and natural science research on information technology. Decis. Support Syst. **15**, 251–266 (1995)
13. Gregor, S., Müller, O., Seidel, S.: Reflection, abstraction and theorizing in design and development research. In: ECIS 2013 Completed Research, Paper 74 (2013)
14. Simon, H.: The Sciences of Artificial, 3rd edn. MIT Press, Cambridge (1996)
15. Gregor, S., Hevner, A.R.: Positioning and presenting design science research for maximum impact. MIS Q. **37**(2), 337–355 (2013)
16. Hevner, A.R., Chatterjee, S.: Design Research in Information Systems, Integrated Series 9 in Information Systems, vol. 22. Springer, New York (2010)
17. Heeks, R.B.: Actor-network theory for development. Actor-network theory for development working. Paper no. 1, Centre for Development Informatics, University of Manchester, Manchester, UK. http://www.cdi.manchester.ac.uk/resources/ant4d (2013). Accessed 30 May 2014
18. Avgerou, C.: Discourses on ICT and development. Inf. Technol. Int. Dev. **6**(3), 1–18 (2010)
19. Walsham, G.: Development informatics in a changing world: reflections from ICTD2010/2012. J. Inf. Technol. Int. Dev. **9**(1), 49–54 (2013)
20. Lorini, M.R., Van Zyl, I.J., Chigona, W.: ICTs for inclusive communities: a critical discourse analysis. In: International Development Informatics Association (IDIA) Conference 2014, Port Elizabeth, Cape Town, 3–4 Nov 2014
21. Diaz Andrade, A.D., Urquhart, C.: The affordances of actor network theory in ICT for development research. Inf. Technol. People **23**(4), 352–374 (2010)
22. De Silva, A., Fernandez, F.: Beyond free lunch: building sustainable ICT4D. In: Proceedings of the 21st European Conference on Information Systems (2013)

23. Puri, S.K., Byrne, E., Nhampossa, J.L., Quraishi, Z.B.: Contextuality of participation in IS design: a developing country perspective. In: Proceedings of the 18th Conference on Participatory Design, pp. 42–52 (2004)

24. Korpela, M., Mursu, A., Soriyan, H.A., De la Harpe, R., Macome, E.: Information systems practice for development in Africa: results from INDEHELA. In: Trauth, E.M., Howcroft, D., Butler, T., Fitzgerald, B., DeGross, J.I. (eds.) Social Inclusion: Societal and Organizational Implications for Information Systems. IFIP TC8 WG8.2 International Working Conference, pp. 15–36. Springer, New York (2006)

25. Tiihonen, T.: Information Systems in Context: Building a Tool for Analysing the Sociotechnical Context of Organisational Information Systems. University of Eastern Finland, Kuopio (2011)

26. Kickbusch, I., Pelikan, J.M., Apfel, F., Tsouros, A.D. (eds.): WHO: Health Literacy The Solid Facts. The World Health Organisation, Copenhagen (2013)

27. Norman, C.D., Skinner, H.A.: eHealth literacy: essential skills for consumer health in a networked world. J. Med. Int. Res. **8**(2), e9 (2006)

28. Mirza, F., Norris, T., Stockdale, R.S.: Mobile technologies and the holistic management of chronic diseases. Health Inf. J. **14**, 309–321 (2008)

29. Norris, A.C., Stockdale, R.S., Sharma, S.: A strategic approach to m-health. Health Inf. J. **15**(3), 244–253 (2009)

30. Mechael, P., Searle, S.: Barriers and gaps affecting mHealth in low and middle income countries : policy. White Paper, pp. 1–79 (2010)

31. Winters, N., Toyama, K.: Human-computer interaction for development: mapping the terrain. Inf. Technol. Int. Dev. **5**(4), iii–viii (2009)

32. Orlikowski, W.J.: Material works: exploring the situated entanglement of technological performativity and human agency. Scand. J. Inf. Syst. **17**(1), 183–186 (2005)

33. Díaz Andrade, A., Urquhart, C.: Mavericks, mavens and social connectors: computer mediated information seeking behaviour in rural societies. In: Proceedings of the 10th International Conference on Social Implications of Computers in Developing Countries, Dubai (2009)

34. Dervin, B.: Users as research inventions: how research categories perpetuate inequities. J. Commun. **39**(3), 216–232 (1989)

35. Robson, A., Robinson, L.: Building on models of information behaviour: linking information seeking and communication. J. Doc. **69**(2), 169–193 (2013)

36. Dearden, A.: See no evil? ethics in an interventionist ICTD. Inf. Technol. Int. Dev. **9**(2), 1–17 (2012)

37. Sabiescu, A., David, S., Van Zyl, I.J., Cantoni, L.: Emerging spaces in community-based participatory design: reflections from two case studies. In: Participatory Design Conference 2014, Windhoek, Namibia, 6–10 Oct 2014

38. Yancey, A.K., Ortega, A.N., Kumanyika, S.K.: Effective recruitment and retention of minority research participants. Annu. Rev. Public Health **27**, 1–28 (2006)

39. Woodsong, C., Karim, Q.A.: A model designed to enhance informed consent: experiences from the HIV prevention trials network. Am. J. Public Health **95**(3), 412–419 (2005)

Emerging IS History Research and Design for Preservation and Usability

A Consideration for Researcher Career Retrospectives in Information Systems and Organization Studies

Arto Lanamäki[✉]

Department of Information Processing Science, University of Oulu, PO Box 3000,
90014 Oulun Yliopisto, Finland
arto.lanamaki@oulu.fi

Abstract. This essay considers the researcher career retrospective (RCR) as an emerging publication genre in information systems (IS) and organization studies (OS). I assess two recent career texts, by/of Daniel Robey and John Van Maanen, as representative exemplars of this genre. I outline the genre, and identify resemblance between this and three genres of academic writing – namely career studies, IS history, and tribute. RCR fills an important niche within IS/OS publishing, and is especially needed in the Scandinavian IS research, in which it is currently absent. The 38 years of the IRIS conference, and 27 years of the SJIS journal, coincide with the careers of dozens of researchers. Reflection on these careers would provide much value for younger researchers and for the whole research community.

Keywords: Career · IS history · Ethnography · Genre · Scandinavian IS tradition

1 Introduction

Information Systems scholars have increasingly begun to debate about the established set of publication genres in our journals and conferences [1]. Does the range of genres limit creativity and relevance? To put it figuratively: are we directed to using maps that do not capture our terrain? [2, 3].

In this essay I outline the researcher career retrospective (RCR) as an emergent genre of publication. This genre is novel, while at the same time it has family resemblance with several existing genres.

Identifying RCR as a distinct scholarly genre (or a subgenre) is of great importance. First of all, this type of writing has existed for a long time, but it is under various labels. Giving this genre a name and thus placing it under a distinctive label will raise its status and guide future work. Recognizable labels establish consistent expectations [4]. Consequently, genre identification helps writing a more insightful, persuasive, and honest text. By acceptance of a genre, there is neither a need to apologize for deriving from scholarly conventions [4], nor a need for masking a research text to represent something that it is not [e.g., 5].

The outline will help a seasoned researcher's life work to be written as reflective analysis, and thus help the career to be understood backwards. This genre involves the

© Springer International Publishing Switzerland 2015
H. Oinas-Kukkonen et al. (Eds.): SCIS 2015, LNBIP 223, pp. 77–91, 2015.
DOI: 10.1007/978-3-319-21783-3_6

researcher as an active observer, thinker, and writer. It is thus an autoethnographic project involving fieldwork, headwork, and textwork [6]. More precisely, the fieldwork is the research career, the headwork concerns building connections to the literature, and the textwork is about writing it all up. The result is a narrative that ties together decades of scholarly work. Published RCRs will then help younger scholars in contextualizing their work, and living their researcher career forwards.

I have chosen two recent works as representative exemplars of this genre. The first one is by John Van Maanen [7], while the second one is an article by Daniel Robey that he wrote together with two of his former doctoral students [8]. The Van Maanen piece represents an organization studies career, and the Robey piece represents an information systems career. My discussion is more oriented towards information systems scholarship, but may also resonate outside of its boundaries.

The remainder of this article has materialized in the following presentational structure. Section 2 presents Van Maanen's and Robey's career texts and argue for their family resemblance. The Sect. 3 outlines what the RCR genre looks like. The Sect. 4 discusses the linkages of RCR to other genres of scholarly writing. Section 5 offers potential avenues for RCR texts, and the last Sect. 6 concludes the essay.

2   Two Exemplars of Researcher Career Retrospectives

In this Section I first summarize Van Maanen's storyline in's and then proceed to Robey's. Subsequently, I argue for the family resemblance between these two texts.

2.1   Van Maanen (2015)

John Van Maanen's article [7] is an elaboration of his Hughes Award Lecture that he held at the *Academy of Management* meeting in August 2014. This article was published in the January 2015 issue of the *Human Relations* journal.

The article is written largely as a first-person narrative. In this article, Van Maanen writes about his career, from the very beginning to the recent times, comprising a total of fifty years of scholarship. He first entered the academia as a social science student at UC Irvine in 1965.

Van Maanen conducted his first ethnographic fieldwork in the Seattle police department in 1969. A year afterwards, he entered his first academic conferences, first in the American Sociological Association and American Psychological Association meetings, and much later in the newly-established Academy of Management meeting. In the article, Van Maanen describes several events and anecdotes with his rich narrative.

While he writes about his career, he also writes about the (imagined) reader's career as well. He provides a tenure track -like narrative in which he contemplates on the peculiarities a young scholar may encounter in the process of becoming an academic with a known name and identity.

Van Maanen identifies himself as an ethnographer "interested in various worlds of work" (p. 36). He ends up conceptualizing career as circular: "moving to the margins to the center to the margins" (p. 38). He contemplates on his retirement from academia and "becoming old" (p. 38). In those parts I sense some sadness in his tone. Like, how he used to know almost everyone at the *Academy of Management* meetings, but now he knows barely few. He writes: "when I do spot a familiar face, I am relieved and likely to rush to hug and embrace them as a long lost friend even though our relationship may have been distant, even frosty, in the past." (p. 38).

Van Maanen is concerned how some of his work "has somehow fallen off the field's radar" (pp. 38–39). He discusses his "now-forgotten" work on socialization and careers that he had done in his early career. He said that early on he had "a delusion" that he had been able to capture some phenomenon conclusively through his studies, but now he understand that there "was and is always far more to learn" (p. 39).

He also confesses that most of his career he has had a "privileged" position within MIT – a role in which he has had a large degree of freedom and stability (p. 39). This position has enabled his to spend an occasional year or so conducting ethnographic fieldwork in various workplaces.

An interesting point was also the positioning of himself in the continuum of "MIT ethnographers" from the 1970s to the 2000s. He says that he, among most if not all of his fellow MIT'ers, derived much influence from the Chicago School of Sociology. He namedrops many known names from the Chicago School, but the "most brilliant of them all [is] Erving Goffman" (p. 42).

Stylistically the whole article flows beautifully with rich language. Van Maanen uses self-citations quite sparingly: the reference list contains only three of his articles. In contrast, his use of footnotes is plenteous.

Regardless that I much appreciate Van Maanen's [7] text, I would have preferred that the section titled "Plus ça change, plus c'est la même chose" was omitted or revised. That part looks like a rehashed version of a section titled "Plus ça change, plus c'est pareil" in his 2010 article [9], and a section titled "And … on the other hand" in his 2006 article [10]. This kind of redundancy may work well in a lecture (such as the one this article is based on), but it is not that effective in text. Regardless of this minor flaw, I think Van Maanen's career text is highly insightful.

2.2 Robey et al. (2013)

An article of Daniel Robey's career [8], written by Robey together with two of his former doctoral students (Chad Anderson and Benoit Raymond), was published in 2013 in the *Journal of the Association for Information Systems*. Robey's entire career is assessed in this "professional odyssey" through his publications over several decades.

The article is written mostly as a first-person singular "I" narrative, but it also occasionally uses the first-person plural "we" narrative when speaking of all the three authors.

Robey's career entry happens by him getting introduced to contingency theory, which is (or was) one frame to study IT effects in organizations. This occurred when he was a doctoral student in the early 1970s.

The assumptions behind contingency theory became challenged before long. This then directed Robey to work under the banner of process theory, while still continuing to address the research program of IT effects.

Robey summarizes his 40 years of scholarship of IT effects as follows (p. 384):

"IT influences organizational change through its implication in social processes. Among these processes are politics, learning, institutionalization, enculturation, and others. Although social process theories are indeterminate, they provide important explanations of change by focusing on sequences of events, stages, or phases of IT initiatives."

I must say that compressing the contributions of a whole research career into such a compact presentational format is certainly worth applauding.

Robey et al. however state that the quest is far from over. The offer future directions for the study of IT effect, by hinting towards affordance theory and organizational routines.

In this article, Robey does not contemplate much on his career exit. There is however a certain ethos of "passing the torch" to his now-coauthors Anderson and Raymond, who were his last doctoral students.

As a whole, the article is very self-referential, featuring a total of 33 citations to his own previous work. I think this self-citing style is a virtue, and helps the reader in locating previous work much like in a comprehensive literature review.

2.3   Family Resemblance Between the Exemplars

Following Wittgenstein's notion of family resemblance [11], I aim to draft the larger "family" in which both career texts are members.

Craig Fox [12] defines family resemblance as "a particular feature of the way we use (at least some) words: there are words such as 'game' that we use to name a variety of kinds of things people do, even though there is no one feature common to all of these activities" (p. 54). Thus, the notion of family resemblance helps us to group things and activities with "no one common feature to all and only these activities" (p. 61). The point is that Van Maanen's and Robey's texts are similar but not identical.

Let's start with the structure. Both articles have unusual structural choices, and both also justify these choices in the beginning. Robey et al. state that the article is "unconventionally self-referential", and thus they "beg the reader's indulgence for departing from convention" (p. 380). Van Maanen states his article is based on a speech in which he emphasized the spirit not the words, but now "text is all I can offer", but "words alone cannot carry the message I wish to pass on. The spirit, however, just might." (p. 36).

The structure in both contain a chronological career narrative. In Robey's text these are reserved for Sects. 2–5, while Van Maanen does most of this in his second section. Both start their career narrative with the career entry and then proceed to various events throughout the career. Robey's in-career narrative stays closely in his stream of publications, while Van Maanen provides a looser thematic framing.

Both articles address broader themes. Robey et al. explicitly address the research program of IT effects, and provide implications for the affordance theory and the study of organization routines. Van Maanen's trick is more based on thick description, through which he argues that his career bears similarities to other academic careers.

Both articles are mostly written as a first-person narrative: Van Maanen's through-and-through in first-person singular, while Robey's varies between first-person singular and first-person plural. While both have their personal authority presented in writing,

Robey's position to his research subjects seems more detached than the close ethnographic fieldwork type of Van Maanen.

A big difference is that Robey's story is very self-referentials with 33 self-citations, while Van Maanen has only 3 references to his own publications. Both authors use footnotes, but Van Maanen is more footnote-heavy.

These similarities and differences are summarized in the following table (Table 1).

Table 1. A comparison of elements in these two career texts.

Issue	Robey et al. (2013)	Van Maanen (2015)
Contribution to knowledge	IT effects, materiality	Career studies, ethnographic fieldwork
Career entry	Being introduced to contingency theory as a doctoral student in the early 1970s	Social science student at UC Irvine in 1965, first ethnographic fieldwork in the Seattle police department in 1969
In-career	Challenging the assumptions of contingency theory, moving to process theory	Self-identification as an ethnographer of work, participating in the profession of research
Identification of "legacy"	A formulation of how IT influences organization change	There is always more to learn. Recognition from younger scholars.
Pointing future directions	Addressing materiality through the lens of affordances, and in the theory of organizational routines	Reflecting between the origins and the current scholarly work of ethnographic fieldwork and career studies
Institutional conditions	Not reported	"privileged institutional position" at MIT (p. 39)
Boundary-crossing in the career	Not reported	Academic position has allowed several temporary ethnographic inquiries into various professions
Apprenticeship	Entering the study of IT impact while doctoral student in the early 1970s, first within the frame of contingency theory	Influence from the Chicago school of sociology
Mentorship continuum	Positioning Robey as the mentor how passes the torch to Anderson & Raymond	Positioning himself in the continuum of "MIT ethnographers" from the 1970s to the 2000s
Career exit	Mentioned in passing, present implicitly throughout the text	Present in the text. Conceptualizing career as circular: "moving from the margins to the center to the margins" (p. 38).
Amount of self-citations	33	3
Tense	First-person singular and first-person plural	First-person singular

3 An Outline of Researcher Career Retrospectives

In this Section I envision the researcher career retrospective as a publication genre. While moving the paintbrush on the canvas to sketch this outline, I take on not only from Robey's and Van Maanen's career texts. As in Sect. 2.3, I continue to follow Wittgenstein's notion of family resemblance [11]. The purpose is to draft the larger "family" in which both texts are members.

The need for identifying RCR as a distinct genre is of great importance. First of all, this type of writing has existed for a long time, but without a clear identity. Giving this genre a name and thus placing it under a distinctive label will raise its status and guide future work. Otherwise interesting papers might not survive the peer review process because the reviewer does not have a point of reference, i.e. the paper crosses the limits of transgression [13]. According to Sarker et al. [4], recognizable labels "have the advantage of reviewers, authors, and readers having consistent expectations" (p. vii). Consequently, genre identification helps writing a more insightful, persuasive, and honest text. Through community acceptance of a genre, there is neither a need to apologize for deriving from scholarly conventions [4], nor a need for masking a research text to represent something that it is not [5].

An example of such masking is provided by Sutton [5], who wrote of his experiences as a "closet qualitative researcher". He had found many uses for qualitative research, but was not reporting his work as such. This was, at least partly, due to the fear of rejection from journal gatekeepers holding to their variables-centric hypothetico-deductive mantra. My wish is that researchers would not take this path of masking, but instead prefer transparency and honesty in their writing.

I do not wish to make too narrow definitions. All genre definitions have restricting and enabling power at the same time. I aim that this outline will be a generative one. As Finnish poet Aaro Hellaakoski [14] has formulated: "You are a prisoner of the road you follow. Only the untrodden snowdrift is free."[1] Thus the genre should not make the writer a proverbial prisoner, but allow her/him to provide an interesting insight of the career lived and experienced.

I propose that RCR writing follows these five core principles:

1. Career as the unit of analysis
2. First-person autoethnographic writing
3. Publications as points of reference
4. Selective plot for relevance and interestingness
5. Dual-mission of the particular and the general

3.1 Career as the Unit of Analysis

It may come as a surprise that 'individual' is not the unit of analysis in RCRs. Instead, both of the exemplary articles evaluate the whole academic career from the beginning to the point of retirement. Thus, career is the unit of analysis in RCRs.

---

[1] The Finnish original text is as follows: "Tietä käyden tien on vanki. Vapaa on vain umpihanki."

A career is simultaneously objective and subjective [15]. In the words of Hughes, [15] a career is objectively "a series of status and clearly defined offices ... [consisting of] sequences of position, achievement, responsibility, and even of adventure" (p. 409). Subjectively, a career provides "the moving perspective in which the person sees his life as a whole and interprets the meaning of his various attributes, actions, and the things which happen to him" (pp. 409–410).

A career has a beginning and an end, and lots of stuff in between. Therefore writing an RCR suits best for a researcher with decades of work experience – who has retired, is retiring, or is somehow anticipating an "exit from the field". This does not mean, of course, that an RCR is the last text a scholar writes during her/his career. The point is that an RCR fits best when the writer can somehow reflect on the exit as well – a requirement that is most often not feasible to in early or mid-career stage.

3.2 First-Person Autoethnographic Writing

An RCR is an autoethnographic enterprise. "Auto" in that way that it is about the writer's own career, written either alone or together with fellow scholars. This thus departs from the ethnographic convention of capturing the "native's point of view". Self-centeredness is not a fault, but a feature of this genre. Autoethnographic research is an established approach in general [16], and is gaining ground in IS scholarship as well [17]. RCR is "ethnographic" in that way that it involves field-work, headwork, and textwork [6]. This fieldwork just happens to be unusually long for an ethnography, usually for several decades. The "headwork" concerns building connections to the extant literature. Some of those are the scholar's own previous publications, some of them are others' published work. Then finally the "textwork" is what really makes ethnography ethnography [18]. Tony Watson [19] has argued that ethnography is not a process – i.e. not a research method – but the written outcome. He defined ethnography as a *"style of social science writing which draws upon the writer's close observation of and involvement with people in a particular social setting and relates the words spoken and the practices observed or experienced to the overall cultural framework within which they occurred"* (pp. 205–206).

Both of the exemplar articles share first-person narrative. I see this as a good practice. A person's career is best written with the strong presence of the author. Or as Van Maanen [20] has depicted, the purpose is to put forth a "personalized author" who refuses "to cloak a writing in anonymity" (p. 136).

3.3 Publications as Points of Reference

I very much prefer the heavily self-referential style of Robey [8]. Plotting the article using a chronology of published work is a useful way to guide the reader towards additional texts. Some of these texts might have already fell from the radar of younger scholars, but the career plot places them in the larger picture.

Publications will thus work are points of reference, and form the backbone of an RCR text. The author can also use several additional sources. Unpublished sources, such as peer review results, diary entries, selected interview quotes, etc., may provide rich context to the whole story. Lots of the story may also depend on the author's own memory. Collaborating with fellow scholars, and iterative writing, may provide deep insights. For example, Rudy Hirschheim told in February 2015 that their 2012-article "A Glorious and Not-So-Short History of the Information Systems Field" [21] was under development since ICIS 1999, and went through seven iterations.[2]

3.4   Selective Plot for Relevance and Interestingness

Even one single work day may bring forth events and surprises that take a thick book to elaborate on thoroughly. How it is then possible to compress a decades-long career within the word limits of, say, 10000 words?

Writing an impactful RCR requires selectivity. The consideration involves thinking about the core career plot. How would that plot constitute into an inspiring story that would engage even those readers who are not familiar with the author's work previously? Of course, the story might involve some side tracks and useful anecdotes. Van Maanen especially has a very footnote-heavy writing style that at times forms rather hypertextual compositional structures.

Both of the exemplary articles demonstrate selectivity, either implicitly or explicitly. Robey [8] mentions that the plot he tells "excludes almost all of the work on other topics throughout my career", pointing out that in his early career he "was engaged with the discourse on IS development … [treating] it as a social process rather than a methodology" (p. 383).

A scholarly audience comes to read career texts from different backgrounds and expectations. I am quite familiar with Van Maanen's published work, and I can say I've been (and still am) a long-time fan of his writing. A reader's background knowledge provides some expectations of which events are included within the career plot. In my knowledge, a key event for Van Maanen's scholarship in the nineties was his "paradigm feud" with Jeffrey Pfeffer. This started from Pfeffer's 1992 Academy of Management Distinguished Scholar Address calling for a strict Organization Theory paradigm. Van Maanen held the Address the next year and completely put out Pfeffer's call (in Van Maanen's own words: for a "Pfefferdigm"). This continued in Pfeffer's essay [22], in a reply from Van Maanen [20], in a reply to a reply from Pfeffer [23], and so forth [24]. The whole saga has been chronicled ever since in top management and organization studies journals [25–27], and even by Daniel Robey in *Information Systems Research* [28]. Regardless, this saga is absent in Van Maanen's career text. The reason might be that maybe Van Maanen does not see the 90 s paradigm feud to have importance in the larger scheme of things. Or maybe that is part of some other story, just not this one.

3.5   Dual-Mission of the Particular and the General

Although both of the exemplary articles discuss a career of a particular person, they differ in their tactics of addressing the general. Robey et al. take very explicit general target by addressing the research program of IT effects. They also provide implications

---

for the affordance theory and the study of organization routines. Van Maanen in turn applies the thick description tactic. Through thick description, he argues, readers realize "what is important, problematic and central in any given career is quite likely to show up in others as well" (p. 43).

In sum, an RCR should be more than a biography. A career story should provide implications to a broader context, not just details about a particular human being. Different tactics for deriving the general from the particular may exist. The tactics applied by Robey et al. and Van Maanen may be just two among many.

4   Family Resemblance of the Genre

The researcher career retrospective is tied to various scholarly developments in science. Next, I discuss resemblance to three genres: career studies, IS history, and tribute.

4.1   Career Studies

Career studies (or career theory) is a banner that is logical to start with, because that is where Van Maanen located his own career text at [7]. Career studies, as the name suggests, are studies that focus on careers. The notion of a career is surprisingly recent in common vocabulary. Moore, Gunz, and Hall [29] identified that the word career as "one's professional life course" gained its meaning in the 19th century in Britain, and was first mentioned in the *Oxford English Dictionary* in 1933.

The study on careers as a distinct branch of social science research is just some decades old phenomenon. The most usually identified start for career studies is in the 1970's of US-based researchers. Two handbooks of career scholarship have been published thus far. *The Handbook of Career Theory* [30] was published in 1989, and the *SAGE Handbook of Career Studies* [31] in 2007.

Career studies have increasingly shifted their focus on two main outliers: employability and career success [32]. For example, a recent study by Hogan et al. [33] compared psychological determinants (e.g. cognitive abilities, personality) with employer expectations (e.g. willingness and ability to work). While that kind of work has its place, it is quite alien to the provided outline of RCR. Career researchers also seem to be quite a united community, and very much separate from the scholars who study the development and use of IT in organizations. Thus the career studies banner does not hold that much weight within IS and OS.

4.2   IS History

Students of IT and organizing have shifted their interest increasingly towards history [34–37]. Historical reflection is probably natural development of a field that has matured through different phases [i.e. 21]. Historical methods can also be applied in studying an information system as a system, not just Information Systems as a research field [35].

The point in which RCR departs from IS history is General History's detached researcher position and its "systematic" rhetoric [35]. I don't see any point to chronicle a researcher's own career through any other way than through a first-person (singular) narrative which provides a strong authorial presence.

I would however be happy to place RCR as an IS history subgenre – while it may be a subgenre of some additional genres as well, including research essay and literature review. What is important to acknowledge is that RCR has its own characteristics, of which some have connections to the broader IS history thematic, while some don't. (See also Porra et al. [38] for a comparison between the historical research method and other research approaches.)

4.3 Tribute

Tribute is a seemingly marginal, but in fact a surprisingly prominent genre of scholarship. With tribute I refer to that class of articles where other scholars are writing – often with an admiring tone – of some researcher's life work. This literature can be roughly categorized in two main types depending on whether the tribute is addressed to a person alive or deceased.

An example of a tribute text to a living scholar is an essay written by Dennis Gioia [39]. This essay is titled "On Weick: An Appreciation". In this essay, Gioia chronicles Karl Weick's research contributions. The narrative starts from Gioia's remembrance of his first encounter with Weick's work. At that time he felt this style was "cryptic and arcane, and also as rooted in ideas that seemed obscure and esoteric" (p. 1710). Later on Gioia acquired a taste for Weick. The essay ends in Gioia's "rule of thumb": "If Weick wrote it, I'll read it" (p. 1719).

A posthumous tribute – which might also be called an obituary, in memoriam, or postmortem – is relatively often seen is OS/IS journals. In IS, such texts have been written of, e.g., Claudio Ciborra [40], Heinz Klein [41], and Alessandro D'Atri [42].

While the tribute genre bears similarities to the RCR, the main difference is that RCRs are written by the person themselves. Tribute texts also seem to vary a lot in their length and depth. Some tributes are very thorough investigations in a scholar's life work, while some are shorter acknowledgements of the loss of a friend.

One observation about tribute texts is that many of them remain quite minimally cited. It is purely speculation to guess the reasons to this state of affairs, but perhaps this is due to a perceived lack of "rigor." I hope that initiating a solid foundation for RCRs will provide the emerging genre a more impactful future.

5 Potential Avenues

In this Section I provide two ideas for drafting future RCRs. These ideas are called (1) addressing a research program, and (2) re-interpretation and re-positioning.

5.1 Addressing a Research Program

Similarly to how Robey [8] positioned his article towards the study of IT effects, an RCR can be designed to address any larger research program. Robey et al. depict that a large research program addresses even a larger "intellectual puzzle". They attribute intellectual puzzles to be so "difficult to solve and large enough in scope … that [they] may stimulate research and theory for decades" (p. 380). Robey says (p. 380) that for him, "attempting to solve the intellectual puzzle of IT impacts has consumed over 40 years of sustained effort, and it is still not yet completed."

A potential stub for such address could be Juhani Iivari's recent "behind-the-scenes" story [43] of the process that eventually resulted in his article "Distinguishing and contrasting two strategies for design science research" [44]. The "backstory" chronicles how his role as the *MIS Quarterly* associate editor for the Action Design Research article submission [45] got him pondering the article's relationship to Design Science Research [46]. While this Iivari's "backstory" [43] is framed in the context of the peer review process, the story could be extended and reframed as a timeline of Iivari's career within the research program of systems design. There's certainly a rich story to be told [47–49].

5.2   Re-Interpretation and Re-Positioning

Ideas, things and actions change their meanings when observed in retrospect. Spandex trousers were a big fashion statement in the 1980s, but many would now consider them ridiculous. Your early-career articles might have seemed exciting at the time you wrote them, but now those may appear premature. In addition, ideas find their audience within a particular window of opportunity. For example, systems thinking suited well in the Zeitgeist of the early 1970s [50], and e-commerce had its momentum in early 2000s [51].

Robey's story has many elements of re-positioning, particularly associated with his shift from contingency theory to process theory. Robey [8] states (p. 384):

> *"I believe that organizational changes attributed to technology originate in the process of developing and implementing systems. This observation now seems self-evident, but I only realized this connection in the 1980s"*

To provide another example of re-positioning, consider how Karl Weick has been retrospectively defined as a process theorist. This is a label he did not attach to himself, but it was provided by others [52]. He says he came to identify process theorizing only much later than he had actually done it. Weick notes that the word 'process' was not in the index of his of his 1995 book [53], while in retrospect that book can be seen to have a process orientation [52]. That idea is at the core of Weick's sensemaking recipe: "How can I know what I think, until I see what I say?"

The point is that a career plot helps putting everything in (a new) perspective. How did one thing lead to another? Especially, it becomes possible to assess the chains of impact and refinement of ideas through an interpretive lens: what did others cite from your work, and what did you cite from theirs – and most importantly, what kinds of chains do these reciprocal patterns form? Which ideas never took off, and why?

6   Conclusion and Future Directions

The often-quoted words of Danish philosopher Søren Kierkegaard offer an important guidance: life "must be lived forwards", while it is "understood backwards". In this article I have argued for the recognition of researcher career retrospectives (RCR) that is one way to narrate life-lived-forwards in retrospect. This emergent genre forms an autoethnographic plot that ties together decades of scholarly work. RCRs can help younger scholars in their work, and living their researcher careers forwards.

In this article I have outlined the "family" of the RCR, and positioned two researcher career texts, by/of John Van Maanen and Daniel Robey, as its family members. I have also provided a genre outline – which may be revised in the future – that involves five principles: (1) career as the unit of analysis, (2) first-person autoethnographic writing, (3) publications as points of reference, (4) a selective plot for relevance and interestingness, and (5) dual-mission of the particular and the general.

In addition to discussing the family resemblance within the RCR genre, I have discussed resemblances to other established genres. I have also provided potential avenues to fuel inspiration to write RCR texts.

If we agree that RCR has its own place within IS/OS scholarship, then how could we attract more RCRs in our publication outlets? This question is linked to a broader question of how any novel genre gains acceptance within academia. Indeed: How do new scholarly genres get established and accepted within a research community? The answer is inconclusive, but some clear evidence exists that journal special issues have a big role in introducing new pathways to a research. If we consider how qualitative research has gained ground in organization studies, then the 1979 *Administrative Science Quarterly* special issue on Qualitative Methods [54] is a major cornerstone. Similarly, the 1999/2000 *MIS Quarterly* special issue on Intensive Research [55–57] paved way for many qualitatively oriented IS researchers. Considering these encouraging experiences of the emancipatory power of special issues, I think a special issue on RCRs is needed.

Maybe we need a *Scandinavian Journal of Information Systems* special issue on (Scandinavian) Researcher Career Retrospectives? If we consider just the 27 years of the journal, that in itself involves a lot of history that various careers have crossed. Maybe some of the authors of the early *SJIS* issues would now be interested in writing their career texts? Or perhaps some of the forefathers (as well as mothers) of the IRIS conference would like to share their story? My plea is to get more of this stuff! Make way for researcher career retrospectives!

Acknowledgments. I would like to thank Harri Oinas-Kukkonen, Daniel Robey, Rudy Hirschheim, all participants of the Seinäjoki IS doctoral seminar in April 2015, and three anonymous reviewers for their constructive and encouraging comments.

References

1. Rowe, F.: Toward a richer diversity of genres in information systems research: new categorization and guidelines. Eur. J. Inf. Syst. **21**, 469–478 (2012)

2. Ågerfalk, P.J.: Insufficient theoretical contribution: a conclusive rationale for rejection? Eur. J. Inf. Syst. **23**, 593–599 (2014)
3. Avison, D., Malaurent, J.: Is theory king?: questioning the theory fetish in information systems. J. Inf. Technol. **29**, 327–336 (2014)
4. Sarker, S., Xiao, X., Beaulieu, T.: Guest editorial: qualitative studies in information systems: a critical review and some guiding principles. MIS Q. **37**, iii–xviii (2013)
5. Sutton, R.I.: Crossroads—the virtues of closet qualitative research. Organ. Sci. **8**, 97–106 (1997)
6. Van Maanen, J.: Tales of the Field: On Writing Ethnography. University of Chicago Press, Chicago (2011)
7. Van Maanen, J.: The present of things past: ethnography and career studies. Hum. Relat. **68**, 35–53 (2015)
8. Robey, D., Anderson, C., Raymond, B.: Information technology, materiality, and organizational change: a professional odyssey. J. Assoc. Inf. Syst. **14**, 379–398 (2013)
9. Van Maanen, J.: A song for my supper: more tales of the field. Organ. Res. Meth. **13**, 240–255 (2010)
10. Van Maanen, J.: Ethnography then and now. Qual. Res. Organ. Manag. Int. J. **1**, 13–21 (2006)
11. Wittgenstein, L.: Philosophical Investigations. MacMillan, New York (1953)
12. Fox, C.: Wittgenstein on family resemblance. In: Jolley, K.D. (ed.) Wittgenstein: Key Concepts, pp. 51–62. Routledge, Abingdon (2014)
13. Barley, S.R.: When I write my masterpiece: thoughts on what makes a paper interesting. Acad. Manag. J. **49**, 16–20 (2006)
14. Hellaakoski, A.: Huojuvat keulat. WSOY (1946)
15. Hughes, E.C.: Institutional office and the person. Am. J. Sociol. **43**, 404–413 (1937)
16. Jones, S.H., Adams, T.E., Ellis, C.: Handbook of Autoethnography. Left Coast Press, Walnut Creek (2015)
17. O Riordan, N.: Autoethnography: proposing a new method for information systems research. In: Twenty Second European Conference on Information Systems, Tel Aviv (2014)
18. Van Maanen, J.: Ethnography as work: some rules of engagement. J. Manag. Stud. **48**, 218–234 (2011)
19. Watson, T.J.: Ethnography, reality, and truth: the vital need for studies of 'how things work' in organizations and management. J. Manag. Stud. **48**, 202–217 (2011)
20. Van Maanen, J.: Style as theory. Organ. Sci. **6**, 133–143 (1995)
21. Hirschheim, R., Klein, H.K.: A Glorious and not-so-short history of the information systems field. J. Assoc. Inf. Syst. **13**, 188–235 (2012)
22. Pfeffer, J.: Barriers to the advance of organizational science: paradigm development as a dependent variable. Acad. Manag. Rev. **18**, 599–620 (1993)
23. Pfeffer, J.: Mortality, reproducibility, and the persistence of styles of theory. Organ. Sci. **6**, 681–686 (1995)
24. Van Maanen, J.: Fear and loathing in organization studies. Organ. Sci. **6**, 687–692 (1995)
25. Weick, K.E.: Drop your tools: an allegory for organizational studies. Adm. Sci. Q. **41**, 301–313 (1996)
26. Glick, W.H., Miller, C.C., Cardinal, L.B.: Making a life in the field of organization science. J. Organ. Behav. **28**, 817–835 (2007)
27. Alvesson, M., Kärreman, D.: The closing of critique, pluralism and reflexivity: a response to Hardy and Grant and some wider reflections. Hum. Relat. **66**, 1353–1371 (2013)
28. Robey, D.: Research commentary: diversity in information systems research: threat, promise, and responsibility. Inf. Syst. Res. **7**, 400–408 (1996)

29. Moore, C., Gunz, H., Hall, D.T.: Tracing the historical roots of career theory in management and organizational studies. In: Gunz, H., Peiperl, M. (eds.) Handbook of Career Studies, pp. 13–38. Sage Publications, Thousand Oaks (2007)

30. Arthur, M.B., Hall, D.T., Lawrence, B.S.: Handbook of Career Theory. Cambridge University Press, Cambridge (1989)

31. Gunz, H., Peiperl, M. (eds.): Handbook of Career Studies. SAGE Publications, Thousand Oaks (2007)

32. Baruch, Y., Szücs, N., Gunz, H.: Career studies in search of theory: the rise and rise of concepts. Career Dev. Int. **20**, 3–20 (2015)

33. Hogan, R., Chamorro-Premuzic, T., Kaiser, R.B.: Employability and career success: bridging the gap between theory and reality. Ind. Organ. Psychol. **6**, 3–16 (2013)

34. De Vaujany, F.-X., Mitev, N., Laniray, P., Vaast, E.: Materiality and Time: Historical Perspectives on Organizations, Artefacts and Practices. Palgrave Macmillan, Basingstoke (2014)

35. Oinas-Kukkonen, H., Oinas-Kukkonen, H.: What every information systems (IS) researcher should know about IS history (ISH) research. In: Thirty Fifth Conference on Information Systems, Auckland (2014)

36. Paakki, J.: Opista tieteeksi – Suomen tietojenkäsittelytieteiden historia. Tietojenkäsittelytieteen Seura ry (2014)

37. Heinrich, L.J., Riedl, R.: Understanding the dominance and advocacy of the design-oriented research approach in the business informatics community: a history-based examination. J. Inf. Technol. **28**, 34–49 (2013)

38. Porra, J., Hirschheim, R., Parks, M.S.: The historical research method and information systems research. J. Assoc. Inf. Syst. **15**, 536–576 (2014)

39. Gioia, D.A.: On Weick: an appreciation. Organ. Stud. **27**, 1709–1721 (2006).

40. Braa, K., Dahlbom, B., Hanseth, O.: Our antenna in the south is gone. Scand. J. Inf. Syst. **17**, 197–200 (2005)

41. Truex, D., Cuellar, M., Takeda, H., Vidgen, R.: The scholarly influence of Heinz Klein: ideational and social measures of his impact on IS research and IS scholars. Eur. J. Inf. Syst. **20**, 422–439 (2011)

42. Spagnoletti, P., Baskerville, R., De Marco, M.: The contributions of Alessandro D'Atri to organization and information systems studies. In: Baskerville, R., De Marco, M., Spagnoletti, P. (eds.) Designing Organizational Systems, vol. 1, pp. 1–18. Springer, Heidelberg (2013)

43. Iivari, J.: How to improve the quality of peer reviews? – Three suggestions for system-level changes (2014)

44. Iivari, J.: Distinguishing and contrasting two strategies for design science research. Eur. J. Inf. Syst. **24**, 107–115 (2015)

45. Sein, M.K., Henfridsson, O., Purao, S., Rossi, M., Lindgren, R.: Action design research. MIS Q. **35**, 37–56 (2011)

46. Hevner, A.R., March, S.T., Park, J., Ram, S.: Design science in information systems research. MIS Q. **28**, 75–105 (2004)

47. Iivari, J.: A paradigmatic analysis of information systems as a design science. Scand. J. Inf. Syst. **19**, 39–64 (2007)

48. Iivari, J., Lyytinen, K.: Research on information systems development in Scandinavia—unity in plurality. Scand. J. Inf. Syst. **10**, 135–185 (1998)

49. Iivari, J.: A paradigmatic analysis of contemporary schools of IS development. Eur. J. Inf. Syst. **1**, 249–272 (1991)

50. Järvinen, P.: Oppikirjan sisällön säilymisestä ajankohtaisena: Esimerkkinä Systemointi II. In: Iivari, J. (ed.) Alussa oli mies, metsä – ja innostus. Juhlakirja emeritusprofessori Pentti Kerolan 80-vuotispäivänä, pp. 27–46. Juvenes Print, Tampere (2015)
51. Baskerville, R.L., Myers, M.D.: Fashion waves in information systems research and practice. MIS Q. **33**, 647–662 (2009)
52. Weick, K.E.: The poetics of process: theorizing the ineffable in organization studies. In: Hernes, T., Maitlis, S. (eds.) Process, Sensemaking, and Organization, pp. 102–111. Oxford University Press, Oxford (2010)
53. Weick, K.E.: Sensemaking in Organizations. Sage, Thousand Oaks (1995)
54. Van Maanen, J.: Reclaiming qualitative methods for organizational research: a preface. Adm. Sci. Q. **24**, 520–526 (1979)
55. Markus, M.L., Lee, A.S.: Special issue on intensive research in information systems: using qualitative, interpretive, and case methods to study information technology – foreward. MIS Q. **23**, 35–38 (1999)
56. Markus, M.L., Lee, A.S.: Special issue on intensive research in information systems: using qualitative, interpretive, and case methods to study information technology – second installment, foreword. MIS Q. **24**, 1–2 (2000)
57. Markus, M.L., Lee, A.S.: Special issue on intensive research in information systems: using qualitative, interpretive, and case methods to study information technology – third installment; foreword. MIS Q. **24**, 473–474 (2000)

Integrating Contemporary Content Management and Long-Term Digital Preservation: A Design Problem

Tero Päivärinta[✉], Parvaneh Westerlund, and Jörgen Nilsson

Luleå University of Technology, Information Systems, Luleå, Sweden
{tero.paivarinta,parvaneh.westerlud,jorgen.nilsson}@ltu.se

Abstract. The fields of long-term digital preservation (DP) and enterprise content management (ECM) have remained, until recently, rather separated. Along with increasing amounts of digital content and evolving DP services, there is a need for maximal automation of preservation processes from ECM systems instead of continuing current resource-consuming practices. This paper aims at a design problem definition on the integration of ECM and DP solutions. In order to motivate and to define the problem in more detail, we conducted a review on ECM and DP literatures touching the issue. The review reveals a research gap addressing a need for designing new middleware solutions for interactive processes between ECM and DP. We suggest a general-level model of three such processes between ECM and DP: preservation administration, pre-ingest, and access. The article concludes with avenues for future research on novel solutions for integrating DP with contemporary ECM and other information systems in organizations.

Keywords: Long-term digital preservation · Enterprise content management · System integration

1 Introduction

The field of digital preservation (DP) focuses on keeping digital information objects, which involve benefit for organizations and the society [9], to be ready for access and use over "long periods" of time [9, 27]. DP includes the tasks of maintaining the semantic meaning of the digital object and its content, its provenance and authenticity, and retaining information about contexts of information production and use [39]. A "long period" here means "[a] period of time long enough for there to be concern about impacts of changing technologies, including support for new media and data formats" [9, p. 1-1]. The related topics of research and development include DP strategies [30, 34, 39], systems, solutions and services [46], and processes to preserve digital information objects [23]. Beyond the sectors with long traditions of information preservation, such as (mostly governmental) archiving institutions, culture institutions, and libraries, the penetration of digital preservation practices is still low and few organizations are willing to use resources on the preservation activities [39]. Therefore, also research on digital preservation in organizational contexts in the field of information systems is still in its infancy [7, 49]. At the same time, the issue of digital preservation is emerging especially

H. Oinas-Kukkonen et al. (Eds.): SCIS 2015, LNBIP 223, pp. 92–107, 2015.
DOI: 10.1007/978-3-319-21783-3_7

in the field of e-government [11]. For example, in Sweden alone, investments in electronic archiving solutions and services including 117 state-level government organizations are expected to rise up to between 1,1 and 1,7 billion SEK between 2014 and 2016 [40], while this estimate does not cover the rest of Swedish state-level organizations or municipalities and regions, which have similar challenges [38].

While the amount of digital content to be preserved expands, the diversity of methods to capture, store and organize the content for preservation raises a challenging problem [42]. Moreover, modern preservation tasks may involve rather complex digital objects, such as relational databases [18], advanced product data and models [22] and even whole workflows with business semantics [30, 34]. As a result, modern preservation systems need to operationalize both advanced data models for the content to-be-preserved and rich (and varying) models for managing metadata, i.e., add-on data about the content [9] itself. Hence, current information systems and their repositories rarely, if ever, provide methods for automated preservation workflows or support for preservation metadata. This makes digital preservation, still, a manual and labor-intensive task [42]. This issue is right now rather acute among governmental organizations, which plan for intermediate digital preservation repositories and jointly developed electronic archiving services [11, 45]. However, manual or tailored preservation of the rapidly increasing volumes of digital content has already become practically unsustainable [32] and digital preservation should thus be as transparent and automated as possible. Tailored preservation projects from contemporary information systems to preservation services are also costly. For example, it is estimated that each one-time preservation project to transform information from an enterprise system to a DP solution will cost between 100 and 400 kSEK [39]. While an example from ten Swedish municipalities alone revealed hundreds of systems from which such preservation project would be needed sooner or later, a need for innovative solutions for automated preservation from organizational information systems to DP solutions is obvious [39].

Aiming for such automation causes a need to develop the contemporary information systems as well. In the field of information systems, enterprise content management (ECM) has been suggested as an integrative concept of information management, which highlights the management of structured, semi-structured, and unstructured information content altogether [23, 37, 44, 49]. While longer-term issues of information preservation, such as records management and archiving, have sometimes been mentioned as areas of enterprise content management [e.g. 49], actual digital preservation challenges have been largely left out from the ECM research discussions and frameworks [49]. The same applies also vice versa [25] – the prevailing standards for digital preservation, such as the OAIS (Open Archival Information System) reference model [9], address little, if at all, the issue of integration between information systems and digital preservation. In order to contribute to this gap of research and development between ECM and digital preservation [25, 49], our study focuses on reviewing and summarizing existing academic research on the problem of integrating digital preservation with ECM systems. Below, we will discuss about literature on ECM and digital preservation which has suggested at least partial concepts, models and solutions to this issue. We form a general-level model for conceptualizing the problem further and relate the existing pieces of research to the model. As such, this article represents a literature-based problem identification and motivation phase of a wider design research project [35] developing synergetic solutions for digital preservation from ECM systems to DP services [1, 17].

The rest of this article is organized as follows. The next section elaborates our understanding of the current gap between ECM and DP giving motivation for our research. Section 3 declares the literature review method and Sect. 4 describes the resulting integrative general-level model between ECM and preservation systems. Section 5 discusses about the contributions of the review and outlines potential areas of future research. Section 6 concludes the article.

2   Background: Gap Between ECM and DP

In the field of ECM, preservation and records management are mentioned as relevant functional areas of interest from early on [49]. However, preservation issues have rarely been demonstrated or evaluated as parts of the reported cases of implemented ECM systems [20] or analysis methods [51]. In the reviews on the field of ECM, digital preservation of enterprise content is barely visible [2, 20, 21].

From the viewpoint of digital preservation, Korb and Strodl [25] have identified and highlighted gaps between ECM systems and OAIS-compliant preservation systems. On one hand, the OAIS reference model does not determine how other information systems are technically supposed to interact with preservation systems. As human intervention in digital preservation decreases, most of the actions to preserve and to utilize preserved information are expected to take place automatically, and most likely initiated through actively used ECM systems. On the other hand, ECM systems still need to be prepared for integration to DP services because such integration does not readily exist [25].

Moreover, contemporary ECM systems provide little or no preservation planning functionalities [25]. It remains unclear how to integrate the long-term preservation planning with administration of ECM systems. In records management, records need to be migrated over time to new media and sometimes to new formats. In ECM-related records management systems, migration has mostly taken place in the form of migration of data from one storage medium to another, and focused less on the problem of migrating file-formats when the old ones have become obsolete due to a change in an ECM system [25]. Hence, there is a gap between the administration of ECM systems in relation to preservation services. In ECM systems the functions which capture content to the system often also gather metadata (automatically, in a few systems). However, the capture functions of ECM systems rarely, if at all, provide metadata for preservation, which could be utilized later on by a preservation system [25]. While an ECM system has captured and collected context-related metadata, the digital preservation system needs to add it to the preservation-related metadata [25]. This should be based on preservation planning and administration policies [15]. The preservation system needs to store descriptive metadata separately from the actual content. In ECM systems, these are often tightly coupled [25]. Moreover, ECM systems are rather integrated in the organizational IT-infrastructure [20, 33], while preservation services often are less intertwined with the operational systems [13]. Organizational information systems and external preservation services thus also lack administrative alignment [25].

Figure 1 illustrates this gap. On the ECM side, Fig. 1 depicts the general-level functional areas of an ECM system [20, 44]. Access relates to channels and functions of accessing an ECM system for information retrieval. The ECM process usually includes further elements of workflow management, collaboration, and data analysis. The service component includes capture, management, use, and publication functionalities. Finally, the repository component involves auditing support, content storage, metadata, taxonomy, and version management functionalities [20].

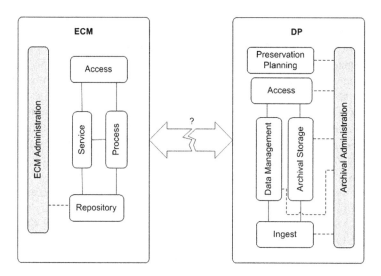

Fig. 1. Gap between ECM and DP

In OAIS-compliant preservation systems, the ingest component represents a collection of tasks that together have the responsibility for accepting submitted information package and preparing it for storage in archive [29]. Currently, creation, configuration and transfer of information packages from enterprise systems to the OAIS-compliant ingest function requires tailor-made and relatively expensive projects [38, 39]. Services by which users of an archive locate the information that resides in archival storage, request it, and receive delivery, are managed by access process [19, 27]. Data management and archival storage are responsible for maintenance of databases of descriptive metadata and management of long-term storage, respectively [27]. Data management also manages the administrative data that supports OAIS's internal functionality [27]. Preservation planning arranges OAIS's preservation strategy [28]. Finally, archival administration is needed to coordinate tasks of the five above-mentioned processes, in addition to manage OAIS's daily operations [27].

As indicated above, the gap between ECM and DP systems has been identified in the literature [25] but the problem has remained largely unsolved. However, a few potential parts and elements of workflow solutions that provide seeds for better integration of ECM and preservation in a few domains have been suggested. This initial observation provided us a further motivation for conducting a literature review to collect the pieces of research related to interaction between ECM systems and DP into an integrative, general-level framework, which will be presented below.

3   Literature Review Process

We conducted a literature review with the following question in mind: What processes and solutions for integration between ECM and DP systems have been discussed and suggested? Aiming at identifying the relevant literature for our purpose, we followed the review approach introduced by Webster and Watson [52]. We investigated literature and articles in such areas as digital preservation workflow and content management, looking for discussions about integration of ECM systems into DP systems. We obtained a list of relevant scholarly articles through three stages, each starting by a search session. We chose Google scholar as the search engine due to the multi-disciplinary nature of the area of study allowing us to access multiple journals and conference proceedings from different research areas at the same time. Search for articles, identifying relevant articles, and making the concept matrix has been done by one of the authors and the results have been discussed with other authors in group at every stage in the process.

First, we searched the literature by using such words as "content management system" (657 hits), "enterprise content management" (195 hits), and "long term digital preservation" (87 hits) as keywords in the title of articles since year 2000. Out of these, we identified 15 as useful. We identified an article as useful if it contained information about one or more of the following issues: DP components, ECM components, DP components in relation to ECM and the other way around. We first read the abstract and conclusion of an article. In case that those parts were unclear, we read the whole text. The first review round led us to identify an additional number of keywords that we found relevant to our topic. On the second search session, we used a similar procedure and identified 14 useful articles (out of 84 hits) when the additional keywords were "digital preservation workflow" (9 hits), "digital preservation architecture" (16 hits), and "digital preservation metadata" (59 hits). Finally, we identified 10 useful articles with such keywords as "digital preservation management" (71 hits) and "digital preservation outsourcing" (1 hit). We added recent European research projects on digital preservation that were identified by Strodl et al. [46] where they tried to consider all major contributions of the recent research projects in the area of digital preservation. While the major proportion of the "preservation workflow" articles focused on the digital preservation workflows *inside* an OAIS–compliant archival system, being thus outside of our scope and therefore excluded, we found altogether 39 articles and project reports (among the hits with the above-mentioned keywords) that focus on interaction between archival services and ECM. In total, our review includes articles that are published at latest in September 2013.

Referring to the OAIS reference model [9] and the functional areas of ECM [20], we identified seven thematic areas of interaction between DP and ECM systems to organize our analysis (Preservation administration, Repository, Pre-ingest, Ingest; Access (in DP), Access (middleware), and Access (ECM) (Table 1). We followed also the idea introduced by the Protage [41] and SHAMAN projects [e.g. 6], which have reported conceptual frameworks and prototypes for middleware to be placed between preservation services and ECM systems. We categorized each of the two processes that lead interactions from ECM to a DP system, and back, under "Communication from ECM to DP" and "Communication from DP to ECM" (Table 1), respectively. We continued to identify the scopes of suggested contributions in each article. To create the concept matrix [52] of our review, we analyzed each article or report and labeled each according to the type of the suggested contribution as our analysis suggested. Twelve articles simply mentioned (Men) one or more areas of our interest without addressing much scrutiny on solutions or challenges. Furthermore, we identified articles representing a literature review (Rev) on one or more areas of interaction, or propositions (Prop) for, methods (Meth) of, models (Mod) of, applications (App) for, or evaluations (Eval) of suggested solutions (Table 1).

4   Results

In this section, we suggest first a model for interaction between ECM and DP. Secondly, we provide an overview on current solutions, models, and suggestions for the problem based on the reviewed articles and reports. As depicted in Table 1, many of the contributions in the literature remain at the level of the mention, while only a few of them introduce a model or method, and only one runs an evaluation of current models. Moreover, we found only 13 academic journal articles related to these issues, while the major part of the literature consists of technical conference and workshop papers (19) or plain project reports (7). Altogether, this addresses the relative immaturity of academic literature on the problem.

As mentioned above, we follow the idea of Protage [41] and SHAMAN [6] projects for a middleware to be placed between preservation services and ECM Systems. For example, the SHAMAN [6], project, Lavoie and Dempsey [27] and Wittek and Daranyi [54] define and discuss about processes and sets of preservation activities that would either precede the ingest process or succeed the access to preserved information in an OAIS-compliant preservation system. We called such processes as pre-ingest and access (middleware), respectively.

In addition, we identified a group of processes that are needed for management of communications between ECM and DP, and we decided to name this group of processes as preservation administration (Fig. 2). Altogether, we thus suggest three areas of interactive processes, which a middleware between ECM and DP needs to support. Figure 2 illustrates on a general level how our suggested middleware's processes are supposed to communicate with the components of ECM and DP. SIP (submission information package) is an information package that is delivered by the producer of information to the preservation system [9]. DIP (dissemination information package) is an information package that is sent by an archive to a consumer in response to a request to the preservation system [9].

Table 1. Concept matrix, categorization of literature

Article	Preservation administration	Interaction between DP and ECM					
		Communication from ECM to DP			Communication from DP to ECM		
		Repository	Pre-Ingest	Ingest	Access [DP]	Access [middleware]	Access [ECM]
[1]			Prop	Prop			
[3]			App	App			
[5]	Prop						
[6]	App		App	App	App	App	
[7]	Prop						
[8]			Mod			Mod	
[9]	Mod		Mod				
[10]	App			Men	Men		
[12]	App		App	App			
[13]				Mod	Mod		
[14]				Men	Men		
[16]	Men		Men	Men	Men	Men	
[18]				Prop	Prop		
[20]		Rev & Mod					Rev & Mod
[21]		Mod					Mod
[22]			Men	Men	Men		
[23]			Men			Men	
[24]				Prop			
[25]	Men						
[26]	App		App	Men			
[27]				App & Meth	App & Meth		
[29]				App, & Eval			
[30]			Men	Men			
[31]	Mod						
[32]			Mod	Mod	Mod	Mod	
[34]				Mod	Mod		
[36]			Men	Mod	Mod		
[39]	Men			Men			
[41]	Mod						
[42]	Mod		Mod			Mod	
[43]	Men			Men	Men		
[45]	Prop		Prop		Men	Prop	
[46]	Men		Men	Men	Men	Men	
[48]	Men		Men			Men	
[49]		Mod			Prop		
[50]				Men	Men		
[51]	Men						
[54]	Prop		Prop			Prop	
[55]	Men			Men	Men		

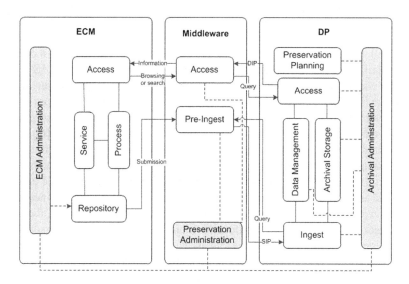

Fig. 2. Model for interaction between ECM and DP

The three areas of middleware processes, namely preservation administration, pre-ingest, and access, should automate interactions between ECM systems and DP services to the extent possible. When information is communicated from ECM to DP, a piece of information starts its journey from repository in an ECM system through pre-ingest in the middleware, which prepares the information for preservation and sends a SIP forward to the ingest component of digital preservation. On the way back, the access component of the preservation system packs the information object and metadata to a DIP which the middleware access function delivers to the access function of ECM. In addition to the ingest and access processes, we also need to plan and administrate for integrating (potentially more than one) ECM systems with (potentially more than one) preservation services [4]. In the following, current research on these areas of interactive processes is declared in more detail.

Pre-Ingest. DP research has mainly focused on particular techniques for packaging and ingesting information into a digital preservation system. However, less research has covered preparations for the ingest process before the preservation system would take over the SIP. As shown in Table 1, 17 out of 39 reviewed articles relate to processes and tasks of pre-ingest. Three articles suggest a model or method aiming for an enhancement in this area, two articles report an application developed for pre-ingest purposes, whereas 12 articles stay at the level of reflecting on existing literature. In the field of ECM, we need to keep in mind that contemporary ECM systems provide little, if any, support for producing preservation description information and implementing longer-term preservation appraisal in the active production/storage systems [25]. The content management interoperability (CMIS) standard [8], however, provides a specification for sharing information objects between ECM repositories, which could be potentially usable also in connection to DP services.

In the field of DP, a few targeted and automated techniques have been developed to extract preservation metadata from particular types of content [e.g. 29]. The PAIMAS standard [9] was created already a decade ago to recommend practices for a producer-archive interface communications. The definition of "consumer" in PAIMAS refers to persons or client systems, which implies the necessity of a human actor to interact with a DP system [9]. The PLANETS project has provided a set of pre-ingest and preservation workflow support techniques. PLANETS provides also testbeds for pre-ingest processes and tools for data/metadata management [43]. The SHAMAN project [6] has also created initial workflow support and tools from creation of objects and context data, through assembly of objects with metadata to form submission information packages. In addition, Heutelbeck et al. [22] highlight the definite need for automatic extraction of metadata and validation of manually entered metadata in the field of engineering and design. However, as an approach contradicting the goal of full automation, the Prome-theus project [12] has continued to develop tools for easing human interaction with archival services during pre-ingest and ingest workflows, especially for the needs of libraries.

Access. Alike in the case of ingest, few DP studies address an access concept beyond the OAIS specification that represents a viewpoint of one archival service or system. Hence, few studies discuss how other systems could have an integrated access to digital preservation services in general. At such a general level, Nguyen et al. [32] suggest architecture of a system of concept servers to enhance scalability and flexibility of access to differentiated service levels of long-term preservation. As well, ECM systems usually pay little, if any, explicit attention for receiving and processing DIPs automatically [25]. Altogether, 10 articles (out of 39) discussed the access-related tasks and processes. Three of those articles develop models for access, whereas the others simply mention or discuss about the area at a more general level.

The CMIS standard [8] provides several useful specifications for enhancing access between ECM repositories. As above in the context of pre-ingest, CMIS can also become a potential approach to enhance the system integration for access from DP to ECM. After the early focus on preservation and preservation planning workflows, the SHAMAN and PLANETS projects have as well provided their own toolsets, such as PLANETS Digital Object manager, graphical user interfaces and pluggable access components [43] and SHAMAN's "Multivalent browser" [6] to access preserved information resources. SHAMAN also provides tools for "adoption" of objects, including their descriptive metadata, context metadata, and preservation metadata through a graphical user inter-face so that the objects can be processed for reuse [6].

Preservation Administration. As Korb and Strodl [25] addressed, research and devel-opment on integrating preservation planning and ECM administration are rare. In order to make such integration take place, we suggest that an additional middleware element and a set of tasks for preservation administration are necessary (Fig. 2). This element is important especially in any environment where one organization could use more than one DP services. Within our review results, a half of the articles at least mentioned the issue of preservation administration, whereas 75 % of those remained merely at the level of initial conceptual reflections or propositions. Nguyen and Lake [32] and Schmidt et al. [42] suggest models for interactive processes in this area. Archival storage could be chosen to be implemented with delayed access and near-line storage or rapid access and high-performance storage [32]. Content servers could be implemented to function either just-in-time or to be always active [32]. The decision of the preferred service level furthermore will impact the actual workflows, tasks, and the experienced seamlessness of the preservation and access workflows. Here, the design details will depend on the application demand.

The workflows of preservation planning, administration and policy implementation have not been comprehensively discussed in the literature. However, we could recognize a few elements in the previous research which are worth considering while designing more detailed workflow solutions in the future. The SHAMAN project [6] developed a preservation management and planning interface to manage the pre-ingest phase. The PLANETS infrastructure provides a web portal framework that integrates a set of end user applications with a number of data repositories and a federation of grid/web and other services [43]. Tarrant et al. [48] discuss about possibilities of connecting the preservation planning element of the PLANETS project, Plato, and digital repository interfaces. Laleci et al. [26] introduce a semantic backend for ECM Systems, which could be useful for creation of relevant ontology mapping between content repositories, including ontologies for preservation.

All in all, the currently suggested ideas and solutions for pre-ingest, access, and preservation administration processes between ECM systems and DP remain, at best, at the level of prototypes which are so far (reportedly) created mainly in research projects for research purposes. As the analysis of the literature (Table 1) suggests, no single solution covers all of the necessary processes for integration between ECM and DP. Especially, it remains unclear how the distribution and execution of the preservation administration in relation to pre-ingest and access processes should be organized.

5   Discussion

Our review suggests three types of processes needed for integrating ECM systems with DP services. The review provides an overview on the existing literature. The literature mostly only mentions issues of ECM-DP integration. Very few research efforts suggest concrete methods, models, applications, let alone evaluations, and no suggested method, model or solution so far covers all of the identified integration aspects (Table 1). The most, if not all, arguments for better integration between ECM and DP have been provided by the DP scholars. In the field of ECM, DP-related issues are sometimes mentioned, but the field lacks concrete methods, models and solutions for proceeding with the integration between ECM and DP. The field of information systems seems still to largely ignore the research focus on long-term aspects of information as well.

In addition to addressing the design problem, our work contributes by suggesting a general-level model for processes and middleware for bridging (potentially many) ECM systems with (potentially many) preservation services. The model combines the previously separated perspectives of DP and ECM. The previous literature has mainly focused on the DP side of the model (Table 1). For example, Nguyen, Lake and Huber [31], focus on increasing flexibility and scalability of a DP solution in itself. We argue for a need to go beyond the plain focus on preservation and add to the scalability and flexibility of all interactions that are needed between ECM and DP. Our work also highlights that in addition to focusing on archival administration inside *one* OAIS-compliant DP solution [9], *preservation administration as a whole* needs to become an intermediary process that will need to "plug-and-play" among potentially several information systems and DP services over time. One organization can, on one hand, use many DP services, while, on the other hand, a particular preservation service can accept submissions and access requests from several ECM applications [3]. The suggested middleware to support such processes should be able to link preservation administration, pre-ingest and access among ECM systems and DP services as seamlessly as possible in the future. This represents a new design challenge in the field of digital preservation.

As such, the identified design challenge suggests a complementary view also to our understanding of ECM functionality [20, 47] by addressing the need for making a clear distinction between contemporary content management repositories and long-term DP solutions. That is, we suggest that a separate logical layer of "long-term digital preservation" going beyond the simple repository or storage component should be added to the functional ECM frameworks and architectures, such as the one proposed by Grahlmann et al. [20]. Our work also addresses the need for designing preferably standardized solutions for integrating and interfacing the DP layer to the repository and access layers [20] of operational ECM solutions.

Designs of specific solutions for pre-ingest, access and preservation administration processes depend a lot on the actual domain of information and the related metadata standards and models. Hence, the subsequent development may require several application processing interfaces between the middleware and particular types of ECM and other information systems. Having that in mind, and to provide impetus for the development of more detailed studies in digital preservation field, we suggest a stream of design research related to such middleware in the future.

Hence, our study altogether suggests a motivation and problem definition for a significant and timely design research program [35] on ECM-DP integration and supporting middleware. We suggest that future design research and development efforts of such middleware should focus on the challenges of linking several ECM systems to several DP services since the need for implementing this many-to-many system interaction pattern is ultimately expected. Specific integration and interaction challenges between particular types of content production systems and digital preservation services create another path for future research. In addition to "ordinary" ECM systems, we may also need to preserve data from other organizational information systems, for example, product life-cycle management (PLM) systems [53], enterprise resource planning (ERP) systems [45], engineering systems [22] or e-health systems. Information systems and DP systems will both change over time. A stream of future research should thus aim at solving challenges and design issues for seamless integration and enhanced automation related to continuing management of changes in information systems and preservation services [1]. This issue is addressed, e.g., in a large, on-going European design research project [17].

Our review has also its limitations. A closer technical evaluation of the software prototypes and evaluation results was not in focus within this review. More detailed models of tasks and workflow implementations and analyses of the existing partial solutions within the particular functional areas need still to be conducted. We aim at creating a more detailed task list under each of the process types of our preliminary model. Actual implementation of the middleware will still need considerable design research and development efforts. Another shortcoming is our dominating focus on the academic literature. Specialized vendors of ECM systems and cloud-based preservation services may already provide solutions for the interaction between information systems and preservation services, which are not covered by our review.

Plain construction of middleware between DP and ECM per se guarantees no automation of system interaction. Even in the near future, interactions between ECM and DP will remain challenging without a human actor who is in charge of configuring the middleware workflows and, especially, taking care of the preservation administration process. In contemporary practice, this requires rather expensive and tailored projects [38]. In the contemporary research prototypes, the integrations will still continue to be developed in a tailored manner for a while in order to create the first pilots of more automated pre-ingest and access workflows. Several inter-system queries, such as a request generated by ECM for deletion of an object in an archive, may still need to be checked by a human intermediary. However, alongside the first prototypes for better integration of pre-ingest and access between ECM and DP, the research efforts should pursue systematically towards more generic solutions to support the overall preservation management as well. Addition of intelligence to automated processes or services that could ease tasks of preservation administration and decrease human intervention thus continues to be an important subject for further research.

6   Conclusion

The rapidly increasing amount of digital content that needs to be preserved and accessed over long time poses new challenges for system integration between enterprise content management and long-term digital preservation systems. Enterprise content management and digital preservation have been so far established as relatively separate research fields, whereas the need for integrating organizational content management and digital preservation services in practice has started to emerge. To concretize and to position the problem in relation to contemporary research, we identified and analyzed 39 articles and suggested a general-level model of ECM-DP interactions based on the literature. The model conceptualizes a novel design problem and argues further for three types of interaction processes which need to exist between ECM and DP systems (From ECM to DP, From DP to ECM, and preservation administration). Based on the model, we propose five avenues for future research and development:

- middleware which could connect (potentially many) ECM systems and (potentially many) DP systems to each other with increasingly automated functionality of pre-ingest, access, and preservation administration,

- standardized interfaces to integrate the DP layer architecturally to the repository and access layers [20] of ECM,
- solutions for integrated interactions among DP services and also other types of systems than traditional ECM, such as ERP, engineering, PLM, and e-health systems,
- solutions and practices for preservation administration to manage changes that will take place unavoidably in information systems and DP services over time in order to sustain the established system interactions, and
- intelligence and automation to decrease hitherto necessary human intervention in ingest, access and preservation administration among information systems and DP services.

As modern DP systems and services need to deal with rapidly increasing amounts of digital content and increasingly complex and heterogeneous digital objects, such as relational databases, product data, and digital workflows, the design research and development efforts on enhanced interactions between digital preservation and information systems will remain as a non-trivial field within the foreseeable future.

Acknowledgement. This work was partially funded by the European Commission in the context of the FP7 ICT project ForgetIT (under grant no: 600826).

References

1. Afrasiabi Rad, P., Nilsson, J., Päivärinta, T.: Administration of digital preservation services in the cloud over time: design issues and challenges for organizations. In: Endicott-Popovsky, B. (ed.) Proceedings of the 2nd International Conference on Cloud Security Management, ACPI, Reading, pp. 1–8 (2014)
2. Alalwan, J.A., Weistroffer, H.R.: Enterprise content management research: a comprehensive review. J. Enterp. Inf. Manag. **25**(5), 441–461 (2012)
3. Andersson, I., Lindbäck, L., Lindqvist, G., Nilsson, J., Runardotter, M.: Web archiving using the collaborative archiving services testbed. In: e-2011 Conference proceedings (2011)
4. Andersson, I., Randers, F., Runardotter, M., Nilsson, J., Päivärinta, T.: Design principles for a quality model supporting the selection of a cloud-based preservation solution. In: Proceedings of the 36th Information Systems Research Seminar in Scandinavia (IRIS), 11–14 Aug 2013. Oslo, Norway (2013)
5. Becker, C., Faria, L., Duretec, K.: Scalable decision support for digital preservation. OCLC Syst. Serv. **30**(4), 249–284 (2014)
6. Birrell, D., Menzies, K., Maceviciute, E., Wilson, T., Wollschläger, T., Konstantelos, L., Zabos, A.: Shaman: D14. 2-report on Demonstration and Evaluation Activity in the Domain of Memory Institutions. Borås Academic Digital Archive (BADA), Högskolan (2011)
7. Burda, D., Teuteberg, F.: Towards an understanding of needs, capabilities and alignment mechanisms in digital preservation: results from an explorative case study. In: Wirtschaftsinformatik Proceedings, pp. 785–799 (2013)
8. Choy, D., Müller, F., McVeigh, R.: Content Management Interoperability Services (CMIS) Version 1.1 OASIS Content Management Interoperability Services (CMIS) TC (2011)
9. Consultative Committee for Space Data Systems: Recommendation for Space Data System Practices, Recommended Practice for a Producer-Archive Interface Methodology Abstract Standard, Washington DC/St. CCSDS Secretariat / Magenta Book, Hubert (2004)

10. Constantopoulos, P., Dritsou, V.: An ontological model for digital preservation. In: International Symposium in Digital Curation DigCCur April 2007, Chapel Hill, NC (2007)
11. Decman, M., Vintar, M.: A Possible Solution for Digital Preservation of E-government. Aslib Proc. New Inf. Perspect. **65**(4), 406–424 (2013)
12. del Pozo, N., Elford, D., Pearson, D.: Prometheus: managing the ingest of media carriers. In: National Library of Australia Staff Papers (2009)
13. Digital Curation Centre: Digital curation lifecycle model, (2013). http://www.dcc.ac.uk/resources/curation-lifecycle-model. Accessed Feb 2013
14. DigitalNZ: Make it digital - getting started with digitisation (2013). http://www.digitalnz.org/make-it-digital/getting-started-with-digitisation. Accessed April 2013
15. ERPANET: Policies for digital preservation. In: ERPANET Training Seminar, Paris, 29–30 Jan 2003 http://www.erpanet.org/events/2003/paris/ERPAtraining-Paris_Report.pdf (2003)
16. Farquhar, A., Hockx-Yu, H.: Planets: integrated services for digital preservation. J. Ser. Community **21**(2), 140–145 (2008)
17. ForgetIT: Concise preservation by combining managed forgetting and contextualized remembering, (2015) http://www.forgetit-project.eu/ Accessed Feb 2015
18. Freitas, R.A.P., Ramalho, J.C.: Relational databases digital preservation. Doctoral thesis, University of Porto (2009)
19. Giaretta, D.: Advanced Digital Preservation. Springer, Dorset, ISBN: 978–3-642-16808-6 (2011)
20. Grahlmann, K.R., Helms, R.W., Hilhorst, C., Brinkkemper, S., Van Amerongen, S.: Reviewing enterprise content management: a functional framework. Eur. J. Inf. Syst. **21**(3), 268–286 (2012)
21. Haug, A.: The implementation of enterprise content management systems in SMEs. J. Enterp. Inf. Manag. **25**(4), 349–372 (2012)
22. Heutelbeck, D., Brunsmann, J., Wilkes, W., Hunsdörfer, A.: Motivations and challenges for digital preservation in design and engineering. In: InDP 2009, Austin, TX (2009)
23. Hitchcock, S.: Setting institutional repositories on the path to digital preservation. Final report to JISC Keepit project, (2011). http://repository.jisc.ac.uk/553/1/finalreport-keepit10.pdf. Accessed Feb 2013
24. Hunter, J., Choudhury, S.: Implementing preservation strategies for complex multimedia objects. In: Koch, T., Sølvberg, I.T. (eds.) ECDL 2003. LNCS, vol. 2769, pp. 473–486. Springer, Heidelberg (2003)
25. Korb, J., Strodl, S.: Digital preservation for enterprise content: a gap-analysis between ECM and OAIS. In: proceedings of the 7th International Conference on Preservation of Digital Objects (iPRES 2010), Wien, pp. 221–229 (2010)
26. Laleci, G.B., Aluc, G., Dogac, A., Sinaci, A., Kilic, C., Tuncer, F.: A semantic backend for content management systems. Knowl. Based Syst. **23**(8), 832–843 (2010)
27. Lavoie, B., Dempsey, L.: thirteen ways of looking at… digital preservation. D-Lib Mag. **10**(7/8), 1082–9873 (2004)
28. Levy, D.M.: Heroic measures: reflections on the possibility and purpose of digital preservation. In: proceedings of the third ACM conference on Digital libraries, pp. 152–161 (1998)
29. Mao, S., Kim, J.W., Thoma, G.R.: A dynamic feature generation system for automated metadata extraction in preservation of digital materials. In: Proceedings of the first International Workshop on Document Image Analysis for Libraries, pp. 225–232 (2004)
30. Mayer, R., Proell, S., Rauber, A.: On the applicability of workflow management systems for the preservation of business processes. In: Proceedings of the 9th International Conference on Preservation of Digital Objects (iPRES 2012), Toronto, pp. 58–65 (2012)

31. Nguyen, Q.L., Lake, A., Huber, M.: Evolvable and scalable system of content servers for a large digital preservation archives. In: 4th Annual IEEE Systems Conference, pp. 306–310 (2010)

32. Nguyen, Q.L. Lake, A.: Content server system architecture for providing differentiated levels of service in a digital preservation cloud. In: IEEE International Conference on Cloud Computing (CLOUD), pp. 557–564 (2011)

33. Nordheim, S., Päivärinta, T.: Implementing enterprise content management: from evolution through strategy to contradictions out-of-the-box. Eur. J. Inf. Syst. **15**(6), 648–662 (2006)

34. Page, K., Palma, R., Holubowicz, P., Klyne, G., Soiland-Reyes, S., Cruickshank, D., … Gomez Perez, J.: From workflows to research objects: an architecture for preserving the semantics of science. In: Proceedings of the 2nd International Workshop on Linked Science, Nov 2012, Boston, USA (2012)

35. Peffers, K., Tuunanen, T., Rothenberger, M.A., Chatterjee, S.: A design science research methodology for information systems research. J. Manag. Inf. Syst. **24**(3), 45–78 (2007)

36. Portico: Preservation Step-by-Step, (2013). http://www.portico.org/digital-preservation/services/preservation-approach/preservation-step-by-step#step1. Accessed June 2013

37. Päivärinta, T., Munkvold, B.E.: Enterprise content management: an integrated perspective on information management. In: Proceedings of the 38th Annual Hawaii International Conference System Sciences, HICSS'05, pp. 96–106 (2005)

38. Päivärinta, T., Samuelsson, G., Jonsson, E., Swensson, E.: Nyttorealisering av FGS:er: Delprojekt 2, Project report (in Swedish). Riksarkivet, Stockholm (2014)

39. Ross, S.: Digital preservation archival science and methodological foundations for digital libraries. New Rev. Inf. Netw. **17**(1), 43–68 (2012)

40. Rydberg, J.: Staten Bygger E-arkiv för En Halv Miljard, Computer Sweden, 19 Aug (2014)

41. Saul, C., Klett, F.: Conceptual framework for the use of the service-oriented architecture-approach in the digital preservation. In: Proceedings of The Fifth International Conference on Preservation of Digital Objects, pp. 229–234 (2008)

42. Schmidt, R., King, R., Jackson, A., Wilson, C., Steeg, F., Melms, P.: A framework for distributed preservation workflows. Int. J. Digit. Curation **5**(1), 205–217 (2010)

43. Schmidt, R., Lindley, A., King, R., Jackson, A., Wilson, C., Steeg, F.: The planets IF: a framework for integrated access to preservation tools. In: Proceedings of the 1st International Digital Preservation Interoperability Framework Symposium, New York, pp. 10:1–10:8 (2010)

44. Smith, H.A., McKeen, J.D.: Developments in Practice VIII: enterprise content management. Commun. Assoc. Inf. Syst. **11**, 647–659 (2003)

45. Stewart, C.: Preservation and access in an age of e-science and electronic records: sharing the problem and discovering common solutions. J. Libr. Adm. **52**(3–4), 265–278 (2012)

46. Strodl, S., Petrov, P., Rauber, A.: Research on Digital Preservation within Projects Co-Funded by the European Union in the ICT Programme. Vienna University of Technology, Wien (2011)

47. Svärd, P.: Enterprise content management and the records continuum model as strategies for long-term preservation of digital information. Rec. Manag. J. **23**(3), 159–176 (2013)

48. Tarrant, D., Hitchcock, S., Carr, L., Kulovits, H., Rauber, A.: Connecting preservation planning and plato with digital repository interfaces. In: 7th International Conference on Preservation of Digital Objects (iPRES2010). pp. 153–161 (2010)

49. Tyrväinen, P., Päivärinta, T., Salminen, A., Iivari, J.: Characterizing the evolving research on enterprise content management. Eur. J. Inf. Syst. **15**(6), 627–634 (2006)

50. Upward, F.: Modelling the continuum as paradigm shift in recordkeeping and archiving processes, and beyond - a personal reflection. Rec. Manag. J. **10**(3), 115–139 (2000)

51. Vom Brocke, J., Simons, A., Cleven, A.: Towards a business process-oriented approach to enterprise content management: the ECM-blueprinting framework. Inf. Syst. E-Bus. Manag. **4**, 475–496 (2011)
52. Webster, J., Watson, R.T.: Analyzing the past to prepare for the future. Writ. Lit. Rev. MIS Q. **26**(2), xiii–xxiii (2002)
53. Wilkes, W., Brunsmann, J., Heutelbeck, D., Hundsdörfer, A., Hemmje, M., Heidbrink, H.U.: Towards support for long-term digital preservation in product life cycle management. In: The Sixth International Conference on Preservation of Digital Objects (iPRES 2009), pp. 211–219 (2009)
54. Wittek, P., Darányi, S.: Digital preservation in grids and clouds: a middleware approach. J. Grid Comput. **10**(1), 133–149 (2012)
55. Wolski, M., Simons, N., Richardson, J.: ECMs and institutional repositories. The case for a unified enterprise approach to content management. In: THETA: The Higher Education Technology Agenda, Hobart, Tasmania (2013)

Procuring Usability: Experiences of Usability Testing in Tender Evaluation

Sirpa Riihiaho[1]([✉]), Marko Nieminen[1], Stina Westman[2],
Ronja Addams-Moring[1], and Jukka Katainen[3]

[1] Department of Computer Science, Aalto University, 00076 Aalto, Finland
sirpa.riihiaho@aalto.fi
[2] Department of Media Technology, Aalto University, 00076 Aalto, Finland
[3] IT Services, Aalto University, 00076 Aalto, Finland

Abstract. Comparing software systems for a purchase decision in a highly regulated public procurement process is a new domain for usability testing. We performed a comparative summative usability evaluation of Current Research Information Systems (CRIS) as a part of a public procurement process in Finland, EU. The evaluation method had to provide objective and unbiased results for comparison and it had to be defined in detail already in the invitation to tender. In this paper, we report the details of our successful procedure that enabled straightforward and quick decision making in selecting the winning system. Additionally, we present calculations to legitimate the potentially higher investment costs through estimated savings and increased income.

Keywords: Usability evaluation · Public procurement · Research information system · Test user · Test task · System usability scale

1 Introduction

Since the emergence of usability engineering [26], usability testing has been an integral part of user-centred software development [14]. Typically, usability testing is applied in development projects to discover defects in the user interface with the aim to improve its functionality and performance. This type of formative evaluation [4, 12] has long been applied, and performs well in software development surroundings.

However, in commercial-off-the-shelf (COTS) software system procurement, formative usability testing is not applicable. Instead, a comparative approach emphasizing the use of summative evaluation [4, 12] is needed. Public procurement of information systems must be done according to legislation and regulation on public contracts. In European Union, the directive 2004/18/EC on *"the coordination of procedures for the award of public works contracts, public supply contracts and public service contracts"* defines constraints and requirements for activities that take place in such procurement projects [9]. This is reflected in the national legislation e.g. in the Finnish Act on Public Contracts (348/2007) [11]. At the same time as these regulations aim at improving the transparency and equality of tenders, they introduce challenges on how to deal with usability issues in such projects. Even though usability has long been

© Springer International Publishing Switzerland 2015
H. Oinas-Kukkonen et al. (Eds.): SCIS 2015, LNBIP 223, pp. 108–120, 2015.
DOI: 10.1007/978-3-319-21783-3_8

acknowledged as an important factor in operational benefits in information systems [3], we still lack proper methods and practices to take usability into account in public procurements.

In this paper, we report a case study on applying usability testing in government system procurement. In previous COTS procurement cases in our organisation, inspection methods, such as heuristic evaluations (e.g. [22]), had been used, so real users had not been involved in the evaluations. However, in this case, inspections were considered as too subjective, and their ambiguous results (see e.g. [20]) were considered to generate complaints to the Market Court. Furthermore, in cases where a major impact of the system is expected in the operative organisation, the involvement of real users is of utmost importance to ensure that the system meets at least the minimum requirements of the key user groups. Therefore, usability tests with users were selected over usability inspections.

In this case, three universities were purchasing a Current Research Information System (CRIS) at the same time. Thousands of researchers and administrative personnel were expected to use this system in these universities, as the coordinating university alone had more than 2500 researchers. The participating two other universities committed to procure their system according to the decision of the coordinator.

The CRIS system has a very straightforward impact to university funding: a substantial part of the university funding from the Ministry of Education and Culture rests on the activities and publications reported through this system. Therefore, the information need to be complete, correct and easy to enter even for casual users. Typically, researchers use the system once or twice a year, emphasising the need for a straightforward and easy-to-use system. By applying user testing already in the procurement process, we could address critical usability issues beforehand to support the decision making and selection of this central system.

The local and international regulations i.e. procurement directives and law, give strict legal requirements for procuring. These requirements apply in organisations governed by public, if the service contract exceeds a threshold value. This type of public contracts in the EU are to be awarded based on objective criteria to ensure transparency, non-discrimination and equal treatment, and effective competition [9]. Moreover, the current legal practice in Finland involving procurement is very strict. EU public procurement law, Finnish Act on Public Contracts [11] and both EU and Finnish case law thus pose considerable challenges for usability evaluation in public procurement.

These regulatory constraints indicate that usability criteria may be used to compare tenders, as long as they are [11]:

- linked to the object of contract
- relevant to choosing the economically most advantageous tender
- measurable
- objective
- non-discriminatory
- published in the invitation to tender.

There are very few reported examples of using usability evaluations as selection criteria in public procurement [17]. Despite Carey's [8] opening on "Usability Requirements

Model addressing public procurements" already in 1991, this academic discussion and research did not continue and attract broader academic interest until Buie & Murray's book on Usability in Government Systems in 2012 [6]. In order to evolve this practice, it is important to understand the ways in which user-centred methods may be utilised in such a highly regulated context.

The research question in this paper is, how to integrate usability testing into a public procurement process so that the results significantly contribute to the decision making when selecting the new system. As a result of our study, we argue that usability evaluations can be successfully used as selection criteria in public procurement. Our results inform practitioners of organising systematic comparisons in information system procurement. For academic readers, we introduce initial experiences of summative usability testing in a regulatory context, in contrast to non-regulated private software development.

2   Case Description

A Current Research Information System (CRIS) is an information system used to store and manage data about research conducted at a university. It supports researchers, administrative personnel and management at all levels in documenting, managing, reporting, sharing and evaluating research activities. The information reported through CRIS gives the basis for university funding from the Ministry of Education and Culture. In late 2012, three Finnish universities started collaboration between their projects to procure current research information systems. These modern off-the-shelf software solutions were sought to replace existing, outdated research registers. By 2013, Aalto University was chosen as the party to procure a system on behalf of the three universities.

As all the factors used to compare tenders need to be described in the invitation to tender, also usability criteria and evaluation methods needed to be specified in advance without knowing how many tenders had to be compared. The evaluation criteria had to be objective, and the metrics needed to be well-established and relevant. Furthermore, the procedure had to be identical for all the tenders.

The methods were selected, designed and carried out collaboratively with usability researchers in the university, the project staff at the three universities, and the procurement specialists. After assessing alternative methods [16], a typical usability test was finally selected as the evaluation method. This way, the future users could be involved as test participants, and we could ensure that the new system would meet the minimum requirements of the key user groups. In addition to usability, also accessibility was considered in the evaluation by including one visually impaired test participant using a screen reader.

In spring 2013, an advance notice about the CRIS procurement was published at the national public procurement announcement site. Five suppliers indicated their interest in the procurement. Separate from the discussions with the companies, the usability evaluation methods were defined and documented in autumn 2013. In November 2013, technical dialogues with the interested vendors were organised to get feedback on the draft documents that included also the usability criteria. Based on these dialogues, two or three tenders were expected, and the potential system providers were promised unofficial feedback from the tests to be freely used in their further development. The final usability evaluation methods were then described in two appendices to the invitation to tender, published in December 2013. Table 1 presents the timeline of the CRIS procurement.

Table 1. Schedule of the CRIS procurement with usability planning and implementation.

Time	Phase and activities
05/2012	**Project started** - requirements - market study - definition of usability methods
05/2013	**Advance notice to vendors** - indication of interest from vendors
08-11/2013	**Definition of usability methods and criteria** - user groups: researchers and administrative personnel - test tasks: 5 relevant tasks per group - metrics: effectiveness, efficiency, satisfaction
10-11/2013	**Investment decision** - technical dialogues - joint procurement decision
12/2013	**Invitation to tender** - usability evaluation methods described in detail
02/2014	**Tender submissions** - finally, tenders from 2 vendors
03-04/2014	**Usability tests** - tests with 12 users (2 groups; 6 + 6 users)
06/2014	**Procurement decision** - usability test results as the main selection criteria

3   Method

Finnish Act on Public Contracts [11] requires the evaluation of competing tenders and systems in a procurement project to be measurable, objective, and non-discriminatory. Therefore, the outcome from the comparison must provide clear evidence on the preference over the offered systems.

As an internationally acknowledged standard, ISO 9241-11 was selected as the framework for the usability metrics [13]. The standard defines the measurable parameters as effectiveness, efficiency, and satisfaction. Usability test is a well-established method that has been widely used to measure and provide answers to these parameters. In our case, the available resources, including the tight procurement schedule and the limited demonstration systems, did not leave room for longitudinal studies. Therefore, traditional usability tests in controlled settings were selected. The usability metrics were then selected on the basis of the Common Industry Format (CIF) for usability test report in ISO/IEC 25062 [15]. Bevan et al. presented already in 2002 that the Common Industry Format for usability test reports *"provides a platform on which to evaluate potential competitive products from a number of supplier organisations during the procurement of a new system/product"*, and integrates consumers' requirements with objective user performance and satisfaction metrics [2].

Extensive simulations on the possible results of effectiveness, efficiency, and satisfaction related to the investment price were run to find limits and weights for the metrics. The simulations revealed that an aggregated single-score metric on usability would not provide sufficient and clear information for decision making despite such attempts [23]. Finally, the weights of the different parameters were set so that higher than minimum satisfaction could compensate the price of the tender. For effectiveness and satisfaction, there were minimum levels that had to be reached for the tender to be considered in the procurement. The weight assigned to usability in the scoring of the tenders was 30 % (efficiency 10 %, satisfaction 20 %).

The absolute results of time on tasks and users' satisfaction were not of main interest, but the differences between the systems, so a within-subjects design was selected over between-subjects [18]. Additionally, this within-subjects evaluation enabled calculations on the differences in the return on investment (ROI) between the compared systems. These calculations, on their part, made it easy to argue for a higher investment price as the ROI could be estimated.

The usability tests were conducted in a usability laboratory in order to minimize disruptions and to ensure equal working conditions for the evaluated systems. Representatives of the key user groups performed a sample of tasks with demonstration systems offered by the tenderers. Thinking aloud was not used due to performance time measures. A test moderator sat next to the users and helped if technical problems arose, but otherwise followed a predefined test procedure without giving guidance on the use of the systems or answering the users' questions.

Users. Two user groups were defined to reflect the use cases: researchers and administrative personnel. In order to ensure the equality of the tenderers, the recruiting protocol was described in the invitation to tender, although the actual test users were not known at that time. Representative researchers and support staff were then recruited through the university intranet.

Finally, 6 users were recruited for both user groups. Although Lewis [19] presents a detailed equation to estimate an appropriate number of test users for certain problem coverage, we were not interested in the usability problems as such. Thereby, the strict test schedule and considerable preparations for each test user restricted the number of test users into 6 for both groups. Even so, this number is in conformance with the studies by Virzi [25] and Nielsen [21] showing that 4–5 users reveal 77–85 % of the problems, as well as the recommendation by Dumas and Redish [10] to use 6–12 users from each studied user group.

Researchers and postgraduate students from the case university were recruited for the first group including one visually impaired user. Research support staff from the university was recruited for the other group. CVs with publications were collected from the first group and prepared before the tests to make the test tasks as realistic as possible.

Tasks. The test tasks were selected from predicted use cases based on current key tasks with similar systems and most common new tasks planned with the new system. The use of one system in the test session was not to take longer than 90 min, so only five tasks were defined for each user group. These tasks were iteratively developed within the project groups at the three universities to make sure they matched real user needs and that the wordings were clear. For each task, a maximum time of 15 min was reserved in the test procedure. Thereby, we could ensure that each user tried to perform all the tasks. The essential contents of the five test tasks for the researchers were the following: (1) Enter the article details manually in the system, (2) Create a description of a research visit to another university, (3) Modify your research profile, (4) Construct a CV with publications and activities from your profile, (5) Import previous publications to the system from a BibTeX file.

Several test tasks required the user to input data. Example entries were given in the invitation to tender but all users were able to input their own data to make it easier for the users to assess the usability and also the utility of the systems as they could better relate the tasks into their own work [7].

Measures. The ISO 9241-11 [13] provided the assessed parameters (effectiveness, efficiency, satisfaction), and the Common Industry Format (CIF) for usability test report [15] gave the measurable metrics:

- *Effectiveness* was measured by how many tasks were completed successfully within the maximum time. Total effectiveness was then calculated by summing successful tasks over all the users. Any tasks not finished in time, abandoned by the user, or deemed as not successful either by the user or the evaluators were not counted in.
- *Efficiency* was measured as the average time for a user to complete the tasks. Time for task was measured individually for each task and user. For successful tasks, the actual time for task was used. For non-successful tasks, the maximum 15 min was used.
- *Satisfaction* was measured with the positive version of the System Usability Scale (SUS) [24]. A bilingual questionnaire (Finnish and English) was prepared because the users' language preferences were not known at the time of preparations. The SUS questionnaire was scored between 10 and 50 points in this case due to multiple criteria (price, supplementary requirements, and efficiency) for scoring the tenders. For the purposes of this paper, however, all the scores have been transformed into conventional SUS scores (max 100 points).

Minimum criteria were set both for the total effectiveness (70 % of the test tasks) and for the satisfaction (50 points in the conventional SUS scores). The latter was influenced by the semantic interpretation of the scale [1] where 52 points was the minimum score for the adjective rating "ok".

System. The number of systems to be tested was not known at the time when the evaluation method was defined, so the method needed to be flexible. Therefore, counterbalancing or randomizing any number of systems was defined, as well as potential need to divide the tests into multiple sessions.

Each tenderer was required to make a demonstration system available online as part of their tender. The demonstration needed not to be the complete product, but it had to support all the test tasks and include the university data that were described in the invitation to tender. The tenderers were also asked to include instructions with screen captures for the administrative personnel's test tasks.

4   Procedure and Test Setup

Two systems (named A and B in this paper) were eventually tendered. Each user evaluated both systems in back-to-back sessions, with the order counterbalanced. The tests in the usability laboratory were recorded (audio, video and live screen capture) at the users' consent.

Five senior master's degree students in usability moderated the test sessions, but each test user interacted with only one moderator. A faculty usability expert together with the procurement project manager oversaw each test session from the one-way-mirror-separated observation room, where a second student also took notes.

Three pilot tests were run to provide the moderators practice with the procedure and to solve any technical issues. All the test participants used the same laptop, except for the visually impaired user who had his own laptop with a screen reader software (JAWS) installed.

At the beginning of each test session, the test user was informed of the purpose and procedure of the evaluation. The users then received the test tasks one at a time, first read aloud and then in writing. The representatives of the administrative personnel also received the tenderer-supplied instructions, which they were free to use when doing the tasks. The maximum time of 15 min for each task was also articulated. The users were asked to inform the moderator when they were either done or had decided to abandon a task. The users were free to end a task or the whole test at any time.

All users answered the SUS survey after finishing the test tasks with one system. After that, more feedback on the system was gathered with a short interview. Then, a short break was held. A second session was then conducted for the second system with an identical procedure.

To ensure that both systems and all users were handled equally, all moderators used the same printed script and instructions with all the test users. If test users asked questions that could not be answered without potentially endangering equal treatment, the moderators used scripted answers, such as apologizing for not being allowed to help, empowering the user to make their own decisions, and making sure if the user wanted to continue with the task at hand.

After the second session, there was an exit interview eliciting impressions with the test and the systems as well as providing an opportunity to give feedback on any part of the test. During the exit interview, each user was asked additional questions about their personal preferences, recommendations to the university, and relevancy of the test tasks. The users were thanked and compensated for their time with a voucher.

5 Results

System B scored higher in all measures, passing the minimum limits for effectiveness and satisfaction set in the invitation to tender. System A did not pass either of the minimum limits, so according to the rules set in the invitation to tender, this tender was excluded from the competitive bidding.

Effectiveness: Total effectiveness for System A was 26 and 46 for System B, corresponding to 43 % versus 77 % of tasks being successful (Fig. 1). Thus, a user was able to complete 2.2 tasks on average with System A and 3.8 tasks with System B. Across users, 17 tasks (28 % of all tasks) were abandoned by the users on System A, compared to 1 task (2 %) on System B.

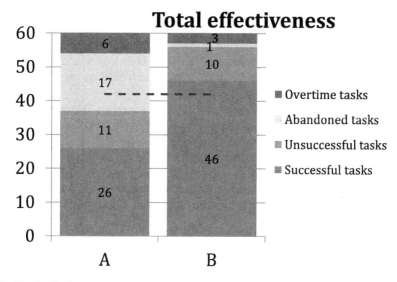

Fig. 1. Total effectiveness out of maximum 60 per system. System A did not reach the minimum acceptable level (42, dotted line), so it was excluded from further competitive bidding.

Efficiency: The average time for the all the test tasks per user was 55 min for System A and 35 min for System B. For System A, the time on task varied from 1:52 to the maximum 15:00, and for System B, from 1:21 to 15:00. The maximum time of 15 min was used for the non-successful tasks.

Satisfaction: The results of the SUS questionnaire were 38 for System A and 62 for System B (Fig. 2). The scores for System A varied from 2.5 to 65, and for System B from 10 to 90.

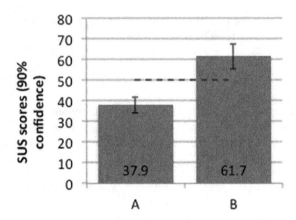

Fig. 2. SUS score averages with a 90 % confidence interval. The required minimum score (50) is illustrated with the dotted line.

All of these differences were in favour of system B in the researcher user group. The screen reader user had considerable difficulty with both systems and managed to complete only one task, on system B. Thereby, the lowest SUS survey scores for both systems were from the screen reader user.

The three usability measures correlated well with each other. The effectiveness and satisfaction survey scores correlated strongly $r(24) = .72$, $p < .0001$, and also efficiency and satisfaction correlated $r(24) = -.62$, $p < 0.001$.

All except one user expressed their personal preference for System B, but all the users preferred it if they were to choose the system for the university. As a measure of validity, according to the feedback from the test users, the test tasks were considered relevant and representative of typical tasks that the users would perform when working with a CRIS system.

6   Discussion

We identified following key benefits on how the usability evaluation contributed to the procurement in this case:

- Pre-defined minimum levels of usability (efficiency, effectiveness, satisfaction) made it possible to leave unacceptable systems out of consideration.
- Detailed pre-defined user tasks in tests leave out "promiseware" i.e. software that aims at fulfilling the requirements in the future. Especially the requirement to deliver a working system for the tests seemed to narrow down the number of tenders, as well as the mentioning of a screen reader test user.
- The usability tests can be repeated for acceptance testing in the introduction of the final system.

- Feedback provided by the test users informs the planning of user support and training.
- Straightforward facts and results supported extremely quick and efficient decision making in management. Estimates on return on investment, on their part, helped in justifying a higher investment price.

At the end, the minimum criteria for usability ended up being the cornerstone in comparing the tenders and selecting the winner. Since the performance of System A did not reach the minimum requirements for usability, it needed not to be included in further considerations, and economic comparisons were not required. Therefore, these usability comparisons and minimum criteria were extremely important in the decision making process, and made it much more straightforward than expected. As a consequence, the remaining decision making process became cheaper than expected due to less analyses and less decision making committee meetings. Thereby, we conclude that the comparative usability tests reached their goals very well.

In a typical multi-disciplinary way, the process required expertise from multiple parties, including system domain experts. Therefore, identifying appropriate participants and coordinating communication between different specialists was crucial in the process, and required strict and clear project management. Rough estimates on the required workload is presented in Table 2.

Table 2. Estimates of workloads for usability evaluation.

Efforts related to usability evaluation	Workload in person days
Specification of evaluation method	30
Documentation for procurement	18
Recruitment and input of user data	10
Test set-up	24
Test sessions	30

Altogether, the estimated amount of working days in the project is 112 days, i.e., 5–6 person months. If conducted through "company internal" work, estimate on the cost would be around 30.000 EUR. With the help of external consultancy the costs would be around 90.000 EUR. However, if we compare these costs to the costs from the actual use of the system over its lifetime in the universities, the costs become very legitimate. For example, the financial benefits of the completed usability comparison come from increased efficiency (i.e. saved working time) as well as from the increased earnings (accurate and timely reporting of results). The 30.000 EUR (the realised internal cost of the comparison) cost may be converted into 1000 h of work (30 EUR/h). As the evaluated system will eventually have more than 3000 users, the costs of the evaluation will be covered through 20 min of saved working time per user. Based on the intensity of use of the system, we argue that the costs will be easily covered within one year. Following calculation illustrates this: If a researcher reports 3 publications, updates her CV and other research activities (e.g. information about a running research project), one can argue that these tasks together correspond to the total time of the test tasks indicating the difference of at least 20 min per person.

In addition to the saved working time, the universities can increase their income through improved reporting of research activities and publications. Taking into account the differences between the amount of unsuccessful and abandoned tasks, the winning system produced 77 % (26 vs. 46) more correct task completions. As 13 % of funding for the university from the Ministry of Education and Culture is based on reported publications, the impact of better reporting could be as high as 20 MEUR (40 % less reported publications with the failing system) from the evaluated total of 50 MEUR (i.e. the 13 % part of the total funding for the university). These savings definitely legitimate the higher investment cost of the winning system.

Furthermore, additional savings would arise from the decreased amount of unnecessary indirect discussions about the defects of the system that often appear in work-related discussions in the organisation. Overall, we argue that the benefits in conducting the usability comparison clearly exceed the costs.

Although successful, the procurement had challenges, as well. For example, this type of comparative testing would not scale easily for several competitors. Therefore, preliminary studies on the market situation and dialogue with the potential tenderers were crucial in estimating the number of tenders and setting the minimum level of usability.

In addition to the positive SUS questionnaire [24], we used the Self-Assessment Manikin (SAM) [5] after each system, although we did not utilise the results in the evaluation. SAM offers a non-verbal pictorial evaluation technique giving the users one more alternative to structure and express their feelings about the systems. In our experience, SAM did not provide much new information compared to the other methods, but it was an important tool for the users in resetting their thoughts before moving on to the next system.

In the exit interview at the end of the whole test session, we also had some general questions comparing the systems. As mentioned in the results, all but one user would have chosen the winning system for themselves, and all the users preferred to have the winning system for the universities. This made us consider, if this overall question could have had more weight in the results or even could have replaced the SUS questionnaire. However, SUS is a very much studied questionnaire [1], and its results are thereby very convincing and trustworthy, so it should not be removed from this type of comparative evaluations.

7   Conclusions

Usability testing provided clear and measurable evidence on the performance of the evaluated systems and enabled extremely smooth decision making. The usability evaluation results were essential and changed the course of the procurement, since only one system scored above the pre-defined minimum levels of usability. The chosen evaluation method suited well for evaluating the CRIS system from the viewpoint of researchers and administrative personnel.

Our calculations on the financial impact of the usability test results indicate that usability testing can detect tiny but crucial differences in the use of the systems. For instance, the 20 min difference in total task time could be converted into 30.000 EUR savings in one year. But even more importantly, the improved reporting of activities and results that have direct financial value (income) for the organisation has substantially greater financial effect, in our case even more than 20 MEUR. So far, these types of calculations have seldom been presented and the financial mechanisms are still unclear. We propose that these types of calculations and estimations would be further studied to reveal new mechanisms on how return on investment could be constructed. Too often, these calculations focus on mere savings on working time.

In general, our experience was positive: in future procurement projects that affect large user populations, we aim to further apply and improve this method. With advance investment in designing an appropriate method into the invitation to tender, usability evaluation can be a key factor in a public procurement process that, also in the long run, result in practically successful and financially viable solutions.

Acknowledgements. We thank all the volunteers who took part in the test sessions as well as the moderators of the tests, and Sampo Teräs for his comments on the first draft of this article.

References

1. Bangor, A., Kortum, P.T., Miller, J.T.: An empirical evaluation of the system usability scale. Int. J. Hum-Comput. Int. **6**, 574–594 (2008)
2. Bevan, N. Claridge, N., Maguire, M., Athousaki, M.: Specifying and evaluating usability requirements using the common industry format: four case studies. In: Proceedings of IFIP 17th World Computer Congress, pp. 149–159. Kluwer, B.V., Deventer (2002)
3. Bias, R., Mayhew, D.: Cost-Justifying Usability. Academic Press, Boston (1994)
4. Booth, P.A.: An Introduction to Human-Computer Interaction. Lawrence Erlbaum, Hove (1989)
5. Bradley, M.M., Lang, P.J.: Measuring emotion: the self-assessment manikin and the semantic differential. J. Behav. Ther. Exp. Psy. **1**, 49–59 (1994)
6. Buie, E., Murray, D. (eds.): Usability in Government Systems: User Experience Design for Citizens and Public Servants. Morgan Kaufmann, Waltham (2012)
7. Bødker, S., Madsen, K.: Methods & tools: context: an active choice in usability work. Interactions **4**, 17–25 (1998)
8. Carey, T.T.: A usability requirements model for procurement life cycles. In: Carey, J.M. (ed.) Human Factors in Information Systems: An Organizational Perspective, pp. 89–104. Ablex, Norwood (1991)
9. Directive 2004/18/EC of the European Parliament and of the Council of 31 March 2004 on the coordination of procedures for the award of public works contracts, public supply contracts and public service contracts. http://eur-lex.europa.eu/legal-content/EN/TXT/?qid=1434726761459&uri=CELEX:32004L0018
10. Dumas, J.S., Redish, J.C.: A Practical Guide to Usability Testing. Ablex, Norwood (1993)
11. Finnish Act on Public Contracts (348/2007): http://www.finlex.fi/en/laki/kaannokset/2007/en20070348.pdf
12. Hartson, H.R., Andre, T.S., Williges, R.C.: Criteria For evaluating usability evaluation methods. Int. J. Hum-Comput. Int. **1**, 145–181 (2003)

13. ISO 9241–11: Ergonomic requirements for office work with visual display terminals (VDTs) Part 11: Guidance on Usability. ISO (1998)

14. ISO 9241–210: Ergonomics of human-system interaction. Part 210: Human-centred design for interactive systems. ISO (2010)

15. ISO/IEC 25062: Software engineering – Software product Quality Requirements and Evaluation (SQuaRE) – Common Industry Format (CIF) for usability test reports. ISO (2006)

16. ISO/TR 16982: Ergonomics of human-system interaction – Usability methods supporting human-centred design. ISO (2002)

17. Jokela, T., Laine, J., Nieminen, M.: Usability in RFP's: the current practice and outline for the future. In: Kurosu, M. (ed.) HCII/HCI 2013, Part II. LNCS, vol. 8005, pp. 101–106. Springer, Heidelberg (2013)

18. Lazar, J., Heidi, J., Hochheiser, H.: Research Methods in Human-Computer Interaction. Wiley, Glasgow, 426 p. ISBN: 978–0-470-72337-1. (2010)

19. Lewis, J.R.: Sample sizes for usability studies: Additional considerations. Hum. Factors **2**, 368–378 (1994)

20. Molich, R., Dumas, J.S.: Comparative usability evaluation (CUE-4). Behaviour and Information Technology, vol. **27**, No. 3, pp. 263–281. ISSN: 0144929X, DOI: 10.1080/01449290600959062. (2008)

21. Nielsen, J.: Estimating the number of subjects needed for a thinking aloud test. Int. J. Hum-Comput. Stud. **3**, 385–397 (1994)

22. Nielsen, J., Molich, R.: Heuristic evaluation of user interfaces. In: Chew, JC., Whiteside, J. (eds.). Proceedings of the ACM CHI'1990 Conference on Human Factors in Computing Systems (CHI1990). ACM, New York, pp. 249–256. ISBN: 0-201-50932-6, DOI: 10.1145/97243.97281. (1990)

23. Sauro, J., Kindlund, E.: A method to standardize usability metrics into a single score. In: Proceedings of CHI 2005, pp. 401–409, ACM Press, New York (2005)

24. Sauro, J., Lewis, J.R.: When designing usability questionnaires, does it hurt to be positive? In: Proceedings of CHI 2011, pp. 2215–2224, ACM Press, New York (2011)

25. Virzi, R.A.: Refining the test phase of usability evaluation: how many subjects is enough? Hum. Factors **4**, 457–468 (1992)

26. Whiteside, J., Bennett, J., Holzbatt, K.: Usability engineering: our experience and evolution. In: Helander, M. (ed.) Handbook of Human-Computer Interaction. Elsevier BV, Amsterdam (1988)

Artifacts, Tools and Generalizing Usability Test Results

Pekka Reijonen and Kimmo Tarkkanen[(✉)]

Information Systems Science, Turku School of Economics, University of Turku,
Rehtorinpellonkatu 3, 20500 Turku, Finland
kimmo.tarkkanen@utu.fi

Abstract. Usability testing has gained a rather stable status as a method for usability evaluation even though it has both low reliability and validity. The sources of result variance are well acknowledged among researchers and practitioners. However, the validity problem has not been explicated or exemplified although it is frequently discussed in the literature how the results of usability tests should be interpreted and to what extent results are generalizable. We employ Activity Theory and a case example to argue that the validity problem is mainly caused by the fact that what we are testing are artifacts and what people are using in their real life activities are tools and these two entities are qualitatively different. Basing on our analysis, the effects of the reliability and validity problems on the application of usability testing and its role as one of the tools in the design process are discussed.

Keywords: Usability testing · Validity · Generalization · Reliability · Activity theory

1 Introduction

Reliability and validity are the measures used in ascertaining the quality of evaluation instruments. Reliability is used in assessing if the measuring tool produces consistent results and validity in ascertaining if the tool is measuring what it is supposed to measure. In the past 20+ years, usability testing has gained popularity in such a manner that some kind of usability testing or evaluation plays some role in practically all software development projects. Usability tests are carried out by different actors during different stages of product's lifecycle with techniques ranging from a heuristic evaluation to laboratory and field tests [1]. The background knowledge of the testers varies considerably from layman to usability experts [2] and even automated asynchronous usability tests have been introduced [3]. When the diversity of usability testing procedures and actors are combined with the fact that there exists also many somewhat different, although overlapping, definitions of the usability concept [4], it is not always clear, how the results of a usability test should be interpreted [5] and to what extent these results are generalizable [6]. Repeatedly, empirical studies wonder why the usability of the system differs in pre- and post-implementation phases despite extensive and varied empirical usability and user research efforts (cf. [6]).

© Springer International Publishing Switzerland 2015
H. Oinas-Kukkonen et al. (Eds.): SCIS 2015, LNBIP 223, pp. 121–134, 2015.
DOI: 10.1007/978-3-319-21783-3_9

In this paper, we attempt to shed light on the interpretation and generalization issues of usability test results. With the activity theoretical support [e.g. 7] we explicate why and how generalizing the results of usability testing to real life situations is not a straight forward procedure. Our exploration is conceptual although as a case example, we refer to the famous empirical study by Suchman [8]. The rest of the paper is organized as follows. In the following section the basic variables of usability testing are listed and their effect on reliability is shortly discussed. The next section is dedicated to the validity issues, i.e. what type of generalizations are made from the usability test results and how justifiable these generalizations are. In the last section, the remarks and arguments about the reliability and validity issues are discussed and a constructive way for using usability test results is outlined.

2   Variables of Usability Testing

According to their use, usability tests can be divided into two broad categories, formative and summative evaluation. Summative evaluation is used, for example, to verify that the delivered product fulfills the usability criteria or to compare the usability of two or more products. The aim of a formative evaluation is during the development process to ascertain that the brewing artifact will meet the predefined usability criteria, i.e. to enhance the usability of the final artifact by helping to remove usability problems. Quite independently of the usability method used or the purpose of the evaluation, the primary output of a usability test is a list of usability problems that form the basis for recommended changes in design [5, 9]. Other often observed dependent variables of usability tests include, for example, time and subjective satisfaction [1]. A usability problem is the most often observed variable in usability tests [2, 5, 10]. In practice, usability problems are identified through the direct observation of users' verbal and non-verbal behavior or indirectly by the evaluator [11]. The trouble with the concept 'usability problem' is that it is elusive and therefore it has no generally accepted definition, i.e. every test administrator seems to use their own criteria. If the definition of the usability problem is vague, all the comparisons based on the number or quality of problems are also vague. This alone partially explains the confusing results attained when different test groups have evaluated the same artifact [9, 12]. Even the broadest possible definition of usability problem, "anything that impacts ease of use - from a core dump to a misspelled word" [13, p. 121], leaves the responsibility to the evaluator. In other words, it does not remove the basic cause of confusion, namely that it is up to the evaluator to decide, what impacts ease of use or hinders use in general [14]. Execution time can be reliably and consistently measured, yet it is less interesting variable, as formative usability tests are mainly used for diagnostic purposes during the development process and aim at design changes. User satisfaction, gathered in interviews and standardized questionnaires, is important not only in detecting usability problems, but specifically in interpreting the causes of the problems. However, data gathering methods are mostly used rather informally and inconsistently as explicated in the analysis of the thinking aloud method by [15].

The tested artifact is the main independent variable in a usability test as all the variation observed in the dependent variables is supposed to be caused by the attributes of the artifact [16–18]. The attributes of the artifact are not, however, the only independent variable causing variation in the dependent variables. Although the artifact is kept constant, different subjects detect and experience different usability problems [9, 10]. Interpretation of test results becomes additionally trickier when two remaining independent variables, test task and test arrangement are also taken into account. At the minimum, the attributes of the test task include the number of tasks (count), type, and coverage, which affect the number and quality of problems found [19]. Despite the fact that there exist numerous general recommendations [1] on how to run usability tests, test arrangements and procedures are far from standardized. Attributes like administrator, testing premises (laboratory, field), observation method (think aloud, observation, video recording), and test situation (pairwise or single subjects or a group), and training before the test session are sources of variability and low reliability (see [20, 21]).

It must be kept in mind that a typical usability test lacks control group so it does not qualify even as the simplest possible experimental design [22]. In practice this means that one must be very careful when interpreting any causal relations between the variables.

3   Generalization of Test Results

As shortly discussed above, there are many variables that can cause uncontrolled changes in the output of the test, i.e. lower its reliability and in principle unreliable results should not be generalized at all [22]. Usability tests are, however, reliable in one respect; they all consistently produce a list of problems with accompanying recommendations. Generalizations are based on the expectation that the external validity of the study is high, i.e. the results hold for other test situations, subjects, times, and environments [23]. Four types of generalizations are routinely done from usability test results (Table 1). The first one is the generalization from the used test tasks to all possible test tasks. For several reasons, often economical, only the parts of software that are considered the most important by some influential actor or the test administrator are tested. This selection is often based on the estimated usage frequency, i.e. the most used software features are tested. It is certainly important that the most frequently used features can be used fluently. The paradox here is that during use users get lots of training in the most used features, but the least used features can cause problems later as they are never properly learned because of infrequent use. For this reason precisely the infrequently used but important features should be easy to learn or rather self-explanatory. The other problem with the generalization from the used test tasks to all the possible test tasks is the type of tasks, especially their breadth (from simple tasks with definite answers to more general ones, see e.g. [24]). For example, in the case of simple tasks with definite solutions the subjects do not need to understand the task flow or how a work process is carried out with the artifact. This problem is confounded with the generalization from the artifact test to the tool use and will be discussed farther down.

Even though the effect of the subjects might be less central to the results of usability testing than to those of user experience [25] the representativeness of the test subjects

Table 1. Generalizations of usability test results.

Test attribute	Generalization to
Used test tasks (partial test, task coverage)	All possible test tasks or the whole software
Test subject	All users
One test arrangement	All test arrangements
Artifact test	Tool use

must be considered in every usability test. It is commonly [1] recommended that the test subjects should be selected from the future users. In general, by following this principle, it is rather safe to generalize the test results to the whole user population. The recommendation is based on the assumption that the target user group is homogenous, i.e. all users have about equal IT skills and interpret the work processes in a similar manner. The situation is not, however, always this straight forward. For example, the new artifact can be designed to help in changing the old work process and does not support the existing one, hence the knowledge of the old work process can actually be a hindrance instead of an advantage. For example, home care nurses were puzzled when they did not find a similar detailed list of work tasks on a mobile device as they were used to get in print from the old desktop system [24]. In the study reported by Suchman [8], the new mechanical parts of the photocopier and the change in the way it handled the originals while making double sided copies were one of the main causes of confusion. In other words, a new version of an artifact can be easier to use for a total novice than for a novice who knows the earlier versions of the artifact or the existing work procedures.

Test arrangements, i.e. how the test is actually carried out, can vary substantially and hence can have an effect on the results. In their explorative field research Boren and Ramey [15] studied thinking aloud method by observing seven usability experts in two professional organizations and found that there is considerable variation in how the method is applied even in the same organization. For example, there were variations in how the participants (subjects) were instructed to think aloud, how and in what pace reminders were given, how practitioners intervened, and how verbal test protocols were treated in interpreting the results. This study clearly shows that the widely applied thinking aloud method is used inconsistently and there are differences between practice and theory, but it does not give any hint of the consequences of the differences between the test results. The data collected from research literature by [20] also reveal that there is a considerable evaluator effect in usability testing, i.e. irrespective of the usability evaluation method (cognitive walkthrough, heuristic evaluation, thinking aloud) different evaluators report substantially different sets of usability problems and seem to rank the severity of the problems differently. Basing on the research on usability practice, [26] conclude that usability evaluation inevitably includes a lot of value judgments and hence experience and competence of usability practitioners is crucial and "Regardless of qualifications, success in systems development indicates a high level of intelligence" [26, p. 961].

The most extensive series of studies comparing the usability test results of different test administrators has been carried out by Rolf Molich [9]. The goal of these comparative usability evaluations (CUE) has been, among other things, to find out to what extent the usability evaluation results are reproducible. The number of test teams has varied from four (CUE-1) to seventeen (CUE-4) and the number of usability issues reported only by single teams has varied from 95 percent (128 of 141 issues) to 60 percent (205 of 340 issues). For example, in the CUE-4 study, none of the issues were mentioned by all teams and 6 of the 340 issues (1.8 %) were reported by the half of the teams (8). In other words, the results of usability evaluations were far from reproducible even though the test teams received the same client scenario describing the main goals of the usability evaluation. The teams were allowed to use their preferred test method so the arrangements varied in many respects, like the number of test sessions, number and type of tasks and scenarios, and the testing premises. The focus of the research was, however, on the results of the tests rather the methods, so it is impossible to infer the effects of the different independent variables from the data.

The most significant, and maybe the least considered, generalization of usability tests is that the results attained in the test are more or less directly applicable to real use situation. This generalization is made commonly implicitly as its rationale lies in the center of the whole idea of usability testing: in (formative) usability testing, usability problems are detected and when these problems are removed, the artifact is more usable. This is admittedly true, if all the other independent variables except the artifact are kept constant when retesting the artifact. In other words, in the retest the subjects, the tasks, and the test arrangements and procedures are the same as in the original test. If any of these independent variables is changed, we do not know any more if the observed changes are caused by the changes in the artifact or the changed independent variable. We maintain that the change of the arrangement, from testing an artifact to using a tool, is so drastic that generalization should be made very carefully. By tool, it is meant "something (as an instrument or apparatus) used in performing an operation or necessary in the practice of a vocation or profession" [27].

Nielsen [17] made in his early usability definition a clear distinction between usability and utility which are the constituents of usefulness, i.e. "whether the system can be used to achieve some desired goal" [17, p. 24]. According to this definition, utility concerns the functionality of the system and usability is the question about how well users can use this functionality. The distinction between utility and usability is not always straightforward and the examples of the benefits of usability engineering given by Nielsen [17, p. 2] point actually more to utility than usability. For example, the damage claim system of an insurance company was designed so that the whole transaction should be carried out completely and if interrupted, the transaction must be started from the very beginning and all previously input data was lost. This caused considerable trouble in the offices and required workarounds, but it is a question about the functionality of the system, not its interface. This example also uncovers two other issues that have to do with the generalization of usability test results to work practices. The first is that the results were not obtained in a usability test, but by observing the use situation and interviewing the users. The second is that the users were not novices as in a typical usability test, but had been using the system long enough to create workarounds for managing the shortcomings of the system. In other words, the observations do not come from artifact testing, as in traditional usability testing, but from tool use in work practices.

4   A Case Example

We explicate the difference between testing an artifact and using a tool by referring to probably the most ever cited single usability test, namely the research carried out by Suchman [8, 28, 29]. This study has not been called a usability test by Suchman, or to our knowledge by anybody else neither, but its empirical part is anyhow a usability test carried out in a laboratory. Actually, 'usability' was not even mentioned, at least not in the original report from the year 1985 [8], and there are at least two reasons for that. First, the goal of the study was not to detect usability problems and hence improve the usability of the artifact but to better understand human-machine communication. Second, at the beginning of the 1980s usability or usability testing had not received the kind of attention as they have today. In fact, this study is one of the first ones that draw attention to the problems the users 'in the field' had when applying computer based artifacts in their work. In that time, actually, "whitewater canoeing" [29, p. 19] was neither called whitewater canoeing, but "to run a series of rapids in a canoe" [28, p. 52].

The actual research was carried out in a laboratory, where a video camera was set up to record the interaction of test subjects with the photocopying machine. All the subjects were novices, i.e. they did not have received training in the use of the machine nor knew its somewhat different functionality in making two sided copies of a bound document. The subjects were given the test task (e.g. make two-sided copies of a bound document) and then left alone to work with the machine. The discussion protocols were transcribed from videotapes and analyzed. When the data is considered as a usability test protocol, it is obvious that the majority of the problems was caused by the fact that the test subjects were novices and could not even recognize the parts of the machine nor know its functions. For example, the subjects did not.

- know what Bound Document Aid (BDA) is [8, p. 91 and p. 111] and if "the latch labeled Bound Document Aid" should be pulled or pushed [8, p. 96] or what is the document cover [8, p. 92 and p. 111]
- find the start button [8, p. 104 and p. 116]
- know that contrary to the older machines, in this machine all pages of a multiple pages unbound document must be loaded at once and not one-at-a-time [8, p. 117].

The study clearly shows that the copying machine was not self-explanatory for a novice user and the evidence from Suchman's pilot studies also throw light on the concept 'novice'. In a video recording, two men try to make two-sided copies of a research to their colleagues and their behavior looks more like a deliberately comic performance than work practice [30]. The men in the video clip were the senior computational linguist at PARC, Ron Kaplan, and one of the founders of the AI (Artificial Intelligence) movement, Allen Newell. In other words, in front of new, computer based equipment nearby everybody is a novice. This example, as well as Suchman's [8] other empirical data, clearly demonstrates the difference between an artifact and a tool: the subjects are obviously trying to make sense of an artifact and not performing a routine work task using a tool. This interpretation is strengthened by the fact that this kind of behavior, i.e. keep trying to make copies for hours, can usually take place only in an experimental setting. In a work setting, i.e. at a quite normal workplace, the workers would have kept trying for a few minutes and then asked for help from their co-workers, help-desk, or invented a functioning workaround.

The difference between testing an artifact and working with a tool can be made explicit by identifying the goal or motive and the actions of the observed behavior. We utilize Activity Theory in clarifying this point as it offers suitable concepts and structures for describing human goal oriented behavior, for example when a human is carrying out work tasks in a specified context using appropriate means like artifacts and/or tools [7, 31]. The basic unit of analysis is an activity that includes a minimal meaningful context for actions, is directed towards an object and turning the object into an outcome is the motive of the activity. The basic activity system consists of a subject (actor), an object, and tools. The actor is not manipulating the object directly, but doing is mediated by the tool (artifact) that is the result of a historical development and also sets limits for doing. An activity is realized by a series of actions carried out by the actor. Every action has a specific goal and the subject is aware of the goal she wants to achieve. Depending on the situation, the same activity can be realized by different actions and the same action can be part of different activities. Through human learning, an action can, and usually will, collapse into an operation, which is a habitual routine that needs less conscious attention than an action and is adjusted to the specific conditions. When an action turns into a routine operation a new, broader action is formed and it includes the operation as a subpart. If the conditions change, for example in the case of a breakdown, the subject can return the operation back to the conscious action, in other words, an operation is not a conditional reflex.

When analyzing the activity system, it can be observed that the subjects in the test situation are test subjects who do not know how the artifact is used, but can be aware of the work practices (Table 2). When a tool is used in a work practice, the subject is a worker who knows how the tool is applied in performing the work practices. The object of the activity in the test situation is the use of the copying machine and the outcome is a pile of double-sided copies of a bounded document created with the copying machine (tool or actually an artifact). In the work situation, the object (motive) of the activity is knowledge sharing and the outcome is information delivered to colleagues. The tool used for knowledge sharing is the copied research paper, not the copying machine.

As the activity systems in these two situations are different also the deeds are different on the different levels of the activity. In the test situation, the activity is solely the making of copies, whereas in the work situation the activity is a collaborative research and copy-taking is just one action in this activity. The actions in the test situation taken by the subject concentrate in sense making, i.e. the subject reads instructions and proceeds step-wise in a trial and error mode. When a worker uses the copying machine as a tool, the action is simply taking two-sided copies of a bounded research paper. The operations used in the actions of the test situation consist of reading instructions in order to identify parts and find appropriate controls and buttons to press. In the work situation, the worker takes copies as usual, i.e. by making appropriate operations in appropriate order and maybe talking on the phone simultaneously. According to our interpretation these two situations, artifact test and tool use, are so profoundly different that the results of the test cannot as such be validly generalized to the real work environment. This issue is further elaborated in the last section.

Table 2. An activity theoretical interpretation of two different behaviors: testing an artifact and working with a tool. Data of Suchman [8, 28] re-interpreted by the authors.

Activity system	Testing an artifact	Working with a tool
Subject	Test subject, knows how to behave in a test situation, may know the work practices, tool is typically novel	Worker, knows how a tool is used in work practices
Object (Motive) → Outcome	Use a copying machine → A pile of double-sided copies	Share knowledge → Information delivered to colleagues
Tool	Copying machine	Copied research paper
Level of activity		
Activity	Taking two-sided copies of a bounded research paper	Taking part in a collaborative research endeavor
Action	Reading instructions and trying to make sense of the interface	Taking two-sided copies of a bounded research paper
Operation	Identifying controls and parts, pressing buttons	Making appropriate operations in appropriate order

5   Discussion

Usability testing has obtained a rather stable status among the methods applied in systems design and development process. The rationale and justification of testing is rather straight forward: when the flaws of the design detected in usability testing are removed the designed artifact suits better its purpose. This is a logically sound conclusion and on some level also an appropriate interpretation but at a closer look there are several factors that must be taken into account when interpreting the results of a usability test and generalize the results to other environments than the test situation.

To begin with, considerable variation in the results of usability tests is introduced by the variations in the independent variables, i.e. artifact, subject, task, and test arrangements and procedures. As the CUE-series of experiment [9] show keeping two variables, the artifact and testing methodology, constant, does not much reduce the variability of the results. This is understandable as the two other independent variables can vary freely. For example, the subjects' skills and knowledge may be very different and the tasks can vary from simple small tasks to longer work processes.

The typical dependent variables, i.e. the measured or observed things, are usability problems, execution time, and different subjective measures like satisfaction. From these variables, only execution time can be reliably and repeatedly measured and compared with the presupposition that the independent variables, at least tasks and test procedures, are kept constant. There have been efforts to define the concept of usability problem more precisely [18] and systemize the extraction of usability problems from test data [32] but their effects on practices have been meager. The same holds for test procedures, as there seems to be differences, for example, in the use of think aloud method even inside the same organization [15].

As the analysis of the usability test variables show (Sect. 2), they are all potential sources of variation in the results of a usability test, thus the variability of results found in the CUE studies [9] is understandable. Despite the fact that different usability tests produce different recommendations, the recommendations are meant to be applied in the design process in order to improve the usability of the tested artifact. It is further expected that following the recommendations has some positive effect on the actual use situation of the tested artifact [6]. This generalization means that the test tasks, subjects, and arrangements are taken as a representative sample of their respective universe. If the subjects are selected carefully, the test tasks are formed sensibly, and the tests are carried out following the recommended procedures, the generalization can be justified. There is, however, one generalization which is more questionable: how the results from testing an artifact can be generalized to the use of a tool.

As pointed out earlier (see Table 2), there is a qualitative difference between the test situation and the use situation. This difference is based on the difference between an artifact and a tool. According to the dictionary definition, an artifact is "something created by humans usually for a practical purpose" and a tool is "something (as an instrument or apparatus) used in performing an operation or necessary in the practice of a vocation or profession" [27]. This difference was insightfully described by Butler in the late 1800-hundreds [33]: "Strictly speaking, nothing is a tool unless during actual use. Nevertheless, if a thing has been made for the express purpose of being used as a tool it is commonly called a tool, whether it is in actual use or no. We see, therefore, matter alternating between a toolish or organic state and an untoolish or inorganic. Where there is intention it is organic, where there is no intention it is inorganic." According to our interpretation, it is exactly this alternation of a product between the untoolish and toolish states that make the direct generalization of the test results to the use situation in many cases unjustified or at least somewhat difficult.

In order to clarify the problem of the contextual generalization we refer to the case study reported by Riemer and Vehring [6], where the use of an IP-based telephony system was observed and the users were interviewed in their workplace context. The aim of the study was to enhance the functionality and especially the usability of the system as the changes made according to the recommendations of a recent laboratory based usability test were not received well by the users. It turned out that in different contexts the functions of the software were utilized in a varying degree and hence also the hardware varied from conventional phones to wireless headsets. As there was no single unified use context or hardware configuration the authors conclude that in this case "establishing a notion of usability as a characteristic of the software turned out an impossible task" [6, p. 7]. Based on the observations and interpretations it is further maintained that laboratory based usability test can be "counterproductive, as it might produce results that are detrimental to the ways in which usability manifests in the sociomaterial use context" and "usability should be treated as a distinctly contextual phenomenon" [6, p. 13]. This study clearly explicates the problem of contextual generalization, but the offered solution, the development of contextual usability testing methods, also has several drawbacks.

A widely accepted standard defines usability as "the extent to which a product can be used by specified users to achieve specified goals with effectiveness, efficiency and satisfaction in a specified context of use" [34]. If this definition is taken literally, it means that the results from a usability test are valid only in the testing environment (specified context of use) and not in the actual use environment regardless of how well the subjects or test tasks represent the actual use situation. In this case, the validity and generalizability of the usability test results would be the highest in the situation where the artifact never achieves the status of the tool. This happens when users (1) do not learn to use the artifact properly and (2) never integrate its use into their work practices. This may happen in situations where the artifact is used seldom, like connecting a laptop to the presentation equipment of a lecture room in a strange environment or using a web shop or other web application for the first and only time.

Contextual usability testing would mean that the usability of the same artifact should be tested separately in every sociomaterial use context, because "usability manifests as an aspect of this sociomaterial use context, with which software and hardware become entangled" [6, p. 2]. This would also mean that the UCD-type of software design and development is impossible as usability can be assessed only after the software has been implemented into and is used in a certain environment. In other words, this would be a move backwards to the waterfall model of systems development.

Carrying out usability tests on the field instead of a laboratory, i.e. on use locations, inevitably introduces some additional independent variables that cannot be controlled or even reliably measured. For example, users' skills and knowledge are at different level, the system has been implemented into the work processes in a certain way, division of labor varies according to the organization, workarounds have been formed to overcome obstacles, etc. In other words, the artifact-tool problem can not be generally solved simply by changing the test premises from a laboratory to a work place as an artifact does not turn into a tool when it is placed in a different location but through human learning when the artifact is used in work practice (cf. [35–37]). Testing an artifact or a tool in a certain sociomaterial context would surely produce results that are applicable in that specific environment, but these results are of less value for the artifact vendor as it is (1) impossible to know to what other environments these results apply, (2) laborious to produce and maintain different artifacts for every possible application environment, and (3) expensive and technically difficult to implement changes in the artifact that is already ready and in use.

If the focus of usability testing is changed from the attributes of the artifact to the utility of the artifact's functions in a certain environment, the question is, is that usability testing or something else. Nonetheless, the usability tests of artifacts can still have relevance in the design process and for the usability of the final product. This standpoint presupposes that artifacts have attributes that can be evaluated independently and without a direct connection to all aspects of its future use environment or its future utility in that environment. This kind of usability testing has been practiced for over 20 years and we maintain that most of the results have been more useful than harmful for systems design. For example, with the help of usability testing it is possible to lower the skills and knowledge requirements of the users by changing the attributes of the artifact in a more comprehensive direction, i.e. less resource is required for training the users irrespective of the use environment (learnability, memorability, errors). The same argument holds for the task execution time, i.e. in most environments, it is beneficial to use less time for a given task (efficiency). Similarly, we maintain that observing tool use in a specific context after the product launch has a firm place in the overall product lifecycle. Thus, artifact testing and tool use are not in competition, but should be acknowledged in the development lifecycle as qualitatively different means to obtain better usability.

It is a reasonable requirement that the procedures of testing and the ways conclusions are drawn are made explicit and methods are applied consistently, but this does not make usability testing an exact science as claimed by Nielsen [17, pp. 26–27]: "Only by defining the abstract concept of "usability" in terms of these more precise and measurable components can we arrive at an engineering discipline where usability is not just argued about but is systematically approached, improved, and evaluated (possibly measured)." This approach would possibly increase the reliability of usability testing, but would not solve the problem of validity, i.e. "whether the usability test in fact measures something of relevance to usability of real products in real use outside the laboratory" [17, p. 169]. An easy way to guarantee the validity of a tool is to define the measured construct through the measuring tool as made by Nielsen [17, p. 23]: "I tend to use the term "usability" to denote the considerations that can be addressed by the methods covered in this book". Unfortunately, this is actually about the level the validity of usability testing has been evaluated. The main reason for this is the high face validity of the usability testing methods. In other words, both laymen and most experts agree upon the fact that the tests measure exactly the right concept [38].

As we have explicated earlier, the generalization from artifact testing to tool use is not a straight forward procedure, but if usability tests are planned carefully, the tool use situation can be to a certain extent simulated by testing an artifact. One possibility is to use open ended tasks that force the subjects to create smaller tasks on the fly in the test situation while simulating their work practices [24]. Another approach with at least some face validity is a procedure where the business goals of the system are considered explicitly in planning and reporting usability tests [39]. Direct and reliable evidence of the effects of artifact test findings on real work situations is hard to attain, but it is, however, possible to integrate usability testing into the redesign of an existing system as done by [40]. The rationale is that usability problems should not be addressed in isolation but integrated into the redesign process as one of the sources producing design alternatives. This is extremely important as in order to be beneficial at all the results of the usability tests should be taken into account, which does not seem always happen. For example, [9] noted that two years after the comprehensive series of usability tests of a web site only 4 of the 26 key problem issues had been apparently solved, even though there had been resources for the development as some new features had been added. As a remedy, [9] suggests that the evaluator should interact closely with the designers and not just deliver a test report. This also implies a hint of the way the scope of usability testing should actually be defined, i.e. it should shift from the number of problems to the effects on the design, or as proposed by [41, p. 105], "the true utility of methods lies in their ability to influence the design of the application being evaluated." In other words, usability testing should be comprehended as an inherent part of design that helps to create design alternatives for an artifact and not as an exact method for enhancing the utility or even the effectiveness of a tool. This definition would also be more realistic and easier to verify than the prevailing one, i.e. the results of an artifact test can be generalized to a tool use situation.

In this theoretically oriented paper, we have used second hand empirical data to highlight the qualitative difference between an artifact and a tool. To our knowledge, this difference has not been considered in usability testing literature and in activity theoretical literature these concepts have been applied interchangeably. If this difference is considered as a new independent variable in usability testing, it can to a great extent explain the different results obtained when the same computer based system has been tested in the laboratory (using an artifact to carry out test tasks) and observed in the field (using a tool in routine work tasks). The main problem with the proposed distinction is how we in practice know if something is an artifact or a tool for its user. One way to determine this is to use an activity theoretical approach: when the user carries out conscious actions she is using an artifact and when the actions have collapsed into routine operations she is using a tool, in other words, humans are using tools and not artifacts in their routine work tasks. Basing on this, we can rather safely state that a computer based system is an artifact when an actor uses the system for the first time, like the subject in a conventional usability test. Unfortunately, it is much more difficult to empirically ascertain when an artifact has become a tool for the user. This is one of the questions that should be clarified in the future research.

References

1. Barnum, C.M.: Usability Testing Essentials: Ready, Set… Test! Morgan Kaufmann, Burlington (2011)
2. Hvannberg, E.T., Law, E.L.-C., Lárusdóttir, M.K.: Heuristic evaluation: comparing ways of finding and reporting usability problems. Interact. Comput. **19**, 225–240 (2007)
3. Andreasen, M.S., Nielsen, H.V., Schrøder, S.O., Stage, J.: What happened to remote usability testing? an empirical study of three methods. In: Proceedings of CHI 2007, pp. 1405–1414. ACM Press (2007)

4. Alonso-Ríos, D., Vázquez-García, A., Mosqueira-Rey, E., Moret-Bonillo, V.: Usability: a critical analysis and a taxonomy. Int. J. Hum.-Comput. Interact. **26**(1), 53–74 (2009)
5. Hornbæk, K.: Usability evaluation as idea generation. In: Cockton, G.G., Hvannberg, E.T., Law, E. (eds.) Maturing Usability: Quality in Software, Interaction and Value, pp. 267–286. Springer, London (2008)
6. Riemer, K., Vehring, N.: It's not a property! exploring the sociomateriality of software usability. In: Proceedings of the International Conference on Information Systems (ICIS), Phoenix, Arizona, pp. 1–19 (2010)
7. Kuutti, K.: Activity theory as a potential framework for human-computer interaction research. In: Nardi, B.A. (ed.) Context and Consciousness, pp. 17–44. MIT Press, Cambridge (1995)
8. Suchman, L.A.: Plans and Situated Actions. The Problem of Human-Machine Communication. Thesis, XEROX PARC. ISL-6 (1985)
9. Molich, R., Dumas, J.S.: Comparative usability evaluation (CUE-4). Behav. Inf. Technol. **27**(3), 263–281 (2008)
10. Nielsen, J., Landauer, T.K.: A mathematical model of the finding of usability problems. In: Proceedings of CHI, pp. 206–213. ACM (1993)
11. Følstad, A., Law, E.L.-C., Hornbæk, K.: Analysis in practical usability evaluation: a survey study. In: Proceedings of CHI 2012, pp. 2127–2136. ACM Press (2012)
12. Molich, R., Ede, M.E., Kaasgaard, K., Karyakin, B.: Comparative usability evaluation. Behav. Inf. Technol. **23**, 65–74 (2004)
13. Jeffries, R., Miller, J.R., Wharton, C., Uyeda, K.M.: User interface evaluation in the real world: a comparison of four techniques. In: Proceedings of CHI 1991, pp. 119–124. ACM (1991)
14. Vermeeren, A., van Kesteren, I., Bekker, M.: Managing the evaluator effect in user testing. In: Proceedings of Interact 2003, pp. 647–654. IOS Press (2003)
15. Boren, T., Ramey, J.: Thinking aloud: reconciling theory and practice. IEEE Trans. Prof. Commun. **43**, 261–278 (2000)
16. Molich, K., Jeffries, R., Dumas, J.S.: Making usability recommendations useful and usable. J. Usability Stud. **2**, 162–179 (2007)
17. Nielsen, J.: Usability Engineering. Academic Press, Boston (1993)
18. Andre, T.S., Belz, S.M., McCrearys, F.A., Hartson, H.R.: Testing a framework for reliable classification of usability problems. In: Proceedings of Human Factors and Ergonomics Society Annual Meeting, vol. 44, pp. 573–576. SAGE Publications (2000)
19. Lindgaard, G., Chattratichart, J.: Usability testing: what have we overlooked? In: Proceedings of CHI 2007, pp. 1415–1424. ACM (2007)
20. Hertzum, M., Molich, R., Jacobsen, N.E.: What you get is what you see: revisiting the evaluator effect in usability tests. Behav. Inf. Technol. **33**(2), 144–162 (2014)
21. Duh, H.B.-L., Tan, G.C.B., Chen, V.H.: Usability evaluation for mobile device: a comparison of laboratory and field tests. In: Proceedings of MobileHCI, pp. 181–186. ACM (2006)
22. Drost, E.A.: Validity and reliability in social science research. Educ. Res. Perspect. **38**, 105–123 (2011)
23. Trochim, W.M.: The Research Methods Knowledge Base, 2nd edn. (2006). http://www.socialresearchmethods.net/kb/, version current as of 20 October 2006. Retrieved 20 Jan 2015
24. Tarkkanen, K., Reijonen, P., Tétard, F., Harkke, V.: Back to user-centered usability testing. In: Holzinger, A., Ziefle, M., Hitz, M., Debevc, M. (eds.) SouthCHI 2013. LNCS, vol. 7946, pp. 91–106. Springer, Heidelberg (2013)

25. Arhippainen, L.: Studying User Experience: Issues and Problems of Mobile Services - Case ADAMOS: User Experience (Im)possible to Catch? Acta Universitatis Ouluensis. Series A, Scientiae rerum naturalium (528) (2013)
26. Woolrych, A., Hornbæk, K., Frøkjær, E., Cockton, G.: Ingredients and meals rather than recipes: a proposal for research that does not treat usability evaluation methods as indivisible wholes. Int. J. Hum.-Comput. Interact. 27(10), 940–970 (2011)
27. Merriam-Webster Online dictionary. http://www.merriam-webster.com/dictionary/
28. Suchman, L.: Plans and Situated Actions. The Problem of Human-Machine Communication. Cambridge University Press, Cambridge (1987)
29. Suchman, L.: Human-Machine Reconfigurations. Plans and Situated Actions. Cambridge University Press, Cambridge (2007)
30. Duguid, P.: On Rereading. Suchman and Situated Action. Le Libellio d' AEGIS 8, 2 Été, 3–9 (2012)
31. Bardram, J., Doryab, A.: Activity analysis – applying activity theory to analyze complex work in hospitals. In: CSCW 2011, pp. 455–464. ACM, New York (2011)
32. Cockton, G., Lavery, D.: A framework for usability problem extraction. In: Sasse, M.A., Johnson, C.V. (eds.) Proceedings of Interact 1999, pp. 344–352. IOS Press (1999)
33. Butler, S.: The Note-Books of Samuel Butler. Edited by Henry Festing Jones (1912). http://www.gutenberg.org/ebooks/6173. Accessed 8 Feb 2015
34. ISO 9241-11:1998 Guidance on Usability. International Organization for Standardization, ISO 9241-11 (1998). http://www.iso.org (1998)
35. Kjeldskov, Jesper, Skov, Mikael B., Als, Benedikte S., Høegh, Rune Thaarup: Is it worth the hassle? exploring the added value of evaluating the usability of context-aware mobile systems in the field. In: Brewster, Stephen, Dunlop, Mark D. (eds.) Mobile HCI 2004. LNCS, vol. 3160, pp. 61–73. Springer, Heidelberg (2004)
36. Rogers, Y., Connelly, K.H., Tedesco, L., Hazlewood, W., Kurtz, A., Hall, R.E., Hursey, J., Toscos, T.: Why it's worth the Hassle: the value of in-situ studies when designing Ubicomp. In: Krumm, J., Abowd, G.D., Seneviratne, A., Strang, T. (eds.) UbiComp 2007. LNCS, vol. 4717, pp. 336–353. Springer, Heidelberg (2007)
37. Nielsen, C.M., Overgaard, M., Pedersen, M.B., Stage, J., Stenild, S.: It's worth the Hassle! the added value of evaluating the usability of mobile systems in the field. In: Proceedings of the 4th Nordic Conference on Human-Computer Interaction: Changing Roles, pp. 272–280. ACM (2006)
38. Nevo, B.: Face validity revisited. J. Educ. Meas. 22(4), 287–293 (1985)
39. Hornbæk, K., Frøkjær, E.: Making use of business goals in usability evaluation: an experiment with novice evaluators. In: Proceedings of CHI 2008, pp. 903–912. ACM (2008)
40. Uldall-Espersen, T., Frøkjær, E., Hornbæk, K.: Tracing impact in a usability improvement process. Interact. Comput. 20(1), 48–63 (2008)
41. Hornbæk, K.: Dogmas in the assessment of usability evaluation methods. Behav. Inf. Technol. 29(1), 97–111 (2010)

Creative Design and Development

A Group Creativity Support System for Dynamic Idea Evaluation

Frank Ulrich[✉]

Department of Computer Science, Aalborg University,
Selma Lagerlöfs Vej 300, 9220 Aalborg, Denmark
frank@cs.aau.dk

Abstract. Idea evaluation is necessary in most modern organizations to identify the level of novelty and usefulness of new ideas. However, current idea evaluation research hinders creativity by primarily supporting convergent thinking (narrowing down ideas to a few tangible solutions), while divergent thinking (the development of wildly creative and novel thoughts patterns) is discounted. In this paper, this current view of idea evaluation is challenged through the development of a prototype that supports dynamic idea evaluation. The prototype uses knowledge created during evaluative processes to facilitate divergent thinking in a Group Creativity Support System (GCSS) designed from state-of-the-art research. The prototype is interpretively explored through a field experiment in a Danish IS research department. Consequently, the prototype demonstrates the ability to including divergent thinking in GCSS driven idea evaluation.

Keywords: Idea evaluation · Creativity · GCSS · Group support

1 Introduction

In recent years, creativity has achieved a comeback in Information Systems (IS) research and practice [42]. Creativity as a business trend has also influenced activities in both the private and the public sectors. In the private sector, creativity has become the foremost driver for sustaining the advantages needed to succeed in an increasingly hyper-competitive environment. Creativity supports this objective by forming the foundation for generating innovative products, services, and the redesign of organizational processes [5, 21]. In the public sector, creativity has become key to sustaining the increased economic requirements for delivering innovative products and services to end users in the most efficient way [10, 55].

However, innovation do not magically fall from the sky. Novel product development are, rather, a process where creative and novel ideas are transformed into useful designs, services, and organizational processes [24]. Moreover, many innovations fail due to a lack of business value, resulting in many innovation projects never leaving the initial (and resource-consuming) experimentation stages [18]. Hence, there is a growing need to evaluate both radical and incremental ideas to determine their business value before resources are allocated to them as prototype projects.

© Springer International Publishing Switzerland 2015
H. Oinas-Kukkonen et al. (Eds.): SCIS 2015, LNBIP 223, pp. 137–151, 2015.
DOI: 10.1007/978-3-319-21783-3_10

Traditional approaches to idea evaluation rank ideas according to fixed parameters such as novelty and usefulness to identify the best possible candidate for implementation, e.g., [6, 17, 22]. However, this traditional approach has been heavily criticized for having a negative impact on creative thinking [3, 4, 35]. To counter this view, this paper sheds a new light on the process of idea evaluation. Firstly, by viewing it as the creative ability to add value to novel impressions and secondly, by diversifying knowledge identified in the evaluation process towards creative thinking.

This paper deploys a prototype through an exploratory and interpretive field experiment to explore how managers can utilize idea evaluation in a IS setting to create the fuel for generating novel ideas. To achieve this goal, the prototype presented here and its underlying processes supports a dynamic and iterative process that uses evaluation methods to conceive novelty from identified knowledge. To guide the research the following question is asked: *"How can idea evaluation support creative thinking through a GCSS?"*

The remaining paper is arranged within the following sections. Initially, the paper presents a perspective for idea evaluation built on state-of-the-art research, where the emphasis is on the issues of idea evaluation and the complexity of creativity. Then it deals with the setup of the explorative field experiment. Next, the paper explores a GCSS prototype that encourages creativity through idea evaluation. Finally, lessons learned from the field experiment are provided and implications and avenues for future research are discussed.

2   Related Theory

This section will introduce two ways of creative thinking and elaborate upon two opposite approaches for idea evaluation.

Creativity is commonly separated into thinking patterns considered to be either divergent or convergent [27, 28] While both ways of thinking leads to the production of ideas [15], they are different in structure and output [27, 28]. Divergent thinking is considered to be the production of diversity and novelty whereas convergent thinking is considered to be the result of a review of narrowing solutions [15, 28]. Moreover, divergent thinking handles problem solving through broad searches for requirements using large quantities of ideas, few and lax restrictions through trial-and-error, and loose and vague structures whereas convergent thinking handles problem solving through restricted searches for requirements aimed at forming correct and well-defined solutions, coping with many rigorous and demanding restrictions, and sharp and well-defined structures [27].

IS enhanced creativity is normally divided between Individual Creativity Support Systems (ICSS) for personal use and Group Creativity Support Systems (GCCS) in a collaborative settings [43]. GCSS is moreover, a class of diverse systems that supports sharing of ideas and creative collaboration. For example, Di Gangi and Wasko [22] explains how Dell used an idea portal to collect ideas from their customers while Müller-Wienbergen et al. [43] provided extensive specifications for a GCSS supporting divergent and convergent thinking in a movie location environment by extending the users personal knowledge. However, a full review of the GCSS and CSS literature would be overwhelming. Instead, this paper relies on 43 contributions on the subject from Müller and Ulrich's [42] literature review of creativity in the IS literature.

Idea evaluation consists of two different management objectives. The first is identifying the values suggested by the idea. Such values are identified by creating input upon known quality parameters such as usefulness and novelty [17], hence creating evaluation content or knowledge about the idea. In this context, knowledge is defined by Alavi and Leidner [2] as "the result of cognitive processing triggered by the inflow of new stimuli" (p. 109). Moreover, knowledge can be stored, manipulated, and accessed which enables actors to know, learn, and influence future outcomes through their actions [2]. The second management objective is to identify the best ideas or creating portfolios of valuable ideas that can solve specific problems [12]. Guilford [28] argues that evaluation is a corrective and selective ability that collects feedback from the individuals' memory storage (past practices and experience) to facilitate divergent or convergent production. However, Guilford [27] also claims that formal evaluation was strictly convergent due to its rigorous structuring and its emphasis on deduction and decision-making. In his later work, Guilford [28] further applies this view by stating that evaluation can decrease divergent thinking abilities. Over the last 45 years, Guilford's view on convergent idea evaluation has influenced both research, e.g., [19] and practice, e.g., [45]. However, the introduction of IS has changed the playing field for creative support by providing solutions that are more effective than traditional pen-and-paper techniques [41].

Novel ideas are often identified as rare, unusual, or uncommon [12, 51]. Accordingly, they are an object for subjective testing and judging by others [36]. As such, a clear distinction is needed between creativity and idea evaluation. Where creativity is about generating novel and useful ideas for specific or loosely defined problems [3, 12], idea evaluation is about identifying specific qualities in ideas (e.g., novelty and usefulness) that can provide an implementable and effective solution for identified problems [17]. Hence, where creativity is about producing novel and useful knowledge for specific or loosely defined problems, idea evaluation is about generating knowledge about the quality of the data provided through creative activities. However, recognizing idea quality is not an easy task and idea evaluation has been criticized for demotivating organizational creativity by finding reasons to terminate ideas through rigorous critique [3, 4] and ultimately underestimating truly novel ideas [35].

Using knowledge to enhance creative thinking is not a new research subject. Existing research includes reusing knowledge embedded in existing ideas, management practices, and existing innovations [11, 38]. Moreover, researchers have explored how managers can use knowledge management systems to access diverse domain knowledge across departments [9, 20]. Knowledge created during an idea evaluation process can materialize when users provide comments or numerical values to a given criteria for a specific idea [6, 7]. According to Sternberg [49], participants can use knowledge for creative activities by (1) viewing it in new light (2) reconstructing it (3) redirecting it (4) transferring it (5) extending it to a new domain, (6) migrating within an existing domain beyond its accepted border or (7) radically redefining the knowledge for a completely new domain. Divergent thinking is about shifting context, branching out, and crossing boundaries whereas convergent thinking is about staying within limits, applying what is known, and avoiding risks [15, 27, 28]. Thus, divergent thinking produces ideas from knowledge by shifting or extending the boundaries within an existing domain. Moreover, divergent thinking can extend knowledge to another domain or radically redefine it for a new domain. Due to its focus on explicit requirements, convergent thinking, however, will only produce ideas within a specific and well-defined domain within clear boundaries.

To further explore the concept of knowledge creation in idea evaluation and its influence on creativity, this paper introduce a new and alternative approach that uses idea evaluation to glean knowledge from existing ideas. The purpose of this approach is to use the generated knowledge from the evaluation process to support both divergent and convergent thinking. This approach is coined as dynamic idea evaluation.

Table 1 demonstrates the overall differences between the approach and focus of traditional and dynamic idea evaluation. The table also include the influence from divergent and convergent thinking on the two evaluation approaches. Both traditional and dynamic idea evaluation involves a secondary convergent process of idea selection or consolidation. The focus of this paper is to elucidate how dynamic idea evaluation uses the knowledge creation process intended to facilitate idea consolidation to enhance divergent thinking.

Table 1. Differences between dynamic and traditional idea evaluation

	Traditional idea evaluation	Dynamic idea evaluation
Approach	Focus is on selecting the best idea for a solution	Focus is on creating a working solution iteratively over time
Focus of knowledge creation	Knowledge creation works in a linear fashion by identifying the correct idea that can form a novel solution	Knowledge creation works actively and iteratively by identifying knowledge in multiple ideas that can improve an existing idea, create novel ideas, and form novel solutions from a portfolio of existing ideas
Influence from divergent thinking	Divergent thinking happens beforehand and does not play any role	Divergent thinking plays a key role when creating novel ideas from identified knowledge in the evaluation process
Influence from convergent thinking	Convergent thinking plays a key role when identifying the correct idea for the correct solution	Convergent thinking plays a key role when improving existing ideas and forming novel solutions from knowledge identified in existing ideas

The purpose of traditional idea evaluation is to identify the best ideas that can fix a specific problem [6, 32, 47]. After all creative activities are concluded [19, 44], traditional idea evaluation achieves this goal by collecting specific domain knowledge concerning the qualities of each individual idea. Such knowledge about quality can include the novelty and usefulness [14, 17, 46] of the idea. Hereafter, this knowledge is used convergent in idea selection to separate the valuable ideas from those less valuable [23].

Dynamic idea evaluation is a creative alternative to traditional idea evaluation approaches. First, the purpose of dynamic idea evaluation is to collect the necessary knowledge to support idea consolidation through convergent thinking. Idea consolidation is a process that collates group knowledge from ideas and evaluation content within a common focus or theme [1]. For example, innovation managers can group knowledge from ideas and evaluation content within the focus or theme of a specific innovation. Moreover, identified knowledge can be used to improve existing ideas [12, 30]. Second, dynamic idea evaluation reuses the existing knowledge, e.g., [11, 38] from ideas and evaluation content to enhance divergent thinking processes simultaneous to the evaluation process. Such creativity enhancing activities can be further supported by using creativity techniques in combination with the generated knowledge, e.g., [12, 13]. As such, dynamic idea evaluation is embedded in the creative process, where it iteratively crafts working solutions over time while reusing the generated knowledge to enhance further creative thinking.

3   Research Approach

To explore dynamic idea evaluation, data was collected using a field experiment [8, 31] and interpretively analyzed [53, 54]. The approach for the field experiment and interpretive analysis is presented here.

Universities have previously been used in a variety of different settings when researching creativity and IS [37, 39, 41]. Hence, 15 members of a computer science department at a Danish university were selected to participate in the field experiment. To participate they had to have been employed in the department for at least nine months so that they would have some sense of the organizational structure and culture. Besides 12 research staff members, three administrative personnel participated, including the head of the department. To analyze the influence of practice, two secretaries without research tasks were added to the experiment.

The procedure for collecting data was constructed around five iterations. However, findings identified when using the prototype may cause changes to its underlying construction [52]. For this purpose, an initial Wizard of Oz (WoZ) HTML prototypical initiation [16, 29] was developed, which enabled the experimenter (the "Wizard") to act as the system when collecting user input, see [25]. The two initial iterations also functioned as learning stages to help the subjects become familiar with the system, see [50]. The starting point of the first iteration was a challenge to identify new ice cream flavors and evaluate an idea for a liquorice-flavored ice cream.

Between the first and second iteration a functional prototype was developed in PHP and MySQL. Incremental changes were made from the interaction with the subjects during the first iteration. During the second iteration, the subjects were reintroduced to the new prototype due to its redevelopment. In the third iteration, the subjects were introduced to a specific real-world challenge for a new travel expense system while the subjects controlled the fourth and fifth iteration. When the five iterations were complete, each subject was interviewed using an open-ended approach [48] to identify reoccurring patterns. Finally, the subjects participated in an open focus group meeting to present preliminary results and collect final feedback. Overall, the data collection lasted 14 weeks. Development of the functional prototype took one month between the first and second iteration. Each subsequent iteration lasted around 14 days. Each interaction with the participants took between five minutes and one hour. In total, 35:12 h of experiment and interview data was collected. To emulate real-world applications, the subjects participated randomly in each iteration [31]. Three subjects left the experiment after the first iteration. Two subjects left their position at the university while a third left the experiment due to other time commitments. Table 2 summarize the data collection procedure.

Table 2. Procedure for data collection

Iteration	Objectives	Task
1	1. To deploy an initial Wizard of Oz (WoZ) HTML prototypical initiation 2. To gather information to redevelop the WoZ prototype and provide learning to the subjects about this class of systems	The subjects learned to use the WoZ prototype and provide feedback on its functionality by evaluating an idea for a liquorice-flavored ice cream
2	1. To deploy a redeveloped PHP and MySQL prototype 2. To reintroduce the subjects to the redeveloped prototype	The subjects learned to use the redeveloped prototype by continuing their evaluation of the ice cream idea
3	1. To introduce the subjects to a specific real-world challenge	The subjects iteratively created and evaluated ideas for a new travel expense system
4–5	1. To enable the subjects to act freely when using the prototype	The subjects used the prototype at liberty

Post evaluation

Open-ended interviews followed by a focus group session

Throughout the five iterations, the collected data was continually analyzed using a flowchart. To establish connections between the different ideas or their evaluation content, subjects were asked about the origin of their ideas. Thus, the subjects became the reviewers of the data they provided. However, while some improvement ideas were added correctly, the subjects embedded other improvements in their comments or added them as new ideas. These improvement ideas were extracted from the evaluation content. Following the data extraction, all ideas were compiled into Fig. 2 shown in Sect. 5. Moreover, a field experiment report [56] was used to continuously record data and time duration from each prototype iteration, interviews, and the focus group. The data was then analyzed using an interpretive approach [53, 54] by identifying reoccurring themes [34] in relation to dynamic idea evaluation. Moreover, the interpretive analysis was supplemented with Sternberg's [49] view about knowledge and the concurrent view on divergent and convergent thinking [15, 27, 28]. This approach enabled an in-depth content analysis of the data to understand the prototypes influence on the subjects' creative actions. The prototype is presented in Sect. 4; the analysis is presented in Sect. 5 and further discussed in Sect. 6.

4   The Prototype

The prototype was constructed as an idea portal. In this portal, users could post initial and open-ended problems (listed as challenges in the design) and ideas solving those problems. Figure 1 shows a screenshot of the evaluation module. Once a user posted an idea (cf., top of Fig. 1), other users could activate the evaluation module. From there, they could evaluate the idea by adding comments and suggesting problems and potential benefits (cf., the 'Comment on Idea', the 'Add Benefit', and the 'Add Problem' action buttons in the top right corner of Fig. 1). Moreover, users could comment on submitted benefits and problems, providing additional knowledge to enable other users to create new improvements for the evaluated idea or proposed challenges and ideas (cf., the 'Add new Comment' action button in benefits or problems in Fig. 1). In both benefits and problems, users could propose improvements that suggested solutions for the selected problem or exploited any selected benefit (cf., the 'Add new Improvement' action button in benefits or problems in Fig. 1). Users could also supplement added content with word tags (cf., 'Tags:' in Fig. 1).

For enhancing divergent and convergent thinking, the evaluation module used a creativity technique called force field analysis, which is intended to encourage creativity in idea evaluation by collecting user input [12]. Couger's [12] evaluation technique enables users to provide benefits, and discuss problems around an idea and suggest improvements or novel ideas from the collected knowledge. This technique was modified to fit the design of the prototype. Furthermore, the prototype used words and images creativity techniques [39], which were embedded into the design. Besides the manually added tags, the system automatically generated a tag cloud from the content added by the users (cf., the tag cloud in the top of Fig. 1). When a user clicked on a manually or auto-generated tag, they were transferred to a Google image search for that tag. From this image search, users could find associated images that might improve their creative thinking.

The system supported both convergent and divergent thinking. The users were encouraged to work convergent within existing ideas by generating ideas as improvements to

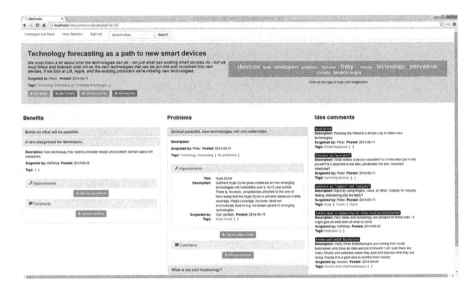

Fig. 1. Screenshot of the idea evaluation module

other ideas. Users could also work divergently by proposing novel ideas for a challenge or by initiating new challenges that might spawn a whole range of ideas (cf., the 'Create new Idea' action button in Fig. 1). When users created any improvement ideas, the prototype would encourage convergent thinking by facilitating knowledge around that content. However, the prototype could also facilitate divergent thinking through knowledge embedded in existing ideas and evaluation of content, enabling users to develop novel ideas with far wider capabilities than being limited to standard idea improvement.

5   Results

During the five iterations, 64 ideas and 10 improvement ideas over 12 challenges were added to the prototype. Three challenges and one idea were added to facilitate the experiment. Moreover, the 15 subjects added 210 entries of evaluation content. Of these, 123 were comments on ideas and challenges, 42 were identified benefits, and 45 were identified problems. From the evaluation content, 26 improvement ideas were extracted during the post-analysis of the data. In total, the subjects added 294 entries to the prototype over the five iterations.

Figure 2 shows the relationships between challenges and ideas created by the subjects during the five iterations. The numbers in Fig. 2 referees to the individual challenges and ideas. The artifact is genetic to different types of user groups. However, it is also designed for the specific purpose of supporting divergent thinking through the exploitation of valuable knowledge added via ideas and evaluation content. The following interpretive analysis will account for the inner workings of the prototype as a platform for knowledge and divergent thinking on the data embedded in Fig. 2. The results are further discussed in Sect. 6.

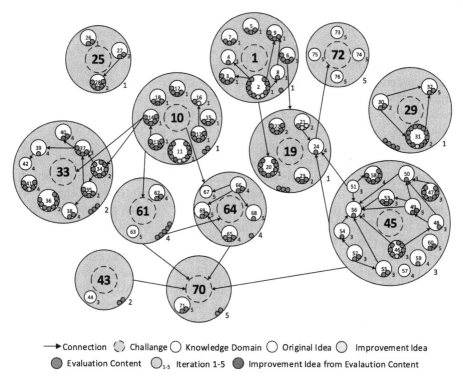

Fig. 2. Context map showing connections between knowledge items and domains (Color figure online)

To illustrate the workings of divergent thinking and the transfer of knowledge, the challenges (blue circles with dashed borders) contains an outer border as its knowledge domain (blue circles with straight borders). These domains contain the ideas for each challenge and evaluation content for the challenge itself (green circles at the edge of the blue circles). The ideas (white circles) have their own knowledge domain of evaluation content (green circles in the white circles) and improvement ideas (yellow and purple circles).

Extracted from Fig. 2, the subjects' divergent production (the result of divergent thinking) has extended the borders of each knowledge domain surrounding the challenges. This divergent production happens when participants act upon a specific challenge by adding novel ideas. For example, one subject created three ideas (47, 59 and 69) over three iterations for the challenge of building a better travel expense system (45). He created these ideas by reflecting on his own experiences and practice and the challenge at hand. Within the same challenge, another subject created two ideas in the third iteration. The subjects identified knowledge embedded in a discussion on efficiency in an existing idea (52), which triggered a reflection of his own practice and enabled him to generate two novel ideas (54 and 55) that could make the travel expense system more efficient.

The subjects' divergent production would also extend a domain by applying missing information. For example, one subject scanned the added ideas in the challenges of the travel expense system (45). Evaluating these ideas helped him to placing value the current knowledge he was experiencing. This process enabled him to reflect on his own practice and propose a new idea (56) that was missing in the domain. In addition, another subject continuously used this technique to add ideas and new challenges. For example, she created the challenge of the Christmas lunch (70) after evaluating newly added challenges and concluding that they were too serious. The production is considered divergent when novel alternatives are provided from the available knowledge [28]. Hence, the subjects used divergent thinking when they evaluating exiting content according to their personal experiences and desire for change and alternative practices.

As shown in Fig. 2, the subjects' divergent production transferred existing knowledge from one domain to another by using the available knowledge in the first domain to create novel ideas in the second. For example, when evaluating the challenge of the travel expense system (45) and an idea on usability (51), a subject related the identified knowledge to an idea about university sports clubs (21) in another challenge (19). He argued that usability is usually associated with websites. First, he combined 'website' with the concept of 'system' from challenge 45. Second, he looked in challenge 19 and found the idea about sports clubs (21). Finally, he argued that there is a department website, but there are also unknown sport clubs at the university. Hence, he created an idea for a website for the university sports clubs (24).

The participants' divergent production also radically redefined existing knowledge from one domain to create an entirely new domain. In the first iteration, one of the younger research staff members evaluated the idea of selling ice cream in each zip code (6). Within this domain, he suggested an improvement idea of having an ice cream vendor on the campus. The knowledge embedded in the improvement and the domain of the original idea made him rethink the concept of having activities on campus. This knowledge he identified during evaluation and his own practice as a former student enabled him to create a new challenge about a way to improve campus life for students (19).

In the idea domains, the participants' convergent production has reconstructed existing knowledge for improvements while maintaining what is safe and within the accepted borders of the original idea. Subjects would generate ideas that improved upon existing ideas, for example by expanding another usability idea (46) by suggesting that usability testing should be done with users. In another example, a subject suggested adding the suggestion of sorbet to the initial liquorice ice cream idea (2).

Two subjects were deliberately inserted into experiment, specifically because they did not share day-to-day duties with the others subjects. The first subject left the experiment after the first iteration. The second subject added a challenge and an idea on improving an administrative system that only she used (43 and 44). This content added by the second subject was largely ignored by the other subjects, as they were unable to correlate that content to their own practice.

Overall, the prototype had the capability to support both divergent and convergent thinking, despite including idea evaluation in the creative process.

6   Discussion

The initial research question was: *"How can idea evaluation support creative thinking through a GCSS?"* To answer this question, a field experiment was deployed and the results were analyzed using an interpretive approach. Throughout the experiment, divergent and convergent thinking patterns were identified.

The results from the field experiment are consistent to Sternberg's [49] view on knowledge. Firstly, divergent production happened when the subjects extended the borders of each knowledge domain surrounding a challenge. In this situation, divergent production happened when the subjects created ideas for challenges from the knowledge they identified in another challenge. Secondly, the ideas clearly shifted context and branched out by deploying existing knowledge in novel ways. Moreover, ideas expanded the knowledge domain of the challenge. Supported by Cropley [15], such production is divergent when it cross boundaries. Thirdly, subjects transferred knowledge from one domain to another by creating novel ideas from one challenge using knowledge identified in another. The activity was divergent when subjects crossed these boundaries. In addition, the participants produced 64 unique ideas during the five iterations. Guilford [27] defines this ability to generate multiple novel ideas for a specific domain as *fluency;* a clear sign of divergent production.

During the field experiment, several signs of convergent thinking were identified, for example, when the subjects suggested improvements to existing ideas. According to Cropley [15], convergent thinking applies what is known and stays within borders. The results are consistent with Cropley [15] and Sternberg [49] views, as the subjects' production was convergent when they remained within the domain of the idea and only applied incremental changes. The experiment demonstrates that supporting divergent thinking is not enough. In his seminal defense of convergent thinking, Cropley [15] explains that divergent and convergent thinking needs to co-exist to be effective. Divergent thinking transforms and reinterprets while convergent thinking prefers simplicity and rules. Thus, divergent thinking can result in overconfident breakthroughs and in worst-case disastrous changes. Convergent thinking used alone can equally result in missed opportunities and stagnation. Hence, convergent and divergent thinking needs to co-exist in a healthy environment to produce both novel and effective solutions. Overall, the field experiment demonstrated that it is possible to create a GCSS that use dynamic idea evaluation to enable the user's divergent thinking. Support of divergent thinking is especially plausible, if designers insert idea evaluation into an iterative creative group process and support it with specialized creativity techniques.

The experiment raises some fundamental question about how current evaluation processes are structured. Guilford's [28] key argument is that formal evaluation may reduce information retrieval from memory storage and should not be included in divergent production. Researchers including Elam and Mead [19] and practitioners such as Osterwalder and Pigneur [45] have taken Guilford's view even further and suggested that idea evaluation can only support convergent thinking due to its emphasis on deduction and decision-making. Without claiming exhaustiveness, current research may have overlooked an important connection between the knowledge creation processes of idea evaluation and divergent thinking. This experiment shows a different side of idea evaluation, where knowledge creation can support retrieval from memory storage for divergent production. It shows how participants evaluated existing ideas on both formal and informal levels, how they identified knowledge from these evaluations, which triggered knowledge from past practices and experiences in their memory storage, and how these triggers result in their divergent production of novel ideas. Moreover, the experiment demonstrates the potential of structuring an iterative creative and evaluative process, which is transferable to a GCSS. Hence, this paper opens up a new branch of research within GCSS that offers a great deal of opportunities for new discoveries.

These findings entail several recommendations for future studies and practice. GCSS researchers and practitioners can use the findings from the experiment to rethink how they deploy idea evaluation in their creative process. Using design science [26, 40] the results from this field experiment can be extended to form novel design requirements, constructs, and principles for this class of systems. Moreover, there is a range of uncertainties connected to this experiment that future research can address. For example, the observations from the field experiment showed how the ranking mechanisms pushed participants to focus around ideas with a high activity and negatively influenced their incentives to explore other ideas. Idea evaluation researchers and practitioners should explore new avenues for placing knowledge on ideas that are based on subjective input from the participants, rather than relying on normative ranking metrics that are best suited for web analytics. In the same context, researchers and practitioners should shift their focus from pursuing one great idea, e.g., [23, 33] by eliminating lesser ideas through normative ranking metrics. Instead, they should focus on developing great solutions by using idea evaluation for collective divergent and convergent production. Such a shift in focus could enable managers and developers to identify novel solutions by collecting best available knowledge from many different ideas and opinions.

7   Conclusion

Existing research in idea evaluation and GCSS have not approached idea evaluation as a divergent process that could create new novel concepts. Instead, the focus has been on supporting evaluation schemes that only included convergent thinking. This paper sought to provide a shift from this traditional view about idea evaluation by presenting an alternative view, where idea evaluation is integrated directly into the creative process. This exploratory field experiment demonstrated a capability to use knowledge collected through dynamic idea evaluation that triggered the participants' memory storage and encouraged their divergent thinking abilities. These results encompass several implications for future research, including rethinking the current views about idea evaluation and suggestions for conducting future empirical research that may advance and guide further development of dynamic idea evaluation. Although the proposed prototype is limited by focusing on the knowledge creation process of idea evaluation and not consolidation, it also presents an interesting shift in research where GCSS driven idea evaluation can be embedded into the creative process. Hence, the design theory and findings from this paper can initiate and guide future research and practice within GCSS and idea evaluation. Researchers are encouraged to investigate the concept of divergent idea evaluation and its implementation in GCSS while practitioners can use the proposed suggestions for idea evaluation to create new features in running GCSS or to develop new state-of-the-art systems.

References

1. Aiken, M., Carlisle, J.: An automated idea consolidation tool for computer supported cooperative work. Inf. Manag. **23**(6), 373–382 (1992)
2. Alavi, M., Leidner, D.E.: Knowledge management and knowledge management systems: conceptual foundations and research issues. MIS Q. **25**(1), 107–136 (2001)
3. Amabile, T.M.: Creativity in Context: Update to the Social Psychology of Creativity. Westview Press, Boulder (1996)
4. Amabile, T.M.: How to kill creativity. Harv. Bus. Rev. **76**(5), 76–87 (1998)
5. Amabile, T.M., Khaire, M.: Creativity and the role of the leader. Harv. Bus. Rev. **86**(10), 100–109 (2008)
6. Blohm, I., Riedl, C.: Idea evaluation mechanisms for collective intelligence in open innovation communities: do traders outperform raters? In: Thirty Second International Conference on Information Systems, Shanghai, 2011, pp. 1–24 (2011)
7. Bragge, J., et al.: Gathering innovative end-user feedback for continuous development of information systems: a repeatable and transferable e-collaboration process. IEEE Trans. Prof. Commun. **48**(1), 55–67 (2005)
8. Bryman, A.: Social Research Methods. Oxford University Press, New York (2004)
9. Candy, L., Edmonds, E.: Creative design of the lotus bicycle: implications for knowledge support systems research. Des. Stud. **17**(1), 71–90 (1996)
10. Castelnovo, W., Simonetta, M.: The evaluation of e-government projects for small local government organisations. Electron. J. e-Gov. **5**(1), 21–28 (2007)
11. Cheung, P.K., et al.: Does knowledge reuse make a creative person more creative? Decis. Support Syst. **45**(2), 219–227 (2008)
12. Couger, J.D.: Creativity and Innovation in Information Systems Organizations. Boyd & Fraser, Danvers (1996)
13. Couger, J.D., et al.: (Un)Structured creativity in information systems organizations. MIS Q. **17**(4), 375–397 (1993)
14. Couger, J.D., Dengate, G.: Measurement of creativity of IS products. In: Proceedings of the Twenty-Fifth Hawaii International Conference on System Sciences (HICSS), 1992, pp. 288–298 (1992)
15. Cropley, A.: In praise of convergent thinking. Creat. Res. J. **18**(3), 37–41 (2006)
16. Dahlbäck, N., et al.: Wizard of Oz studies: why and how. In: IUI 1993, Proceedings of the 1st International Conference on Intelligent User Interfaces, pp. 193–200 (1993)
17. Dean, D.L., et al.: Identifying quality, novel, and creative ideas: constructs and scales for idea evaluation. J. Assoc. Inf. Syst. **7**(10), 646–698 (2006)
18. Desouza, K., et al.: Crafting organizational innovation processes. Innov. Manag. Policy Pract. **11**(1), 6–33 (2009)
19. Elam, J., Mead, M.: Can software influence creativity? Inf. Syst. Res. **1**(1), 1–22 (1990)
20. Faniel, I.M., Majchrzak, A.: Innovating by accessing knowledge across departments. Decis. Support Syst. **43**(4), 1684–1691 (2007)
21. Florida, R., Goodnight, J.: Managing for creativity. Harv. Bus. Rev. **83**(7–8), 124–131 (2005)

22. Di Gangi, P.M., Wasko, M.: Steal my idea! organizational adoption of user innovations from a user innovation community: a case study of Dell ideastorm. Decis. Support Syst. **48**(1), 303–312 (2009)
23. Girotra, K., et al.: Idea generation and the quality of the best idea. Manage. Sci. **56**(4), 591–605 (2010)
24. Govindarajan, V., Trimble, C.: The Other Side of Innovation: Solving the Execution Challenge. Harvard Business School Publishing, Boston (2010)
25. Green, P., Wei-Haas, L.: The rapid development of user interfaces: experience with the wizard of OZ method. Proc. Hum. Factors Ergon. Soc. Annu. Meet. **29**(5), 470–474 (1985)
26. Gregor, S., Jones, D.: The anatomy of a design theory. J. Assoc. Inf. Syst. **8**(5), 312–335 (2007)
27. Guilford, J.P.: The Nature of Human Intelligence. McGraw-Hill, London (1967)
28. Guilford, J.P.: Way Beyond the IQ. Creative Education Foundation, Buffalo (1977)
29. Hajdinjak, M., Mihelic, F.: Wizard of Oz experiments. In: EUROCON 2003, Computer as a Tool. The IEEE Region 8, vol. 2, pp. 112–116 (2003)
30. Isaksen, S.G., Treffinger, D.J.: Creative Problem Solving: The Basic Course. Bearley Ltd., Buffalo (1985)
31. Järvinen, P.: On Research Methods. Opinpajan Kirja, Tampere (2004)
32. Kennel, V., et al.: Creativity in teams: an examination of team accuracy in the idea evaluation and selection process. In: 2013 46th Hawaii International Conference on System Sciences, pp. 630–639. IEEE (2013)
33. Kudrowitz, B.M., Wallace, D.: Assessing the quality of ideas from prolific, early-stage product ideation. J. Eng. Des. **24**(2), 120–139 (2013)
34. Layder, D.: Sociological Practice - Linking Theory and Practice. Sage Publications Ltd., London (1998)
35. Licuanan, B.F., et al.: Idea evaluation: error in evaluating highly original ideas. J. Creat. Behav. **41**(1), 1–27 (2007)
36. Lobert, B.M.B., Dologite, D.G.: Measuring creativity of information system ideas: an exploratory investigation. In: Proceedings of the Twenty-Seventh Hawaii International Conference on System Sciences, pp. 392–402 (1994)
37. Maccrimmon, K.R., Wagner, C.: Stimulating ideas through creativity software. Manage. Sci. **40**(11), 1514–1532 (1994)
38. Majchrzak, A., et al.: Knowledge reuse for innovation. Manage. Sci. **50**(2), 174–188 (2004)
39. Malaga, R.A.: The effect of stimulus modes and associative distance in individual creativity support systems. Decis. Support Syst. **29**(2), 125–141 (2000)
40. March, S.T., Smith, G.F.: Design and natural science research on information technology. Decis. Support Syst. **15**(4), 251–266 (1995)
41. Massetti, B.: An empirical examination of the value of creativity support systems on idea generation. MIS Q. **20**(1), 83–97 (1996)
42. Müller, S.D., Ulrich, F.: Creativity and information systems in a hypercompetitive environment : a literature review. Commun. Assoc. Inf. Syst. **32**(June), 175–200 (2013)
43. Müller-Wienbergen, F., et al.: Leaving the beaten tracks in creative work – a design theory for systems that support convergent and divergent thinking. J. Assoc. Inf. Syst. **12**(11), 714–740 (2011)
44. Osborn, A.F.: Applied Imagination: Principles and Procedures of Creative Thinking. Charles Scribner's Sons, New York (1953)
45. Osterwalder, A., Pigneur, Y.: Business Model Generation: A Handbook for Visionaries, Game Changers, and Challengers. Wiley, New Jersey (2010)

46. Reinig, B.A., et al.: On the measurement of ideation quality. J. Manag. Inf. Syst. **23**(4), 143–161 (2007)

47. Riedl, C., et al.: Rating scales for collective intelligence in innovation communities: why quick and easy decision making does not get it right. In: Thirty First International Conference on Information Systems, St. Louis, 2010, pp. 1–21 (2010)

48. Saunders, M., et al.: Research Methods for Business Students. Prentice Hall, Harlow (2003)

49. Sternberg, R.J.: A propulsion model of types of creative contributions. Rev. Gen. Psychol. **3**(2), 83–100 (1999)

50. Ulrich, F., Mengiste, S.A.: The challenges of creativity in software organizations. In: Bergvall-Kåreborn, B., Nielsen, P.A. (eds.) TDIT 2014. IFIP AICT, vol. 429, pp. 16–34. Springer, Heidelberg (2014)

51. Valacich, J.S., et al.: Idea generation in computer-based groups - a new ending to an old story. Organ. Behav. Hum. Decis. Process. **57**(3), 448–467 (1994)

52. Voigt, M., Niehaves, B., Becker, J.: Towards a unified design theory for creativity support systems. In: Peffers, K., Rothenberger, M., Kuechler, B. (eds.) DESRIST 2012. LNCS, vol. 7286, pp. 152–173. Springer, Heidelberg (2012)

53. Walsham, G.: Doing interpretive research. Eur. J. Inf. Syst. **15**(3), 320–330 (2006)

54. Walsham, G.: Interpreting Information Systems in Organizations. Wiley, Chichester (1993)

55. Warkentin, M., et al.: Encouraging citizen adoption of e-government by building trust. Electron. Mark. **12**(3), 157–162 (2002)

56. Yin, R.K.: Case Study Research - Design and Methods. Sage Publications Ltd., London (2003)

User Experience of Mobile Coaching for Stress-Management to Tackle Prevalent Health Complaints

Marja Harjumaa[1(✉)], Kirsi Halttu[2], Kati Koistinen[2], and Harri Oinas-Kukkonen[2]

[1] VTT Technical Research Centre of Finland Ltd, Kaitoväylä 1,
P.O. Box 1100, 90571 Oulu, Finland
marja.harjumaa@vtt.fi
[2] Faculty of Information Technology and Engineering, OASIS Research Group,
University of Oulu, Paavo Havaksen tie 3, 90570 Oulu, Finland
{kirsi.halttu,harri.oinas-kukkonen}@oulu.fi,
khkoistinen@googlemail.com

Abstract. In recent years, mobile and web-based solutions for health and well-being have become popular. The topic that has been covered the most has been the promotion of physical health, although the importance of mental and social well-being has also been acknowledged recently. Studies have shown that mental health interventions can be successfully designed to be delivered via mobile channels. However, the role of mobile applications in disease prevention and self-management of health is not so well understood. The aim of this study is to explore the need for stress-management solutions by studying the prevalence of health complaints in an academic organization (n = 756). It also describes findings from a field study exploring the user experience of a mobile coaching application for stress-management among the three most prevalent complaint groups (n = 30). The findings show that the three most prevalent complaints are tiredness, depression, and neck problems. All of the 13 complaints were more common among women than men, except loneliness and problems in social life. User experience study showed that most participants found the application useful and they would recommend it to other people. Use activity of the mobile coaching application was highest among the tiredness group. The findings are especially useful in the design new solutions for disease prevention and self-management of health.

Keywords: Disease prevention · Self-management · Health complaint · Occupational health · Mental health · Behavior change support systems

1 Introduction

1.1 Motivation and Background

It is common that people suffer from subjective health complaints or symptoms which are not necessarily signs of a disease or illness. Symptoms such as nausea, pain, and fatigue are experienced by a person, but they are not directly observable by another but instead become known only through the report of the person being assessed [6]. However, these complaints should be taken seriously, as they can decrease people's

© Springer International Publishing Switzerland 2015
H. Oinas-Kukkonen et al. (Eds.): SCIS 2015, LNBIP 223, pp. 152–164, 2015.
DOI: 10.1007/978-3-319-21783-3_11

ability to function and lead to short and long-term sickness absences [15, 33]. When people are experiencing health complaints or symptoms, they often try to get rid of their feelings and thoughts. However, recent cognitive behavioral therapies, such as acceptance and commitment therapy (ACT), emphasize mindfulness and acceptance skills [14]. The core concept of ACT is psychological flexibility, which refers to the ability to focus on the present moment and take actions that are aligned with personal goals and values even in uncomfortable or distressing situations [7, 14]. The development of solutions for mental wellness would be important; ill mental health is a threat for people's health and well-being and as mental health problems progress they are more difficult and costly to treat. People have difficulties to get access to health services and treatment periods may be too short. Results may not be as permanent nor as good if a person is not able to get treatment as long as it is needed [25]. Mental ill health is also becoming a key issue for the well-functioning of OECD's labor markets and social policies. It also causes an enormous economic burden [26].

People are using the Internet more and more in the search for health information. According to Eurostat [10] most Internet users in the age group 25–54 searched for health information (60 %) and it was also popular among users aged 55–74: nearly 60 % searched for information about health. In recent years, also mobile and web-based solutions for supporting health and well-being have become popular. Smart phones and tablet devices provide an excellent access point for digital services, because they are personal and we always carry them along with us. The ability to be connected to the Internet, relatively inexpensive prices, and a high penetration level are among their obvious advantages from a health support point of view. Technologies such as mobile phones, web applications, and social networking tools hold great promise for supporting individuals in health-promoting behaviors [19].

1.2 User Experience Research in Health Context

It has been expected that digital services would lead to greater efficiency and improvements in quality of healthcare. However, in order to realise these promises, digital health services should be operationalized, which concerns the actual introduction, adoption, and employment of the technology in practice [35]. For end-users, such as patients and health care professionals, positive user experience has a central role in operationalization of digital health services. Even subtle elements of an intervention can have strong effects on overall experience and even precede the intended experiences [19, 31]. It has also been stated that behavior change in the traditional clinical sense is not the right metric for evaluating early stage health technologies, but instead randomized controlled trials (RCT) measuring the effectiveness of a technology have a role later when the technology becomes mature [19]. Instead, HCI research should be interested about narrower efficacy evaluations related to behavior change techniques and qualitative studies focusing on people's experiences with the technology [19]. User experience and value are closely intertwined. In order to be successful, health technologies should be designed to be driven by user values [9, 16, 35]. According to Ervasti [9], achieving an understanding of customers' values will greatly help to design and market successful services for target customers.

1.3   Health Behavior Change

Currently, there is a wide selection of personal health technologies. Bardram et al. [5] has divided them into three categories: (1) wellness applications persuading the user to adopt a healthier lifestyle; (2) systems managing chronic illnesses like diabetes; and (3) mental health and illness monitoring systems. However, persuasion, i.e. intention to change people's attitudes or behavior, cannot be assigned only to wellness applications. Any system, whose use has psychological and behavioral outcomes, and is designed to change attitudes or behaviors, can be defined as a Behaviour Change Support System (BCSS); BCSSs provide content and functionalities that engage users with new behaviors, make them easy to perform and support users in their everyday lives [28]. Risk factors for many chronic diseases are behavioural and a successful change in these behaviors is a fundamental aspect of both prevention and effective management of chronic conditions, as well as an important contributor to health and well-being more broadly [19]. BCSS have potential not only to prevent diseases, but also to provide self-management tools that can be used in combination with traditional care. Studies have shown that people can avoid getting face-to-face to therapy, because mental health illnesses and complaints are still a taboo subject for many people [17].

The most covered topic of behavior change applications has been the promotion of physical health [20], although the importance of mental and social wellbeing has also been acknowledged recently. Studies have shown that people's attitudes towards mobile phones as monitoring and self-management tools for mental health are quite positive [30, 34]. Mobile mental health monitoring and self-management are, however, still in the early phases of their development [13].

1.4   Purpose of this Study

The role of mobile applications in disease prevention and self-management of health and well-being is not so well understood. The aims of this study are to (1) explore the need for self-management solutions by studying the prevalence of stress-related health complaints in an academic organization and (2) explore the user experience of an ACT-based mobile coaching application for stress-management among the three most prevalent complaint groups identified in this organization.

Differing from earlier studies reported e.g. in [1] participants were instructed to perform specific exercises that would be especially helpful with regards to their health complaints and symptoms.

The next chapters will describe the methods applied in this work. Then the results are reported separately from the survey and from the user experience study. After this, a discussion and recommendations for further research and design are presented.

2   Methods

The study was consisted of a survey and a short field study studying the user experience.

2.1 Survey

In order to study the prevalence of health complaints in an academic organization students and employees in the University of Oulu in Northern Finland (n ≈ 18,000) were sent an email invitation to participate in the study. In all, 756 individuals were examined with the health questionnaire in December 2013. 42.3 % of them were men (n = 320) and 57.7 % women (n = 436). Their mean age was 33 years (range 18–74). 81 % owned a smart phone (n = 611), which was more common among men (86 %, n = 274) than women (77 %, n = 337).

The health questionnaire enquired information about the frequency of different stress-related *symptoms*, i.e. tiredness, neck problems, sleeping problems, trouble concentrating, feeling tense, headache, abnormal food behaviors/attitudes, difficulties in making decisions related to own life, problems in social life and feeling blocked in getting studies/work done. In addition, *depression* was enquired through two screening questions [2, 3, 37], *anxiety* through Generalized Anxiety Disorder 7-item scale [21, 32, 38], *perceived stress* through one screening question [8], and *perceived loneliness* through one screening question [36].

A person was classified as having tiredness, neck problems, sleeping problems, trouble concentrating, feeling tense, headache, abnormal food behaviors/attitudes, difficulties in making decisions related to own life, problems in social life, and feeling blocked in getting studies/work done, if participant answered questions "weekly" or "daily or almost daily".

A person was classified as having *depression* if participant answered "yes" at least in one of the two questions, *anxiety* if the total score was over 10 meaning moderate or severe anxiety, *stress* if participant answered "quite much" or "very much" and *loneliness* if participant answered "quite often" or "all the time".

2.2 User Experience Study

User experience study was conducted with subgroups of this larger population in February 2014. Inclusion criteria were as follows: age 18 years or more, person is suffering from one of the three most common complaints found in the survey, person owns a suitable smart phone, and person wants voluntarily participate in the field study. 30 people participated and 20 of them were men and 10 women. Their average age was 30 years (range 19–54) (see Table 1).

Table 1. Participant profile of the user experience study

Parameter	Tiredness	Depression	Neck problems	All
Number of participants	10	10	10	30
Men	6	7	7	20
Women	4	3	3	10
Age	29	31	30	30

The field study lasted for two weeks and it was consisted of questionnaires collecting background information, after use feedback and usage log information. After use questionnaire included also open questions. People participated also in a usability test in laboratory settings in the beginning of the use period where they also received instructions for the field study. The usability test is not reported in this article.

The purpose of the user experience study was to mock-up a situation where the system would tailor the content based on user's preferences, in this case the health complaints. Tailoring is one of the methods to increase the effectiveness of information [24]. Tailoring in the context of BCSSs has been defined as follows: "Information provided by the system will be more persuasive if it is tailored to the potential needs, interests, personality, usage context, or other factors relevant to a user group." [29] Thus, differing from earlier studies, participants were instructed to perform specific exercises that would be especially helpful with regards to their health complaints and symptoms. The tiredness group was instructed to perform eight exercises in any order; the depression group was free to perform any exercises they wanted; the neck problems group had three specific exercises.

2.3   System Description

Oiva is a mobile mental wellness training application for stress management. It is designed to increase well-being by teaching skills that increase psychological flexibility and mental wellness. It offers brief acceptance and commitment therapy (ACT) -based exercises that are expected to integrate well into users' everyday lives [1].

The application contains four intervention modules (see Fig. 1) are numbered according to their recommended order, and each path consists of 1–4 subsections that include 5–8 exercises. Each path contains an introduction in the form of text and video, and the exercises are also available as both text and video. Thus, users can choose whether they want to read or listen to the exercises.

In a feasibility study, the application has shown good acceptability, usefulness, and engagement among working-age participants [1]. Its effectiveness has been studied in a randomized controlled trial, the results of which are currently being analysed [22].

3   Results and Analysis

The results include (1) prevalence of stress-related health complaints at the University of Oulu, (2) description of the user experience among the three most prevalent complaint groups and (3) log information about the application use.

3.1   Stress Related Health Complaints

The three most common single complaints reported at the University of Oulu were tiredness (52.8 %), neck problems (32.7 %) and depression (32.1 %). Other popular complaints with over 25 % prevalence were feeling blocked in getting one's studies or work done (27.8 %), trouble concentrating (25.9 %) and sleeping problems (25.1 %). See Table 2 for these data broken down by gender.

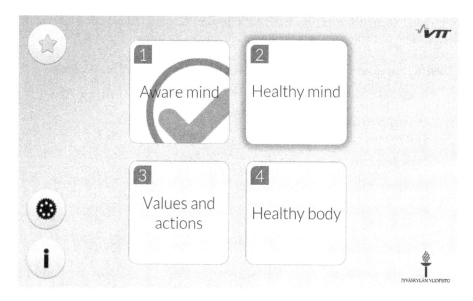

Fig. 1. Oiva application's main screen

Although many people reported these complaints, most of them (90 %) evaluated their own health with a five-point scale as excellent, very good or good. Only 9 % evaluated their health as fair and 1 % as poor. In general, all of the 13 complaints were more common among women than men except loneliness and problems in social life.

3.2   User Experience

The after-use questionnaire showed that most participants (n = 23) found the application useful and most of them would recommend it to other people (n = 23). Less than half (n = 13) of the participants stated that they intend to use the application in the future, but however, as many participants (n = 13) stated that they might use the application in the future (intention to use in the future = maybe).

A comparison between the groups shows that participants in the depression group had the most positive attitudes toward the application; 9 of them found it useful, 9 would recommend it to other people and 6 of them intend to use the application in the future. The other two groups didn't have as positive attitudes and especially the neck group doubted their intention to use the application in the future. See Table 3.

The tiredness and neck problems groups were instructed to perform only specific exercises. In the after-use questionnaire, participants were not enquired about the appropriateness of the pre-selected exercises, but there were some comments: "I feel that the exercises that were recommended for me were the most useful ones" (tiredness group). At least some participants had familiarized themselves also with other exercises: "I noticed that I'm interested also other than the suggested exercises, but I didn't want to use them that much, because I wanted to follow the instructions" (neck problems group) and "Suggested exercises were not a good match, but I found other interesting exercises that I'm going to try in the future" (tiredness group).

Table 2. Percentage of men and women reporting certain stress related health complaints.

Symptom	Men (n = 320)	Women (n = 436)	All (n = 756)
Tiredness	43.1	59.9	52.8
Neck problems	19.1	42.7	32.7
Depression	27.5	35.6	32.1
Feeling blocked in getting studies/work done	24.7	30.0	27.8
Trouble concentrating	21.9	28.9	25.9
Sleeping problems	19.4	29.4	25.1
Feeling tense	12.2	23.4	18.7
Stress	12.5	21.1	17.5
Difficulties in making decisions related to own life	10.3	17.9	14.7
Headache	7.5	16.7	12.8
Loneliness	14.7	10.3	12.2
Abnormal food behaviors/ attitudes	4.7	11.5	8.6
Problems in social life	8.8	8.0	8.3
Anxiety	5.6	10.1	8.2

Table 3. Participants after use attitudes toward the application (usefulness for you = yes, intention to use in the future = yes, recommend to other people = yes) Values are expressed as number of participants.

Parameter	Tiredness (n = 9)	Depression (n = 10)	Neck problems (n = 10)	All (n = 29)
Usefulness	7	9	7	23
Intention to use in the future	4	6	3	13
Referral rate	6	9	8	23

The after-use questionnaire showed that participants had learned new things about themselves: "When you use the application, you notice that how difficult it is nowadays to concentrate even on short 2–3 min exercises" (tiredness group). Participants also felt that application use has had influence on their well-being: "Using the application seemed to relief my stress a bit. Relaxation exercises, especially breathing exercises, helped me to settle down when I had too much stress" (tiredness group), "This is a positive experience, regular use could be useful. Exercises gave new positive insights" (tiredness group) and "This is a convenient way to calm down and relax" (depression group).

The after-use questionnaire showed that barriers of use were feeling of being busy or having lack of time (15x) and forgetting to use the application (5x). People also mentioned that when they have time to relax, they want to do other things that use the application. Some technical problems were reported as well, such as a mobile phone going to sleep in the middle of the exercise, poor sound quality and relatively big size of the application (application content is stored locally and it can be used without the internet connection). Participants suggested that reminders would help them to perform more exercises and changing content would maintain their motivation. Some comments also revealed that the use period was too short for getting enough experience of the exercises as the participants intended to perform more exercises in order to get a better understanding of them.

Interestingly, for some participants their symptoms seemed to have had an influence on their use activity. As participants wrote: "Tiredness influenced me and prevented application use" (tiredness group), "Some days I was so tired after my studies that I wasn't able to think anything" (tiredness group), "Usually I didn't have the energy to do exercises which require concentrating, especially in the evening when I was tired, so I many times I didn't use it although I remembered it" (depression group).

Participants were asked what would be the most suitable place for using the application and does the use environment influence on application's use. The most preferred place to use the application was home (n = 24) whereas school (n = 1), workplace (n = 1) and commuting (n = 1) were not that popular. 2 answered "elsewhere" and the suggestions presented were "in the summer, in the park or elsewhere in the nature" and "everywhere". Most participants (n = 23) stated that use environment has influence on application use. They thought that the application use requires a place where you can concentrate and calm down, such as your own home (mentioned 7 times in open questions). It was also mentioned that the place should be peaceful (5x), no distractions (4x), and quiet and no background noise (2x). Participants considered that in order to use the application you should have a peaceful moment or personal time (3x) and you shouldn't be busy or multi-tasking (3x). It was appreciated that in a peaceful place, you can listen the exercises and you don't necessarily have to read them. (2x) One participant mentioned the use environment depends on the exercise.

3.3 System Use

Altogether 348 exercises were performed during the study. Users preferred exercises in text format (57.5 % of the exercises) over audio format (42.5 %). Comparison between the groups shows that the use activity was highest in the tiredness group where participants performed 18.7 exercises in average (SD 18.3). Participants in the depression group performed 9.6 exercises in average (SD 9.5) and participants in the neck problems group performed 9.3 exercises in average (SD 5.8). See Table 4.

Table 4. Use activity based on amount of exercises performed in each group. Values are expressed as mean (SD).

Exercise format	Tiredness (n = 9)	Depression (n = 10)	Neck problems (n = 9)	All (n = 28)
Text	10.0 (11.9)	7.6 (8.4)	3.8 (2.7)	7.1 (8,6)
Audio	8.7 (24.1)	2.0 (2.4)	5.6 (4.0)	5.3 (7.0)
Both	18.7 (18.3)	9.6 (9.5)	9.3 (5.8)	12.4 (12.6)

4   Discussion and Recommendations

The survey showed that stress-related complaints and symptoms are very common among the employees and students of the University of Oulu and there is a need for self-management solutions. The three most common single complaints reported were tiredness (52.8 %), neck problems (32.7 %) and depression (32.1 %). All of the 13 complaints were more common among women than men except loneliness and problems in social life.

Although 90 % of the respondents evaluated their health as excellent, very good or good, and only 10 % as fair or poor, health complaints should be taken seriously. Earlier studies have shown that at the same time while the prevalence of health complaints has remained relatively stable among working population, sickness absence for health complaints, however, have showed a general increase [15]. There might be several explanations, such as changes in working life and health expectations [15]. The findings indicate that especially women would benefit from learning skills that increase psychological flexibility and mental wellness and help to manage stress better, whereas men could benefit from learning skills that help to manage their social relationships better.

A comparison between the groups shows that participants in the depression group had the most positive attitudes toward the application; 9 of them found it useful, 9 would recommend it to other people and 6 of them intend to use the application in the future. The amount of participants was rather small, but one possible explanation for this finding is that the depression group was free to perform any exercises they wanted. Especially neck group doubted their intention to use the application in the future and they were instructed to perform only three different exercises. Although the depression group had the most positive attitudes toward the application, their use activity, however, was lower than in the tiredness group. The after use questionnaire findings indicated that both tiredness group and depression group experienced that their symptoms prevent them from using the mobile coaching software. It is not possible to make more detailed comparisons between the groups, because of their small size, but it seems that people who suffer from depression or related conditions would benefit from external motivation to encourage them to use self-management solutions for relieving their symptoms.

The participants of this study were instructed to perform only specific exercises that would be especially helpful with regards to their health complaints and symptoms, and it was expected that this "mock-up tailoring" would be make application more persuasive. However, the user experience findings showed that the participants in the depression group had the most positive attitudes toward the application, i.e. those who were allowed to perform any exercises. In other words, providing a recommended set of exercises did not have the expected influence on perceived usefulness, intention to use or referral rate. On the other hand, the use activity of the tiredness group was clearly the highest of all three. It can be discussed if the recommended eight exercises for tiredness group was an appropriate amount of exercises to handle by participants whereas three for neck problems group was too little and 45 for depression group was too many. The findings are interesting and although the number of participants was rather small, the study indicates that a health complaint should not be used as the only nominator in the tailoring of self-care solutions, but factors related to other issues, such as personality and context of use, might also be interesting to study further.

It has been stated that wider adoption of workplace wellness programs could prove beneficial for budgets and productivity as well as health outcomes [4]. ACT-based work stress interventions have been shown to reduce stress and increase well-being and job performance [11, 14, 23], and also psychological flexibility is associated with job performance [18]. Thus, ACT-based solutions have a lot of potential in decreasing stress-related complaints and symptoms in organizations. It was, however, and interesting finding that participants experienced that they would like to perform the exercises preferably at home rather than at school, workplace or when commuting. Designer's expectations (i.e. designer value) concerning the convenient integration of the solution into users' everyday lives was not met in this study, because the participants felt strongly that they want to use the application and perform exercises mostly at home.

In the near future, there will be new services available for disease prevention and self-management of health and well-being. First national initiatives, such as health accounts, medical records and electronic prescriptions, have been launched. It has become possible to manage health information and use health services online. However, until now our health care system has been more physician-centric than patient-centric, which can become a barrier for adoption of these new self-care services. Also, developing new services for disease prevention is challenging as medical services have traditionally weighted towards diagnostic and curative functions rather than preventive functions [12]. Also statistics show this; according to OECD [27] prevention expenditures in health care are 3–4 % of total costs.

Although the service offering is relatively limited at this point, it has been showed that national infrastructures can be established for delivering health services for both disease prevention and management of chronic conditions. As the health care expenditures are continuously rising [12], it is necessary to find new ways to deliver health care services and change the focus from curative functions to preventive functions. Also this study shows that there is a need for the services, but the user experience point of view and user engagement should be acknowledged.

Acknowledgments. This research has been partly funded by a grant from Tekes – the Finnish Funding Agency for Innovation as part of Digital Health Revolution programme. The multi-disciplinary programme is coordinated and managed by Center for Health and Technology, University of Oulu, Finland. This research was part of the OASIS research group of Martti Ahtisaari Institute, University of Oulu.

References

1. Ahtinen, A., Mattila, E., Välkkynen, P., Kaipainen, K., Vanhala, T., Ermes, M., Sairanen, E., Myllymäki, T., Lappalainen, R.: Mobile mental wellness training for stress management: feasibility and design implications based on a one-month field study. JMIR mHealth uHealth **1**(2), e11 (2013)
2. Arroll, B., Goodyear-Smith, F., Kerse, N., Fishman, T., Gunn, J.: Effect of the addition of a "help" question to two screening questions on specificity for diagnosis of depression in general practice: diagnostic validity study. BMJ Br. Med. J. **331**(7521), 884 (2005)
3. Arroll, B., Khin, N., Kerse, N.: Screening for depression in primary care with two verbally asked questions: cross sectional study. BMJ **327**(7424), 1144–1146 (2003)
4. Baicker, K., Cutler, D., Song, Z.: Workplace wellness programs can generate savings. Health Aff. **29**(2), 304–311 (2010)
5. Bardram, J. E., Frost, M., Szántó, K., Faurholt-Jepsen, M., Vinberg, M., Kessing, L. V.: Designing mobile health technology for bipolar disorder: a field trial of the MONARCA system. In: Proceedings of the SIGCHI Conference on Human Factors in Computing Systems, pp. 2627–2636. ACM (2013)
6. Blacklow, R.S.: Signs and Symptoms: Applied Pathologic Physiology and Clinical Interpretation. JB Lippincott, Philadelphia (1983)
7. Bond, F.W., Lloyd, J., Guenole, N.: The work-related acceptance and action questionnaire: Initial psychometric findings and their implications for measuring psychological flexibility in specific contexts. J. Occup. Organ. Psychol. **86**(3), 331–347 (2013)
8. Elo, A.L., Leppänen, A., Jahkola, A.: Validity of a single-item measure of stress symptoms. Scand. J. Work Environ. Health **29**, 444–451 (2003)
9. Ervasti, M.: Understanding and predicting customer behaviour: framework of value dimensions in mobile services. J. Customer Behav. **12**(2), 135–158 (2013)
10. Eurostat: Internet use statistics – individuals (2013). ISSN: 2314-9647 http://ec.europa.eu/eurostat/statistics-explained/index.php/Internet_use_statistics_-_individuals#
11. Flaxman, P.E., Bond, F.W.: A randomised worksite comparison of acceptance and commitment therapy and stress inoculation training. Behav. Res. Ther. **48**(8), 816–820 (2010)
12. Fu, P., Tomines, A., Dickey, L.: Delivery of preventive medicine in primary care. In: Magnuson, J.A., Fu, P.C. (eds.) Public Health Informatics and Information Systems, Health Informatics. Springer, London (2014)
13. Harrison, V., Proudfoot, J., Wee, P.P., Parker, G., Pavlovic, D.H., Manicavasagar, V.: Mobile mental health: review of the emerging field and proof of concept study. J. Ment. Health **20**(6), 509–524 (2011)
14. Hayes, S.C., Levin, M.E., Plumb-Vilardaga, J., Villatte, J.L., Pistorello, J.: Acceptance and commitment therapy and contextual behavioral science: examining the process of a distinctive model of behavioral and cognitive therapy. Behav. Ther. **44**(2), 180–198 (2013)
15. Ihlebaek, C., Brage, S., Eriksen, H.R.: Health complaints and sickness absence in Norway, 1996–2003. Occup. Med. **57**(1), 43–49 (2007)

16. Isomursu, M., Ervasti, M., Kinnula, M., Isomursu, P.: Understanding human values in adopting new technology – a case study and methodological discussion. Int. J. Hum Comput Stud. **69**(4), 183–200 (2011)

17. Järvisalo, J., Andersson, B., Boedeker, W., Houtman, I. (eds.): Mental disorders as a major challenge in prevention of work disability: Experiences in Finland, Germany, the Netherlands and Sweden. Edita Prima Ltd., Helsinki (2005). Kela

18. Kashdan, T.B., Rottenberg, J.: Psychological flexibility as a fundamental aspect of health. Clin. Psychol. Rev. **30**(7), 865–878 (2010)

19. Klasnja, P, Consolvo, S., Pratt, W.: How to evaluate technologies for health behavior change in HCI research. In: Proceedings of the SIGCHI Conference on Human Factors in Computing Systems (CHI 2011), pp. 3063–3072. ACM, New York, NY, USA (2011)

20. Kennedy, C.M., Powell, J., Payne, T.H., Ainsworth, J., Boyd, A., Buchan, I.: Active assistance technology for health-related behavior change: an interdisciplinary review. J. Med. Internet Res. **14**(3), e80 (2012)

21. Kroenke, K., Spitzer, R.L., Williams, J.B., Monahan, P.O., Löwe, B.: Anxiety disorders in primary care: prevalence, impairment, comorbidity, and detection. Ann. Intern. Med. **146**(5), 317–325 (2007)

22. Lappalainen, P., Kaipainen, K., Lappalainen, R., Hoffrén, H., Myllymäki, T., Kinnunen, M.L., Mattila, E., Happonen, A.P., Rusko, H., Korhonen, I.: Feasibility of a personal health technology-based psychological intervention for men with stress and mood problems: randomized controlled pilot trial. JMIR Res. Protoc. **2**(1), e1 (2013)

23. Moran, D.J.: ACT for leadership: Using Acceptance and Commitment Training to develop crisis-resilient change managers. Int. J. Behav. Consultation Ther. **7**(1), 68–77 (2011)

24. Neuhauser, L., Kreps, G.L.: Rethinking communication in the e-health era. J. Health Psychol. **8**(1), 7–23 (2003)

25. Newman, M.G., Szkodny, L.E., Llera, S.J., Przeworski, A.: A review of technology-assisted self-help and minimal contact therapies for anxiety and depression: is human contact necessary for therapeutic efficacy? Clin. Psychol. Rev. **31**(1), 89–103 (2011)

26. OECD: Sick on the Job? Myths and Realities about Mental Health and Work Mental Health and Work. OECD Publishing, Paris (2012). doi:10.1787/9789264124523-en

27. OECD: Health at a Glance 2013: OECD Indicators. OECD Publishing, Paris (2012). doi: 10.1787/health_glance-2013-en

28. Oinas-Kukkonen, H.: A foundation for the study of behavior change support systems. Pers. Ubiquit. Comput. **17**(6), 1223–1235 (2013)

29. Oinas-Kukkonen, H., Harjumaa, M.: Persuasive systems design: key issues, process model, and system features. Commun. Assoc. Inf. Syst. **24**(1), 28 (2009)

30. Proudfoot, J.G., Parker, G.B., Pavlovic, D.H., Manicavasagar, V., Adler, E., Whitton, A.E.: Community attitudes to the appropriation of mobile phones for monitoring and managing depression, anxiety, and stress. J. Med. Internet Res. **12**(5), 64 (2010). http://www.jmir.org/2010/5/e64

31. Schwanda, V., Ibara, S., Reynolds, L., Cosley, D.: Side effects and "gateway" tools: advocating a broader look at evaluating persuasive systems. In: Proceedings of the SIGCHI Conference on Human Factors in Computing Systems (CHI 2011), pp. 345–348. ACM, New York, NY, USA (2011)

32. Spitzer, R.L., Kroenke, K., Williams, J.B., Löwe, B.: A brief measure for assessing generalized anxiety disorder: the GAD-7. Arch. Intern. Med. **166**(10), 1092–1097 (2006)

33. Tellnes, G., Svendsen, K.O.B., Bruusgaard, D., Bjerkedal, T.: Incidence of sickness certification: proposal for use as a health status indicator. Scand. J. Prim. Health Care **7**(2), 111–117 (1989)

34. Torous, J., Friedman, R., Keshavan, M.: Smartphone ownership and interest in mobile applications to monitor symptoms of mental health conditions. JMIR mHealth uHealth **2**(1), e2 (2014)
35. van Gemert-Pijnen, J.E., Nijland, N., van Limburg, M., Ossebaard, H.C., Kelders, S.M., Eysenbach, G., Seydel, E.R.: A holistic framework to improve the uptake and impact of eHealth technologies. J. Med. Internet Res. **13**(4), e111 (2011)
36. Weiss, R.S.: Loneliness: The Experience of Emotional and Social Isolation. MIT Press, Cambridge (1973)
37. Whooley, M.A., Avins, A.L., Miranda, J., Browner, W.S.: Case-finding instruments for depression. J. Gen. Intern. Med. **12**(7), 439–445 (1997)
38. Wittchen, H.U.: Generalized anxiety disorder: prevalence, burden, and cost to society. Depress. Anxiety **16**(4), 162–171 (2002)

Balance of Hedonic and Utilitarian Values in Information Systems Use

Konsta Valkonen(✉), Niklas Lindström, Laura Natunen,
Riina Isoviita, and Tuure Tuunanen

University of Jyväskylä, Jyväskylä, Finland
{konsta.k.valkonen, niklas.o.m.lindstrom,
laura.e.natunen, riina.e.l.isoviita}@student.jyu.fi
tuure@tuunanen.fi

Abstract. This paper investigates the balance of hedonic and utilitarian values in information systems (IS). More specifically, we are interested in the continuum of such values in IS use. The paper reviews a set of literature to investigate the differences of hedonic and utilitarian IS and the role of hedonism in them. Furthermore, we define hedonic and utilitarian values in this context. We propose that the balance between hedonic and utilitarian values varies depending on the nature of the IS, and we present a conceptual model of hedonic and utilitarian values in IS use. The article provides an argument that the nature of the IS influences the balance of hedonic and utilitarian values that the IS provides. Finally, we propose that the nature of the IS is not central in explaining IS use but instead should be considered as a mediator.

Keywords: Hedonic · Utilitarian · Value · Information systems use

1 Introduction

How individuals accept new technology is an important and long-standing branch of study within the field of information systems (IS). This area of research has substantially been rooted in Davis' Technology Acceptance Model (TAM) [2, 3]. Since the publication of the original TAM, the model has been reworked and put into use in multiple ways [4]. Research of user acceptance has widely confirmed that perceived usefulness is the strongest predictor of user acceptance, while ease of use and perceived enjoyment are lesser influences [5–8]. Concerning the latter, the effect of perceived enjoyment has been consistently proven weaker than the earlier literature has expected, see, e.g., [9–11].

Although the above statements have proved factual, many exceptions to the pattern have been reported [e.g., 4, 12–14]. These papers have investigated IS that seem to be accepted more due to perceived enjoyment and perceived ease of use than to perceived usefulness. Reports have been studying systems such as the World Wide Web, home and leisure time related systems, and games and game-based training versions of IS for work.

Generally, literature has focused on utilitarian aspects of IS. Hedonic aspects of systems have not been in the core focus of research. Reasoning for the disregard of

© Springer International Publishing Switzerland 2015
H. Oinas-Kukkonen et al. (Eds.): SCIS 2015, LNBIP 223, pp. 165–176, 2015.
DOI: 10.1007/978-3-319-21783-3_12

systems hedonic side may lie in the origins of IS research in computer science [15] and economic theory [16] literature, which have emphasized natural science, efficiency, and utility rather than hedonic aspects [17]. One milestone in extending the focus to hedonic aspects was Van der Heijden's [4] separation of IS as either hedonic or utilitarian according to their nature. With nature we mean inherent features, character, or qualities of an information system. Van der Heijden found that systems having hedonic natures were more accepted due to perceived enjoyment and ease of use, while the previously dominant role of usefulness weakened. He further discusses that hedonic values can influence the user acceptance of utilitarian IS, too. More specifically, he argues that two types of motivation could determine user acceptance: extrinsic and intrinsic. In other words, if a user is motivated extrinsically, he or she is driven by the expectation of a reward or benefit that is external to the system–user interaction [4]. Davis et al. [9, p. 1112] define extrinsic motivation as a will to perform an activity "because it is perceived to be instrumental in achieving valued outcomes that are distinct from the activity itself, such as improved job performance, pay, or promotions." Perceived ease of use and perceived usefulness have widely been seen as main motivators to use information technology (IT) [10, 18]. Intrinsic motivation is opposite to extrinsic motivation. It mainly is based on the process of a certain activity rather than the enjoyment of using the system [18]. The intrinsically motivated user instead wants to perform the activity "for no apparent reinforcement other that the process of performing the activity per se" [9, p. 1112]. This means that the interaction with the system can be seen as enough reason to use the system.

Phenomena like consumerization and gamification are examples of how users are not totally satisfied with the work-oriented IT. In gamification, game-like elements are added to the software in order to make it more acceptable to users [19], whereas consumerization emphasizes how users rather bring their own devices to work than get frustrated using the IT provided by their employer [20]. We see these as signals that there must be more to utilitarian IS than just means to an end. Furthermore, we expect that in today's mobile application and software market, the role of systems' hedonic nature has become essential in order to deliver appealing and well-accepted software. With this reasoning, it is our goal to find out how features that are considered hedonic in nature could influence the acceptance of utilitarian IS.

Our objective is to investigate how hedonic values are related to utilitarian value. Furthermore, we aim to find out how hedonic values could enhance a utilitarian system's initial value. As is covered in the literature, we propose that hedonic value can enhance user acceptance and therefore the perceived value of an IS, as well as in the case of utilitarian IS. Through mapping out those hedonic attributes that could fundamentally influence how a utilitarian system is accepted, we could extend knowledge regarding the interplay of hedonic and utilitarian natures of IS. Furthermore, this knowledge could extend and support Van der Heijden's [4, p. 701] proposition that "hedonic value can play a pivotal role to increase acceptance of otherwise utilitarian information system." In order to study this, we conduct a literature review. Based on the literature review, we aim to answer the following research question: What is the balance between hedonic and utilitarian values of IS?

The article is structured as follows. We will first define hedonic and utilitarian information systems. We will also review literature on the role of hedonism in information systems. Thereafter, we will look at the literature on the value of information systems and we will more closely define hedonic and utilitarian values. At last the findings and discussion will be outlined together with the conclusion section, where the contributions and limitations will be presented.

2 Hedonic and Utilitarian Systems

Contemporary IS are multifaceted and able to provide value to users in many ways. Information systems can be categorized into three distinctive classes: predominantly utilitarian, predominantly hedonic, and a hybrid being a combination of the latter two [18]. The boundaries of these systems can most clearly be seen in the motivation to use the particular system. The nature of the system can also be identified when assessing the tactics of system developers to encourage the use of the system [1, 4].

According to Van der Heijden [4], utilitarian systems provide instrumental value to the user. The use of such systems is normally productive, goal-directed, and task-performance oriented. When developing utilitarian systems, developers mainly focus on functionality with task requirements. The goal is also to provide as little distraction as possible in order to enhance users' task performance. Utilitarian systems are mostly related to work environments since they encourage efficiency. In utilitarian systems, the extrinsic motivation can be seen as the main driver of the user's intention to use the system. On the other hand, hedonic systems provide self-fulfilling value to the user [4]. Hedonism is strongly connected to pleasure and happiness. Consequently, pleasurable experience and fun are the main frames for hedonic systems [21]. The use of such systems can be regarded as experimental. According to Arnold and Reynolds [23], hedonic systems include positive moods, high levels of satisfaction, and playfulness. Such systems are strongly linked to home and leisure time activities, including games, for example. In hedonic systems, developers mainly focus on visual functions, such as images, colors, sounds, and, in general, aesthetic layouts. Comparing the user values of these two dimensions, hedonic values are more subjective and personal whereas utilitarian values are more rational [22]. Hedonic systems do not have such goals as utilitarian systems, because the use itself and its continuance can already be seen as a goal [4].

Views on hedonic systems emphasize that the usage is driven by users' intrinsic motivation. The emphasis is based on Van der Heijden's [4] statement, which proposes that intrinsic motivation is the dominant predictor of users' intentions to use hedonic systems, which again is based on perceived enjoyment. Intrinsic motivation functions to the expense of extrinsic motivation [4] (Table 1).

A major portion of today's IS literature still takes a narrow view of user experience by concentrating only on work-related use situations [24]. One early attempt to widen the research scope was a longitudinal study of household personal computer (PC) adoption, concentrating solely on adoption outside the organizational context [24]. As a result, Venkatesh and Brown [25] suggest differences between adopters and non-adopters. Adopters were primarily found to be influenced by utilitarian, hedonic, and social determinants, whereas non-adopters were more influenced by fear of obsolescence [25]. Following their definitions, utilitarian determinants relate to

Table 1. Comparing hedonic and utilitarian IS

	Hedonic IS	Utilitarian IS
Motivation	Intrinsic motivation	Extrinsic motivation
Outcome of use	Enjoyment and fun	Efficiency and production
Development focus	Visuals and social	Functionality and task requirements
Value proposition	Instant value	Instrumental value
Objectives	No objectives	External objective
Example	Home, leisure time, games, etc.	Workplace environment, productivity tools

effectiveness in household activities, specifically budget, homework, and work. Hedonic determinants instead relate to pleasure derived from PC use, including games, fun, enjoyment, and pleasure. Finally, social determinants relate to perceived status gains or losses due to· ownership of the technology and the extent to which users' behavior is influenced by their social network [25].

Since users are nowadays more demanding and pursuing a more complete experience with IS than before, Venkatesh and Brown [25] suggest that developers are in a challenging position. Furthermore, they propose how the authors implementing new technology should re-examine the role of non-utilitarian determinants of technology use [25]. These notions have, in a way, foreseen the future. In today's software business, for example, there is demand for IS that address both dimensions, hedonic and utilitarian, by serving basic functions and providing attractive and delightful use [18]. For that, more personalized user interfaces that provide more affective experiences are needed, and those can be fulfilled with hedonic attributes [26]. Customers strive for products that "dazzle their senses, touch their hearts and stimulate their minds" [27, p. 22]. Functional features and benefits are re-positioning themselves as features that users take for granted [18]. According to Fogg et al. [28], users tend to ascribe importance to the design of IS when evaluating the credibility and when assimilating user experience and satisfaction.

Kakar [18] credits the impact of hedonic benefits to the halo effect, which is derived from social psychology. For example, aesthetics, perceived ease of use, and perceived usefulness can be explained by the effect: It describes the tendency of a single attribute of a person to influence other perceptions that that individual makes [18]. According to Eagly et al. [29], people often attribute positive characteristics to attractiveness and negative characteristics to unattractiveness. Due to this, users also associate ease of use (a positive attribute) to attractiveness [18].

Growing evidence within the IS literature supports the significance of hedonic attributes. Seeing the mature markets for mobile applications, for example, shows how product visuals is often the last remaining factor differentiating apps from one another [30]. Users actually expect good-looking things to work better, even without having any knowledge of true performance [31]. Moreover, Schenkman and Jönsson [32] have found that overall preference of websites is influenced by visuals. It has also been suggested that visually more pleasing sites yield enhanced user satisfaction and increased credibility [33, 34]. Venkatesh [35] has proposed that objective usability and perceived enjoyment are determinants to perceived ease of use.

Already in 1998, Norman [36] suggested the idea that when the functionality of IS products meet the users' needs, and while the prices of systems keep decreasing, the competition in software markets takes a turn towards enhancing user experience rather than just improving functionality. Furthermore, Norman [36] proposes that when features of IS reach a mature state in meeting needs, considerations of convenience, reliability, appearance, and even symbolic ownership become more important. Norman's idea functions as a base for the proposed model of balance between hedonic and utilitarian values of IS.

3   Value of IS

In recent decades, a new way to see markets has emerged. Vargo and Lusch [37] state that the dominant view of markets has evolved toward their services. Trade is nowadays the exchange of intangible resources rather than of products for money. Intangible resources include, for example, specialized skills and knowledge that is integrated into the goods. In this service-dominant logic, the firms do not compete with each other for their products, but for the value that the firms offer with the products, such as quality customer service and other innovations. More, consumers determine if the service has any value in use [37]. The firms should thus concentrate on "collaborating with and learning from customers and being adaptive to their individual and dynamic needs," creating a consumer-oriented emphasis [38, p. 6]. The value is defined by and created with the customer in collaboration with the company providing the service. Companies must adapt to consumers' needs and understand what needs must be fulfilled in order to let the consumer perceive value in the product [37].

Kim and Han [39] studied the adoption intention of mobile data services and therefore observed the creation of value in this context. In their study, they argue that perceived value is a combination of tangible and hedonic consequences of use [25, 40, 41]. In this context, the tangible consequences mean the utilitarian benefits that the user has after using the service. Using past research in his study, Kakar [18] combined characteristics of value in both hedonic and utilitarian contexts. These combinations are described in the following sections of the article and summarized in Table 2. Kakar [18] also proposed a conceptual model, which links the value-based view to actual system use via ease-of-use perception. Results in his study support the hypothesis that both hedonic value and utilitarian value of an IS product are positively associated with users' perceptions of ease of use. Our view posits that value of an IS is a combination of two differing value sets: utilitarian and hedonic.

3.1   Characteristics of Hedonic Value

Hedonic values are in general connected to fun, perceived enjoyment, and stimulation [1, 4, 18]. The hedonic value represents the wants, novelties, aesthetics, and

Table 2. Characteristics of hedonic and utilitarian values [18]

Hedonic value characteristics	Utilitarian value characteristics
Represent "wants"	Represent "shoulds"
Novelty, aesthetics, unexpectedness, fun	Functional and practical
Unlimited	Limited
Are ends in themselves	Are means to an end
Represent emotional or affective preferences of the user	Represent cognitive or reasoned preferences of the user
Generate affective delight response when fulfilled	Generate cognitive satisfaction response when fulfilled
Are subjective, experimental	Can be objectively appraised
Represent Maslow's higher-level needs	Represent Maslow's lower-level needs
Represent Herzberg's motivators	Represent Herzberg's hygiene factors
Pleasure seeking	Pain avoidance
Fulfill promotional goals	Fulfill preventive goals
Result in dissatisfaction when unfulfilled	Result in disgust/anger when unfulfilled
Elicitation requires innovation and creativity	Elicitation requires understanding of customer needs

unexpectedness that the user experiences as a human being. These values also represent the user's affective or emotional preferences and are themselves end-values that form as outcomes of activities [18]. They can be viewed as the high-level needs of Maslow's [42] hierarchy of needs and as the motivators in Herzberg's [43] two-factor theory. Hedonic values are pleasure seeking: when fulfilled, they generate an affective delight response. Hedonic values being based on feelings, they are unlimited, subjective, and hard to measure and appraise. They tend to fulfill promotional goals so when unfulfilled, hedonic value expectations result in dissatisfaction. It requires innovative and creative services and product development to successfully fulfill the users' hedonic value expectations [18].

3.2   Characteristics of Utilitarian Value

As stated before, utilitarian value is instrumental for the user and provides the means to an end [1, 4, 18]. Venkatesh and Brown [25] state that the utilitarian value grows from the effectiveness and efficiency that the service offers to the user. The utilitarian value represents what the IS should do and the preferences of users, which by fulfilling generate cognitive satisfaction response [18]. These values can be found in Maslow's [42] hierarchy of needs' lower levels as in Herzberg's [43] hygiene factors. Utilitarian value is functional and practical, but it is also limited, and it can be measured and appraised objectively. Utilitarian value is to fulfill preventive goals: by achieving this value, the user seeks pain avoidance, meaning that he/she is avoiding the consequences of failing a task, and on the other hand, the result is anger if the utilitarian value propositions are unfulfilled. To reach a good proposition of utilitarian value, the needs of the customer must be clear and understood when developing the product or the service implemented in it [18].

4 Findings and Discussion

The interplay of hedonic value (HV) and utilitarian value (UV) still seems like a slightly grey area within IS research. Some discuss hedonic and utilitarian value, while others discuss hedonic and utilitarian natures of IS. It also seems that the relation of HV and UV to use intention is rather lightly established. Furthermore, IS and consumer behavior literature distinguishes consumers and users by hedonic and utilitarian perceptions. Overall, this adds up to at least three entry points to study hedonism and utility in the IS context. It seems like much is understood of how hedonic and utilitarian values individually influence user perception of ease of use. Still, it is rather unknown and hard to distinguish how the two sides of value influence each other and to what magnitude.

Based on the reviewed literature, we argue that the logical explanation of the interaction of hedonic and utilitarian values can be derived from the needs perspective. We suspect that the balance between hedonic and utilitarian value formation varies depending on the nature of the information system. The authors remain skeptical about concentrating on the differing natures of IS and instead suggest concentrating on the differing values the IS drive. We rather support the views that the basic satisfactory level of utilitarian value must be addressed before hedonic value can take a critical role [36, 44]. It is inevitable and necessary for every IS to provide some level of both utilitarian and hedonic values.

When the satisfactory level of functionality and utility (UV) has met the users' basic needs, the critical aesthetics, emotional responses, and graphically appealing interfaces (HV) can be seen. Firstly, we hypothesize a border condition to Van der Heijden's [4] assumption that hedonic attributes can also take a pivotal role in increasing the acceptance of a utilitarian system. We believe that the hedonic attributes cannot take a pivotal role unless the satisfactory level of utilitarian needs is addressed. Secondly, we suggest that the nature of the IS does not directly influence users' perceptions of ease of use, usefulness, or enjoyment, but rather mediates these perceptions via influencing the balance between users' perceptions of hedonic and utilitarian values. The view assumes that UV is not lost during the process of usage. Taking into account these views, we could extend the understanding of how UV and HV can together enhance the perception of ease of use.

We also propose that in the case of utilitarian IS, the critical level of satisfied needs is fairly high. Secondly, in hybrid IS, we suggest that the balance is fairly even. Thirdly, in cases of hedonic IS, we see that the critical level is the lowest. The lines between UV and HV in Fig. 1 illustrate the expected satisfactory level. We argue that this view also applies to IS that possess a predominantly utilitarian nature. We view that the role of utilitarian value can only be seen as dominant until the satisfactory level is achieved. After the satisfactory level is reached, the dominance shifts to the hedonic value propositions offered by the IS. We propose that hedonic value starts to drive the value of utilitarian (and hedonic) information systems when the satisfactory level of

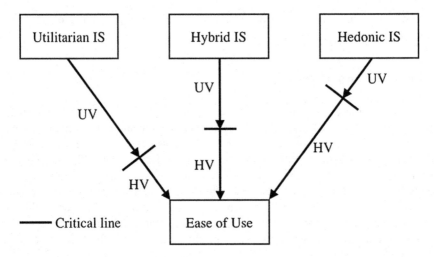

Fig. 1. Balance of hedonic and utilitarian value in information systems use

needs is exceeded. Figure 1 below illustrates the balances between different IS and the satisfactory levels.

We see that our proposition can have a significant impact on future IS research. First of all, although technology acceptance research has recognized the need to understand both hedonic and utilitarian drivers of IS use, the received view does not take account of our argument that there is a varying balance between these different value categories. The lack of recognizing this matter may explain why the literature on the impact of perceived enjoyment [5–8] has been shown to be weaker than the expected [9–11]. Furthermore, this could be a key in explaining the non-consistent findings reported in the literature, [1, 4, 12–14]. Therefore, we see it as important that we further investigate and understand how user values impact [45] user behavior and technology adoption. This in turn should encourage IS researchers to develop new theoretical models that would seek to predict and explain the balance of hedonic and utilitarian values of an IS. This work may lead to further understanding of how the nature of the IS impacts the user experience and what is the preferred balance of hedonic and utilitarian values in a given IS. In addition, this can potentially impact how IS are designed and how requirements are gathered and analyzed [45].

The findings may also impact users' willingness to upgrade or change there is-based products or services. Sääksjärvi et al. [46] have examined the impact of design on user upgrading frequency, and how this differentiates between functional and aesthetic aspects of design when considering mobile phones. In their study, they found that the functional design aspects of mobile phones, such as screen size, keyboard, and width of body, affected perceived ease of use, and that design aesthetics, such as color and thickness of body, moderated the relationship between satisfaction and upgrading frequency. However, they did not find significant results for the relationship between functional design and perceived usefulness. This concurs with our proposition that that the nature of the IS and the underlying balance of hedonic and utilitarian values of users impact the decision making of users.

Vartianen and Tuunanen [47] explored how value is co-created for consumer-targeted information systems. Their study builds on a framework, which argues that value co-creation is the interplay of at least two issues. First, the system makes value propositions to the users, and second, the users have values or goals that drive their behavior [48]. Vartiainen and Tuunanen [47] found that there are recognizable core values that motivate people to co-create value for hedonic IS-enabled activity, such as challenging oneself and others, joy of success, learning, and social relations. They found that this particular activity, geocaching, was distinctively hedonic in nature, as people pursue happiness and utility via geocaching. This concurs with Kakar's [18] findings but also provides an interesting avenue for linking our findings of key determinants of utilitarian and hedonic value and value co-creation. This can potentially also impact service-dominant logic literature [37] and service design in particular. At the moment, there are very few frameworks or models that attempt to predict and/or explain value co-creation.

Finally, we see that our proposed model provides a foundation to assess the balance of UV and HV in information systems of different kinds. The model aims to widen the research scope towards a view that considers utilitarian and hedonic values as equally important but differing in weight as dependent on the system's nature. This view strengthens the reasoning of why, for example, gamification of IS is also important for the work-oriented IS.

5   Conclusion

We have conducted a literature review studying how users perceive, value, and accept information systems of differing natures. An entry point to study user behavior was drawn from motivational theory, which explains basic human behavior. From there, we found how information systems are distinguished in two broad categories: hedonic and utilitarian. We highlighted the role of hedonism in information systems in order to justify the shift to concentrate on hedonic and utilitarian values instead of the nature of the IS. After processing the role of hedonism, we explored how value is and how value should be viewed in the context of IS use. Following the perception of value, we characterized utilitarian and hedonic values.

The key contribution of the article is the assumption that the nature of the IS, whether it is hedonic or utilitarian, influences its balance of hedonic and utilitarian value. We proposed that the nature of the IS is not central in explaining the determinants of use intention but instead should be considered as a mediator of the balance between the hedonic and utilitarian values the IS provides. A model was created in order to illustrate how we see the interaction of systems' natures and the values it generates (Fig. 2). Furthermore, lists of characteristics determining utilitarian and hedonic values were drawn from literature (Table 2).

It was proposed that regardless of the IS's nature, the basic satisfactory level of utilitarian needs must be fulfilled before hedonic characteristics can have significant impact on the system's value. Both the utilitarian and hedonic aspects must be noted when developing a new IS, whether it is for leisure or business use. Kakar [18] highlights how a good design is most likely the aspect that keeps both the form and function in balance.

Further research should be conducted in order to empirically test our propositions. The interaction between an IS's nature and values is only hypothesized in this essay. The theorization in the essay should also be peer reviewed in order to validate the suggestions. Also, which of the views is best when studying a system's acceptance and use—the values the IS offers, the hedonic or utilitarian nature of the IS, or the viewpoints of the user—is still rather unknown. Also, it seems that the research concerning hedonism and the utility of an IS is rather fragmented. Perspectives and views are many, and no comprehensive taxonomy has yet been presented.

"Making things beautiful, interesting, or enjoyable is as important as making them work" [18, p. 433].

References

1. Chesney, T.: An acceptance model for useful and fun information systems. Interdisc. J. Hum. ICT Environ. **2**(2), 225–235 (2006)
2. Davis, F.D.: Perceived usefulness, perceived ease of use, and user acceptance of information technology. MIS Q. **13**(3), 319–340 (1989)
3. Davis, F.D., Bagozzi, R.P., Warshaw, P.R.: User acceptance of computer technology: a comparison of two theoretical models. Manage. Sci. **35**(8), 982–1003 (1989)
4. Van der Heijden, H.: User acceptance of hedonic information systems. MIS Q. **28**(4), 695–704 (2004)
5. Adams, D.A., Nelson, R.R., Todd, P.A.: Perceived usefulness, ease of use, and usage of information technology: a replication. MIS Q. **16**(2), 227–247 (1992)
6. Mahmood, M.A., Hall, L., Swanberg, D.L.: Factors affecting information technology usage: a meta-analysis of the empirical literature. J. Organ. Comput. Electron. Commer. **11**(2), 107–130 (2001)
7. Taylor, S., Todd, P.A.: Understanding information technology usage: a test of competing models. Inf. Syst. Res. **6**(2), 144–176 (1995)
8. Venkatesh, V., Davis, F.D.: A theoretical extension of the technology acceptance model: four longitudinal field studies. Manage. Sci. **46**(2), 186–204 (2000)
9. Davis, F.D., Bagozzi, R.P., Warshaw, P.R.: Extrinsic and intrinsic motivation to use computers in the workplace. J. Appl. Soc. Psychol. **22**(14), 1111–1132 (1992)
10. Igbaria, M., Parasuraman, S., Baroudi, J.J.: A motivational model of microcomputer usage. J. Manage. Inf. Syst. **13**(1), 127–143 (1996)
11. Igbaria, M., Schiffman, S.J., Wieckowski, T.J.: The respective roles of perceived usefulness and perceived fun in the acceptance of microcomputer technology. Behav. Inf. Technol. **13**(6), 349–361 (1994)
12. Atkinson, M., Kydd, C.: Individual characteristics associated with world wide web use: an empirical study of playfulness and motivation. ACM SIGMIS Database **28**(2), 53–62 (1997)
13. Moon, J.W., Kim, Y.G.: Extending the TAM for a world-wide-web context. Inf. Manag. **38**(4), 217–230 (2001)
14. Venkatesh, V.: Creation of favorable user perceptions: exploring the role of intrinsic motivation. MIS Q. **23**(2), 239–260 (1999)

15. Tractinsky, N.: Aesthetics in information technology. In: Zhang, P., Galletta, D. (eds.) Human Computer Interaction and Management Information Systems: Foundations, p. 330. ME Sharpe, Armonk (2006)
16. Simon, H.A.: A behavioral model of rational choice. Q. J. Econ. **69**(1), 99–118 (1955)
17. Tuunanen, T.: Is it time to re-evaluate the connection between bounded rationality and requirements elicitation? In: Proceedings of the Twelfth Americas Conference on Information Systems (AMCIS), Acapulco, Mexico, 4–6 August, pp. 4521–4530 (2006)
18. Kakar, A.K.: When form and function combine: hedonizing business information systems for enhanced ease of use. In: Proceedings of the Hawaii International Conference on System Sciences (HICSS), pp. 432–441 (2014)
19. Huotari, K., Hamari, J.: Defining gamification: a service marketing perspective. In: Proceeding of the 16th International Academic MindTrek Conference, pp. 17–22. ACM (2012)
20. Niehaves, B., Köffer, S., Ortbach, K.: IT consumerization – a theory and practice review. In: Proceedings of the 2012 Americas Conference on Information Systems (AMCIS), Paper 18 (2012)
21. Merriam-Webster: Merriam-Webster's Collegiate Dictionary, 11th edn. Merriam-Webster Inc., Springfield (2003)
22. Babin, B.J., Darden, W.R., Griffin, M.: Work and/or fun: measuring hedonic and utilitarian shopping value. J. Consum. Res. **20**(4), 644–656 (1994)
23. Arnold, M.J., Reynolds, K.E.: Hedonic shopping motivations. J. Retail. **79**(2), 77–95 (2003)
24. Stelmaszewska, H.F., Fields, B., Blanford, A.: Conceptualizing user hedonic experience. In: Proceedings of ECCE-12, the 12th European Conference on Cognitive Ergonomics, Living and Working with Technology, New York (2004)
25. Venkatesh, V., Brown, S.A.: A longitudinal investigation of personal computers in homes: adoption determinants and emerging challenges. MIS Q. **25**(1), 71–102 (2001)
26. Blom, J.O., Monk, A.F.: Theory of personalization of appearance: why users personalize their PCs and mobile phones. Hum.-Comput. Interact. **18**(3), 193–228 (2003)
27. Schmitt, B.H.: Experiential Marketing: How to Get Customers to Sense, Feel, Think, Act, Relate. Simon and Schuster, New York (2000)
28. Fogg, B.J., Kameda, T., Boyd, J., Marshall, J., Sethi, R., Sockol, M., Trowbridge, T.: Stanford-Makovsky web credibility study 2002: investigating what makes web sites credible today. Report from the Persuasive Technology Lab, Stanford University Press (2002)
29. Eagly, A.H., Ashmore, R.D., Makhijani, M.G., Longo, L.C.: What is beautiful is good, but...: a meta-analytic review of research on the physical attractiveness stereotype. Psychol. Bull. **110**(1), 109–128 (1991)
30. Tractinsky, N., Zmiri, D.: Exploring attributes of skins as potential antecedents of emotion in HCI. In: Fishwick, P. (ed.) Aesthetic Computing, pp. 405–422. MIT Press, Cambridge (2006)
31. Norman, D.: Emotion & design: attractive things work better. Interactions **9**(4), 36–42 (2002)
32. Schenkman, B.N., Jönsson, F.U.: Aesthetics and preferences of web pages. Behav. Inf. Technol. **19**(5), 367–377 (2000)
33. Lindgaard, G., Dudek, C.: What is this evasive beast we call user satisfaction? Interact. Comput. **15**(3), 429–452 (2003)
34. Fogg, B.J., Soohoo, C., Danielson, D.R., Marable, L., Stanford, J., Tauber, E.R.: How do users evaluate the credibility of web sites? a study with over 2,500 participants. In: Proceedings of the 2003 Conference on Designing for User Experiences, pp. 1–15. ACM (2003)

35. Venkatesh, V.: Determinants of perceived ease of use: integrating control, intrinsic motivation, and emotion into the technology acceptance model. Inf. Syst. Res. **11**(4), 342–365 (2000)
36. Norman, D.A.: The Invisible Computer: Why Good Products Can Fail, the Personal Computer is So Complex, and Information Appliances are the Solution. MIT Press, Cambridge (1998)
37. Vargo, S.L., Lusch, R.F.: Evolving to a new dominant logic for marketing. J. Mark. **68**(1), 1–17 (2004)
38. Sheth, J.N., Sisodia, R.S., Sharma, A.: The antecedents and consequences of customer-centric marketing. J. Acad. Mark. Sci. **28**(1), 55–66 (2000)
39. Kim, B., Han, I.: The role of utilitarian and hedonic values and their antecedents in a mobile data service environment. Expert Syst. Appl. **38**(3), 2311–2318 (2011)
40. Holbrook, M.B., Batra, R.: Assessing the role of emotions as mediators of consumer responses to advertising. J. Consum. Res. **14**(3), 404–420 (1987)
41. Kim, B., Han, I.: What drives the adoption of mobile data services? an approach from a value perspective. J. Inf. Technol. **24**(1), 35–45 (2009)
42. Maslow, A.H.: A theory of human motivation. Psychol. Rev. **50**(4), 370–396 (1943)
43. Herzberg, F.I.: Work and the Nature of Man. World Publishing, Chicago (1966)
44. Kivetz, R., Simonson, I.: Self-control for the righteous: toward a theory of precommitment to indulgence. J. Consum. Res. **29**(2), 199–217 (2002)
45. Tuunanen, T., Kuo, I.: The effect of culture on requirements: a value-based view of prioritization. Eur. J. Inf. Syst. (2014) (Published online)
46. Sääksjärvi, M.C., Hellén, K., Tuunanen, T.: Design features impacting mobile phone upgrading frequency. JITTA J. Inf. Technol. Theor. Appl. **15**(1), 33–47 (2014)
47. Vartiainen, T., Tuunanen, T.: Co-creation of value for IT-enabled services: a case of Geocaching. In: Proceedings of the 46th Hawaii International Conference on System Sciences (HICSS), pp. 1093–1102 (2013)
48. Tuunanen, T., Myers, M., Cassab, H.: A conceptual framework for consumer information systems development. Pac. Asia J. Assoc. Inf. Syst. **2**(1), 47–66 (2010)

How the Replacement of the Project Manager Unfolds in IS Projects

Tero Vartiainen[✉]

Department of Computer Science, University of Vaasa, Vaasa, Finland
tvartiai@uva.fi

Abstract. Replacement of the Project Manager (RPM) is a known phenomenon in information systems (IS) projects, but scholarly articles on the issue are scarce. To help fill this gap, this study provides an explanation of why RPM occurs in IS projects, how it unfolds over time, and how it affects a project. Based on the analysis of qualitative data, a process model is suggested. The model uses the concept of social mechanisms to explain causal relationships. The activation of deterioration mechanisms initiates the demand or need for RPM, and as a response project healing mechanisms are activated. If RPM is decided upon, handover mechanisms are activated, and after handover, the project experiences post-handover mechanisms. The model is a combination of teleological (goal directed) and dialectical (rival forces) motors, as both the joint and individual goals of the participants motivate RPM. However, the attainment of individual goals in some cases conflicts with others' goals during the RPM process.

Keywords: Project management · IS project · Project manager · Turnover · Process theory · Social mechanisms · Teleological · Dialectical

1 Introduction

The project manager (PM) is perceived as the most important element in a project's success [3, 9]. It is even stated that there is no project management without the manager, who is the glue holding the project together—the mover and shaker [15]. Given this and the anecdotal evidence that replacement of the project manager (RPM) during an ongoing IS project is a known phenomenon, it is surprising that information systems (IS) and project management research are silent on the issue, with five exceptions [1, 6, 12, 16, 20]. The attempt by [12] to explain RPM is based on the concept of contradiction and structural tensions. Their approach offers insight into the reasons for RPM, but they fail to describe how RPM unfolds over time. Other studies offer hints as to possible reasons for RPM in IS projects; for example, uncertainty and variability levels in IS projects are high compared to projects in other areas of business, such as construction, pharmaceuticals, and manufacturing [26, 27]. This should not be a surprise given that elements in IS projects affect each other as well as the existing system [4] and that IS projects suffer from abstract constraints, hidden complexity, and changing business processes [18, 19].

© Springer International Publishing Switzerland 2015
H. Oinas-Kukkonen et al. (Eds.): SCIS 2015, LNBIP 223, pp. 177–189, 2015.
DOI: 10.1007/978-3-319-21783-3_13

To help fill the knowledge gap, in this empirical study I will present a process theory that shows how RPM unfolds and will explain why RPM occurs in IS projects. For the purpose of describing how RPM unfolds in IS projects, I adopt the perspective of process theories. Process theories explain how and why organizational changes, such as organizational reorganization and changes in individuals' jobs and careers, occur [11, 22]. During the analysis process, I realized that there are many causal paths leading to the demand for RPM and to the continuation of RPM after such demands. I also adopt the construct of social mechanisms in considering the phenomenon. Elster [5, p. 45] summarizes mechanisms as intermediate between descriptions and laws as follows: "…mechanisms are frequently occurring and easily recognizable causal patterns that are triggered under generally unknown conditions or with indeterminate consequences." Social mechanisms are used to reveal causal processes that explain how a social phenomenon is created [2]. This means that when we observe that A leads to B in a social setting, social mechanisms describe the processes through which B is generated. There may be one or more social mechanisms that explain the causal relationship. This study discusses a process theory of RPM in IS projects and will show why a PM who is nominated to lead an IS project (A) is replaced with a new PM (B) and what the consequences of this are.

Section 2 describes the process theories and the concept of social mechanisms. Section 3 describes how the data is gathered and analyzed. Section 4 describes the process model of RPM in IS projects, including the social mechanisms explaining what happens during RPM. Section 4 integrates the results with previous research and includes implications for practice and research.

2   Theoretical Framework

The theoretical framework consists of process theories and the concept of social mechanisms. Process theories are used to understand the succession of occurrences during RPM and to hypothesize about the nature of RPM. Social mechanisms are used to explain what happens in these occurrences.

2.1   Process Theories

Process theories explain how and why organizational changes, such as organizational reorganization and changes in individuals' jobs and careers, occur [22]. There are four ideal types of process theories or motors of organizational change [22]: (1) life cycle, (2) teleology, (3) dialectic, and (4) evolutionary process. Life cycle process theories hold that an entity has a predefined logic, program, or law that regulates its development toward a certain predefined goal (e.g., human life). Teleological process theories assume that an entity adapts its behavior either by itself or in interaction with others and correspondingly constructs its own desired end state. According to dialectic process theories, entities live in a pluralistic world facing colliding events and rivalling forces with contradictory values that compete with one another for control or domination. Evolutionary process theories suggest that development occurs through a continuous process of variation, selection, and retention (e.g., biological evolution). There are two dimensions for the process theories—the unit of change and the mode of change [22]. With respect to the unit of change, there is a division into single and multiple entities. Life cycle and teleological theories are concerned with the internal development of a single organizational unit. Dialectical and evolutionary theories relate to the relationships between entities. With respect to the mode of change, life cycle and evolutionary theories represent a prescribed mode of change, which means there is pre-specified direction in the change. Teleology and dialectics are constructive in nature, which means that change is not predictable but that there is novel development in the entity or entities. The four ideal process theories are archetypes that do not exist as such but as combinations of each other [22].

This being the case, RPM as a process has characteristics of teleology, as the RPM phenomenon is part of a larger goal (project success and business success) and is a goal in itself, although possibly an unwanted one. The context of RPM is typically turbulent; IT businesses and stakeholders in an IS project have their own interests in the project. Therefore, RPM likely contains dialectical processes. To understand the reasons affecting the transition from the nomination of a PM to RPM, the concept of social mechanisms offers a promising lens and will be discussed in the following section.

2.2 Social Mechanisms

The concept of social mechanisms is used to explain the relationship between two entities observed to have a systematic relationship [7]. The search for mechanisms means that we have to be able to specify the "machinery" that causes the relationship into existence or in other words the set of statements that create the relationship. This means that we are not interested in the covariance between variables but that the explanation includes a systematic set of statements that created the relationship. In the search for social mechanisms, the causal paths of conditions, actions, and events that generate the outcomes have to be identified [2]. There may be several social mechanisms that explain the phenomenon, and it is possible that some mechanisms are not activated and that some are activated. A single activated mechanism may be enough to create the relationship.

Other constructs related to the construct of social mechanisms are actors, structure, and systemic effects [8]. The construct of actors refers to the specification of actors or casting of mechanism. The structure relates to the scene where actors operate and the stages of the mechanism. Systemic effects relate to what happens to the actors or the structure as a consequence of their combination.

The concept of social mechanisms is helpful in understanding why a PM who is nominated to head an IS project is afterwards replaced by another PM. In the following section, the research design that includes both process theories and social mechanisms is presented.

3   Research Design

Interpretive approaches are recommended for studies involving complex IS phenomena [25]. Such approaches and methods involve examining individuals' understanding of reality and how they interact with the world around them [10, 21]. Given that my research question concerns a complex real-life phenomenon, RPM in IS projects, I adopted an interpretive approach and used open-ended interviews and surveys [17]. Next, I will discuss the data gathering process, followed by the data analysis and development of the RPM process model.

3.1   Data Gathering

Data gathering took place from 2006 to 2014 and consisted of qualitative data gathered through interviews and a survey. Three researchers (including the author) conducted the interviews and surveys, and permission to use the data for scientific studies was obtained [23, 24]. Myers and Newman's [13] interview guidelines were followed, according to which it is important that the interviewees feel free to talk and that the interviewers do not influence the respondents by expressing their own ideas. Given the sensitivity of the topic, it was made clear that the interviewees would not be identified in the interviews. In the surveys, the respondents were also able to freely express their thoughts on the issue. The interview subjects were project managers (17), project supervisors (18), and representatives of middle or top management (5). Data consisted of 12 interviews for 2006, eight interviews for 2009, 18 questionnaire responses for 2010, 10 interviews for 2010, an email response for 2011, and 10 interviews for 2014. Open-ended questions were used in the interviews, and example questions are as follows: "What comes to your mind about replacing a project manager?" and "Explain why a project manager can be replaced during a project." Prompting questions were asked to obtain more detailed answers. Next, I will describe how I analyzed the data.

3.2   Analysis and Development of the Process Model

First, I coded all the transcribed texts to identify perceptions about what happens during RPM and the reasons for RPM. I used Atlast.ti software to support the analysis process. During this process, I started to understand the reasons for RPM, which vary from case to case, but they nevertheless started to saturate. I also started to code other occurrences that relate to RPM, such as what happens during the handover from the outgoing to the incoming PM and what the consequences of RPM are. At this point, I sketched the overall time ordering of what happens in RPM and tentatively identified significant events [14] that occur as RPM unfolds.

I soon realized that the concept of social mechanisms [2] would be helpful in developing an understanding of the process of RPM, as there are a variety of causal paths relating to RPM and what happens during RPM. Following instructions for tracing social mechanisms [2], I started to identify causal paths that lead to replacing a PM. I identified several deterioration mechanisms that lead to problems in a project or even to its failure. As a response to deterioration mechanisms, there are mechanisms that can be used to save the project. For example, when personality problems between client representatives and the PM start to escalate (deterioration), the PM's supervisor may take action, such as discussing the issue with the parties to prevent the failure of the project (project healing). This means that the mechanisms operating when RPM is occurring are dialectical in nature. There are also reasons for RPM that have nothing to do with deficient work performance but that have to do with reorganizing the work to support the firm's larger business goals. However, these situations can be interpreted as deteriorating in nature vis-à-vis the project, and I therefore defined these mechanisms as such. The major motivation for RPM is to guarantee the success of a project or to mitigate its failure as much as possible. In terms of these aims, I identified from the data that there are three episodes that are important from the standpoint of RPM—the episode that relates to the emergence of the reasons for RPM (deteriorating mechanisms), the episode that relates to the reaction to the expressed need for RPM (project healing), and the handover episode. Each of these episodes reveals inherent social mechanisms that affect the overall success of RPM, namely project success and business success of the firm. Next, my interpretation of the trajectory of RPM is described.

4   A Process Theory of RPM

In the process model, an IS project is divided to three phases: (i) set-up, (ii) progression, and (iii) closure (Fig. 1). First, during the set-up, the scene and actors in an IS project are established. The structure of the scene of a single IS project is formed when the actors and their responsibilities are agreed upon in the contract and a board is formed to steer the project. The actors are the PM, the client and their representatives, the PM's supervisor, the project portfolio manager of the provider firm, project team members, and the board and its members. During the set-up of an IS project, it is possible that deterioration mechanisms that eventually lead to RPM are activated.

Second, an IS project progresses through the major tasks or stages, such as requirements definition, design, implementation, and testing. During the progression of the project, it is possible that deterioration mechanisms are activated. These deterioration mechanisms explain why demands for RPM emerge. As a response to the expressed demand for RPM, social mechanisms to correct the situation emerge. If RPM is decided upon, handover mechanisms are initiated; otherwise, RPM is cancelled or an alternative solution is found. After handover, there are social processes that I call post-handover mechanisms.

Third, after deployment there is a closure phase when maintenance contracts are formed. In the following sub-sections, the episodes relating to RPM, including social mechanisms, are discussed.

4.1   Deterioration Mechanisms Activated During Project Set-up

Deterioration During Project Procurement. In the procurement process, the cost of the project in relation to what the client gets is negotiated. According to the interviews, it is possible that IS projects are sold to clients with parameters that make it impossible for the PM to complete the task. This will lead to problems, such as the PM being burdened with excessive stress and not being able to get the work done, which may result in RPM.

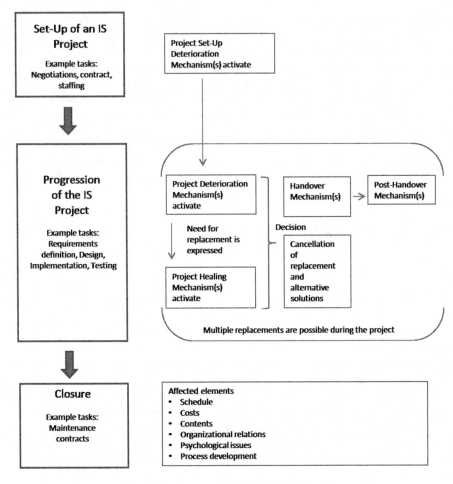

Fig. 1. The process model of RPM in IS projects

Deficient Recruitment Mechanism. The deficient recruitment of key players, such as the board members and the PM, may cause major problems and lead to RPM. The board of an IS project was mentioned by participants as being critical in a project as it represents the most important "steering committee" and makes the most important decisions during the project. In recruiting the PM, recruiters should be able to understand that person's real competencies and guarantee that the PM would be a good fit with the client. However, based on the participant interviews, it is not always possible to predict how a PM, project team, and client will get along during the project.

4.2   Project Deterioration Mechanism(s)

Deterioration of the Management Mechanism. The roles of the steering group and the management of the provider organization are critical in the project and in managing incidents such as RPM. The steering group and management representing the provider organization may have interests at stake in the project, such as in the form of bonuses. However, it is possible that there is deterioration in the practices of the steering group and representative management. Deterioration becomes visible when board members are not interested in the project or the skills of the board members do not match with the needs of the project. One participant stated it is possible that a steering group member not having experience with the realities of IS projects may make too many demands and put stress on the PM, possibly causing the PM to leave the project. Similarly, if the supervisor does not support the PM, the PM may find his or her job untenable. In some cases, the PM recruitment process may have been inadequate, leading to a situation where an unsuitable PM is nominated to head the project, and therefore RPM occurs.

Scapegoating Mechanism. The scapegoating mechanism is where a client aims to get a new PM who benefits the client more than the current one. To initiate RPM, the client blames the PM for any problems with the project or for poor performance, regardless of whether the PM is at fault. The participants explained that in these kinds of situations, the provider side may not have any other option than to agree to RPM, even if the treatment of the PM is unfair. However, one participant said that in their organization any demands for RPM would be carefully studied and discussed and that without any real deficiency in the PM's performance, RPM would not be agreed upon.

Development Mechanism. The development mechanism relates to new experiences and challenges that PMs take on in the form of training and education that entail to RPM as while in training PM may not be available for the project. At the organizational level, it is vital to train and develop employees, and this viewpoint has emerged in supervisors' perceptions. To avoid becoming too routinized in his or her job, it is vital for the PM to gain new experiences and take on challenges.

Mechanism of Evolving Needs for Competencies. Evolving competency needs in IS projects may cause the reallocation of a PM. At the project level, it is possible that needed competencies concerning IT technologies change when solutions to problems are found during the project. This may lead to RPM as the PM does not have the needed competencies for the solutions. At the project portfolio level, the status of projects may change if a senior PM is transferred to a project that requires his/her competencies and a junior PM is nominated to the project.

Deterioration of Performance Mechanism. Deterioration of performance means that the PM starts to implement tasks in a deficient way. These tasks may be any project management tasks, such as guiding project team members or reporting the status of the project. The PM may lose the trust of the supervisor, the client, or the team members when deterioration of performance becomes known. The participants described troubled projects that did not proceed because the board lost their trust in the ability of the PM to complete the project successfully, and therefore RPM occurred.

Deterioration of Relationship Mechanism. Deterioration of the relationship mechanism means that interpersonal relationships between the PM and the stakeholders become dysfunctional to the extent that RPM is necessary to continue the project. The participants explained that chemistry problems were a major cause of RPM. This means that although the PM might be capable of completing the project, the dysfunctional interpersonal relationships between the PM and a critical stakeholder, such as the client, jeopardizes the project.

Individual Balance Seeking Mechanism. For the PM, balance seeking is about searching for balance in his or her life as a whole. Continuing as PM would oppose that end, and therefore RPM is initiated. Some PMs combine private life and work life demands and decide to change jobs, consequently leading to RPM. Life events such as maternity leave or illness can lead a PM to resign from a project or the provider. For example, a project PM may lead a very long project and in order to avoid excessive stress and becoming too tired may seek another job in the organization.

4.3 Project Healing Mechanism(s)

Developing Mutual Understanding Mechanism. When arguments in favour of RPM have been expressed, the mechanism that leads to a better understanding of the situation may be activated. When the client side has demanded RPM, the supervisors first aim to understand the reasons for such demands in case there has been a misunderstanding. When the provider side is about to launch RPM in order to transfer the PM to another project, it is necessary to discuss this with the client and give reasons for RPM. Once an understanding of the situation has been reached, it is possible that the reasons for RPM might vanish.

Development and Support Mechanism. When the arguments for RPM have been given by a stakeholder, such as the client, the supervisors may perceive that the PM is need of training or mentoring. In addition, as the PM's job is typically quite stressful and the work environment is socially complex, the arguments against the PM may be unjustified. Therefore, the PM may require mental support. Thus, many supervisors have the attitude that PMs should be supported.

Successor Finding And Decision-Making Mechanism. Determining successor candidates occurs when the need to replace the PM seems probable. According to some participants, an internal successor may be better as he or she already has knowledge of the project. It is possible that no successor is available and the project has to continue with the same PM or the board has to adopt the role of PM.

4.4 Handover Mechanism(s)

Knowledge Transfer Mechanism. Knowledge transfer is divided into the transfer of formal and informal knowledge. Formal knowledge consists of project documentation. Some participants explained that the more the organization uses standards in documentation the easier the knowledge transfer of formal knowledge is. However, informal knowledge plays a critical role in the PM's job, as during the project the PM makes many decisions and gives promises that are not documented. Information about those decisions and promises should be transferred to the succeeding PM.

Informing Stakeholders. The timing of communicating RPM to stakeholders depends on the individual case. It may occur at the beginning of the RPM implementation or at the end. Many participants emphasized that the client needs to be informed about RPM as soon as possible to maintain trust in the relationship.

Outgoing and Incoming PMs Working in Parallel. Many participants explained that it is important that the outgoing and incoming PMs work together. This not only aids knowledge transfer, but it may help retain the trust of the client when they see that leadership of the project is being smoothly transferred to the new PM.

4.5   Cancel RPM or an Alternative Solution Mechanism(s)

Support Person to Assist PM. Handover may not be necessary, but instead a PM may be provided with a support person for the continuation of the project.

The Board Takes on the Role of PM. It is possible there are no candidates to take over as PM and that the current PM does not continue in that role. In such cases, it is possible that the board takes on the role of PM.

4.6   Post-Handover Mechanism(s)

Relationship Building. When the new PM starts his or her job, he or she must build relationships with all stakeholders. The participants described how in such a situation each team member aims to build a relationship with the new PM. If the relationships with the previous PM were good, functional RPM may cause negative reactions when stakeholders such as the client and team members have to learn to collaborate with the new PM.

Deterioration of Outgoing PM's Self-image and Support and Development of Outgoing PM. Before and during RPM, the PM may deal with mentally difficult situations, such as scapegoating. The outgoing PM may perceive the RPM in different ways. On one hand, the PM may consider it a relief. On the other hand, if the PM has invested his or her resources in the project, RPM may be mentally difficult and his or her self-image as a professional may start to deteriorate. Therefore, supervisors may start supporting the PM and assist with their future development.

Taking Advantage of Discontinuity. RPM causes discontinuity of the project when the outgoing PM leaves and the new PM starts. According to the participants, knowledge is lost during RPM as it is impossible for the PM to transfer all his or her knowledge to the successor. This kind of situation makes it possible for the client to take advantage; for example, the client might falsely claim that certain issues were agreed with the outgoing PM and might insist that the new PM comply with their demands.

Organizational Development. When RPM is initiated, it may harm the provider organization to the extent that it provokes a developmental process in the provider organization. In one case, RPM caused the project to slow down to the extent that it negatively affected other projects that were dependent on it. This led to the development of project processes to avoid such problems in future.

4.7 Consequences of RPM for the Project

Schedule. RPM may prolong the project. In the case that in the original schedule there was enough slack time, prolonging the project may be tolerable.

Costs. RPM may increase the costs of the project. Some interviewees said that in the case of small projects, the costs incurred by RPM are not so critical compared to the cost of RPM in large projects.

Contents. The preceding PM's acts may have negatively affected the results of the project to the extent that only RPM can stop the deterioration.

Organizational Relations. RPM may affect the trust the client has in the ability of the provider to deliver what was agreed upon.

Psychological Issues. RPM may negatively affect the self-image of the outgoing PM.

Process Development. The organization experiencing RPM may have developed its RPM related processes.

4.8 An Example of an Occurrence of RPM

In the following example, the deterioration of relationships mechanism was activated when the relationship between the provider's PM and the client's PM started to decline. As a response to the deterioration, the project healing mechanism of developing mutual understanding was activated and the situation was discussed by the parties. The successor finding and decision-making mechanism was activated when the supervisor started looking for a new PM and made the decision to implement RPM. Then, during the handover, knowledge transfer took place, with the outgoing and incoming PMs working in parallel. Although the extract does not reveal how the stakeholders were informed, this likely occurred. As a result, the situation improved. It is possible that the professional identity of the PM was negatively affected during the RPM, as the PM perceived that s/he was falsely accused. The example is as follows.

> Subject 41: *"In practice it led to the situation that communications between the provider's and the client's project managers did not work. The pal from the provider side said 'OK. This should be done but your environment is not ready', and as a response, the client's project manager said 'I cannot do that because you have not delivered the specifications.' So, this means that from the beginning they got off on the wrong foot ... they were not constructive ... although [the project] proceeded and the board was assured it was going in the right direction, the communication between these two central persons still did not work. Then, when the board found out*

that the project was behind schedule, the project manager from the client's side said it was the fault of the provider's project manager and that he did not know his stuff. The client representative asked, 'What shall we do now?' They were up against a brick wall, meaning that the personal chemistry did not work. What the reason was is very hard to say. We had to get a new person to put things back on track and get the project going. The only option was to replace the project manager. The provider's project manager naturally feels that this was an unjust [decision] as he did his best, but in this situation it did not matter. What happened was that we took a new person into the project, and the preceding project manager ran the new guy in, and after the turnover, the mood in the project changed, and the end result was almost what we wanted, well, not perhaps in terms of the schedule, but it didn't run very late."

5   Discussion

The main contribution of this study is the RPM process model in IS projects. This process model includes dual motor change theory [22] as it combines teleological and dialectical motors. Teleology relates to one entity that has a desired end state [22], and in the case of RPM, the business benefits gained via an IS project and its success can be perceived as a desired end. RPM is used to safeguard those ends, and when RPM is decided upon, it becomes a sub-goal to be attained successfully. RPM is also a dialectical process [22] in that the interests of stakeholders may be contradictory and even a power play between firms may be mediated both during and after RPM. To summarize, RPM in IS projects is a combination of teleological (goal directed) and dialectical (rival forces) motors as it is motivated by both the joint and individual goals of the participants. However, the attainment of individual goals in some cases conflicts with other goals during the RPM process. RPM in IS projects is a constructive process because the end result is not prescribed.

The social processes of the process model explain why RPM occurs, reactions to the demands for RPM, what happens when handover occurs, and what happens after the handover. All these social processes have consequences and as a whole explain the possible paths from initiating an IS project and nominating a PM to the RPM and its consequences.

Implications for Practice and Research. The social mechanisms discussed in this study offer insights for the managerial practices of project-based IT firms in relation to the issue of RPM. For example, the mechanisms highlight the fact that the competencies of all key actors involved in IS projects are important and that attention should be paid to the competencies of PMs, their supervisors, and board members to guarantee they can manage and support IS projects. This means that project portfolio management should better take into account RPM, how to prevent it, and how to manage it when it does occur. In addition, the consequences of RPM should be better understood from the standpoints of economics and professional identity.

Limitations. With respect to the nature of the mechanisms that they are between description and law, it is noteworthy that this study does not show exact causal paths but instead a variety of social mechanisms that affect the emergence of RPM and its consequences. This can be interpreted as both a strength and a weakness of this study.

On one hand, we are not able to predict the consequences of RPM based on the current results. On the other hand, this is the first study that explains what happens during RPM.

6 Acknowledgements

I wish to thank Professor Tuure Tuunanen and Professor Ola Henfridsson for their constructive feedback in this research. In addition, I would like to thank Heli Aramo-Immonen, Kirsi Liikamaa, Maritta Pirhonen, and Arja Salmela.

References

1. Abdel-Hamid, T.K.: Investigating the impacts of managerial turnover/succession on software project performance. J. Manage. Inf. Syst. **9**(2), 127–144 (1992)
2. Avgerou, C.: Social mechanisms for causal explanation in social theory based is research. J. Assoc. Inf. Syst. **14**(8), 399–419 (2013)
3. Cleland, D.: Matrix Management Systems Handbook. Van Nostrand Reinhold, New York (1984)
4. Dekkers, C., Forselius, P.: Increase ICT project success with concrete scope management. In: Proceedings of the 33rd EUROMICRO Conference on Software Engineering and Advanced Applications (EUROMICRO 2007), Lübeck, Germany, 28–31 Aug 2007, pp. 385–392. IEEE Computer Society, Los Alamitos (2007)
5. Elster, J.: A plea for mechanisms. In: Hedström, P., Swedberg, R. (eds.) Social Mechanisms: An Analytical Approach to Social Theory, pp. 45–73. Cambridge University Press, Cambridge (1998)
6. Havelka, D., Rajkumar, T.M.: Recovering troubled projects: prescriptions for sustained recovery. Issues Inf. Syst. **7**(2), 92–96 (2006)
7. Hedström, P., Swedberg, R.: Social Mechanisms: An Introductory Essay. In: Hedström, P., Swedberg, R. (eds.) Social Mechanisms: An Analytical Approach to Social Theory, pp. 1–31. Cambridge University Press, Cambridge (1998)
8. Hernes, G.: Real Virtuality. In: Hedström, P., Swedberg, R. (eds.) Social Mechanisms: An Analytical Approach to Social Theory, pp. 74–101. Cambridge University Press, Cambridge (1998)
9. Kezsbom, D.S., Schilling, D.L., Edward, K.A.: Dynamic Project Management: A Practical Guide for Managers and Engineers. Wiley, New York (1989)
10. Klein, H.K., Myers, M.D.: A set of principles for conducting and evaluating interpretive field studies in information systems. MIS Q. **23**(1), 67–94 (1999)
11. Langley, A.: Strategies for theorizing from process data. Acad. Manage. Rev. **24**(4), 691–710 (1999)
12. Liikamaa, K., Vartiainen, T., Pirhonen, M., Aramo-Immonen, H.: Replacing project managers in information technology projects: contradictions that explain the phenomenon. Int. J. Hum. Capital Inf. Technol. Prof. (2015) (forthcoming)
13. Myers, M.D., Newman, M.: The qualitative interview in IS research: examining the craft. Inf. Organ. **17**, 2–26 (2007)
14. Newman, M., Robey, D.: A social process model of user-analyst relationships. MIS Q. **16**(2), 249–266 (1992)
15. Nicholas, J.: Managing Business and Engineering Projects: Concepts and Implementation. Prentice-Hall, Englewood Cliffs (1994)

16. Parker, S.K., Skitmore, M.: Project management turnover: causes and effects on project performance. Int. J. Project Manage. **23**(3), 205–214 (2005)
17. Patton, M.Q.: Qualitative Evaluation and Research Methods. Sage, Newbury Park (1990)
18. Peffers, K., Gengler, C.E., Tuunanen, T.: Extending critical success factors: methodology to facilitate broadly participative information systems planning. J. Manage. Inf. Syst. **20**(1), 51–85 (2003)
19. Rodriguez-Repiso, L., Setchi, R., Salmeron, J.L.: Modelling IT projects success: emerging methodologies reviewed. Technovation **27**(10), 582–594 (2007)
20. Sauer, C., Gemino, A., Reich, B.H.: The impact of size and volatility on IT project performance. Commun. ACM **50**(11), 79–84 (2007)
21. Trauth, E.M.: Qualitative Research in IS: Issues and Trends. Idea Group Publishing, Hershey (2001)
22. Van de Ven, A.H., Poole, M.S.: Four process theories explaining development and change in organizations. academy of management. Acad. Manage. Rev. **20**(3), 510–540 (1995)
23. Vartiainen, T., Liikamaa, K., Aramo-Immonen, H., Pirhonen, M.: Contract on the use of the data (2013)
24. Vartiainen, T., Salmela, A.: Contract on the use of the data (2014)
25. Walsham, G.: Doing interpretive research. Eur. J. Inf. Syst. **15**, 320–330 (2006)
26. Wirth, I.: How generic and how industry-specific is the project management profession? Int. J. Project Manage. **14**(1), 7–11 (1996)
27. Zmud, R.W.: Management of large software development efforts. MIS Q. **4**(2), 45–55 (1980)

Design with and by Users

Co-Creation of Patient-Oriented Services: Design of Electronic Booking for Norwegian Healthcare

Polyxeni Vassilakopoulou[✉], Miria Grisot, and Margunn Aanestad

University of Oslo, Blindern, Postboks 1080 0316 Oslo, Norway
{xvasil,miriag,margunn}@ifi.uio.no

Abstract. Recent perspectives in service design discuss how it entails a process of co-creation with the active engagement of users. In this paper we take this lens of service design to analyze two empirical cases on the design of two patient-oriented electronic services for appointments with healthcare providers in Norway. Specifically, we focus on how the service concepts were initially conceived, how they were gradually concretized and how different user groups (patients and healthcare providers) were involved in this process. Our findings show how the involved actors gradually realized that the design of appointment services requires more co-production than initially assumed. This realization made the design scope go beyond the interactive artifacts and extend towards the overall shaping of complex interactive relationships.

Keywords: Electronic appointment services · Healthcare · Service design · Users' involvement · Patient centeredness

1 Introduction

The theme of the conference (system design for, with and by users) calls for studies on information systems that become intertwined and embedded in parts of our everyday life. These novel types of systems require reconsidering traditional understandings of systems' use and users' roles. With this paper we respond to the conference call by studying the trajectories followed for the realization of patient-oriented, web-based services.

Specifically, we study electronic services for patients' appointments with healthcare providers in Norway. The new electronic services aim to improve the accessibility and expediency of conventional (i.e. non electronic) appointment services and to contribute in overall efficiency improvements in healthcare delivery. In that sense, this new type of electronic services extends service models that have been successfully introduced during the past two decades in the commercial sector (e.g. in the travel industry) and brings them into healthcare. But new electronic appointment services are not only motivated by practicality and efficiency concerns. More importantly, they are part of a wider ongoing transition within healthcare towards patient centeredness.

Patient-centered care entails keeping patients informed, involving them in decisions and self-health management activities, improving communication and acknowledging

© Springer International Publishing Switzerland 2015
H. Oinas-Kukkonen et al. (Eds.): SCIS 2015, LNBIP 223, pp. 193–207, 2015.
DOI: 10.1007/978-3-319-21783-3_14

their experience of illness and psychosocial context [1–5]. Norway has also embraced this shift towards patient-centeredness; the National Health Plan states: "we want users to know about the services and that they are meant to participate and influence. (...) Users and their relatives are experts concerning their own situations and what they can master. (...) Being taken seriously and feeling that one is respected as a patient is important to everybody – both in the light of human dignity and because we know that users who participate in their own treatment often achieve a better result" [6]. As "patient-centered" care is increasingly becoming part of national healthcare agendas, numerous patient-oriented systems are being put in place and there is a growing body of literature (both practitioner and academic) examining the potential benefits and the challenges related to this new type of systems e.g. [7–9]. With this paper we aim to advance our understanding on how to face the challenges of developing patient-oriented technologies by introducing a perspective that goes beyond a traditional systems' design view: we approach the realization of electronic booking through the lens of service design [10–12].

The paper is structured as follows. First, we lay out the theoretical background, then we provide an overview of the electronic appointment cases investigated and we describe the method used to collect empirical data. Subsequently, we describe and present our analysis and interpretation. Finally, we conclude by discussing insights from our analysis, pointing also to possible directions for further research.

2   Theoretical Background

Researchers of service design, service innovation and service enabling information technologies have argued that the conceptualizations of service that have been imported from economics and tend to reduce service to just an intangible type of good or a unit of output are not useful for understanding services as they obscure significant service's aspects. They should be replaced by conceptualizations that bring forward a relational, interactional, co-creative perspective [10, 13]. For the realization of interactions contact points need to be in place. These points are known as "touchpoints" in the service design literature [14, 15] and usually their purpose is information exchange. Following this line of thinking service has been conceptualized as "socioeconomic exchange" [16, 17], "co-creation of value" [10, 18, 19], "Actor to Actor processes" [20, 21].

The adoption of such a relational perspective makes evident that electronic service design goes beyond the design of interactive artefacts [22] or information systems [23]. Although the use of interactive artefacts is required for the realization of electronic services, service design needs to embrace a wider view that covers also the social relations entailed in the service [24]; a view that goes outside the digitally mediated service touchpoints [21] and entails an active engagement with service actors' practices [11]. Additionally, electronic service design needs to take into account strategic intents that drive design decision [25].

Service designers approach their work as an enquiry in which they and others would construct an understanding of what the service is [11]. This collective construction of understanding has been conceptualized as co-creation and is "not just a question of formal consultation in which professionals give users a chance to voice their views on a limited number of alternatives. It is a more creative and interactive process which challenges the views of all parties and seeks to combine professional and local expertise in new ways" (p. 22) [26]. Hence, service design goes through iterative learning cycles of understanding, framing, exploring, reducing, rationalizing, realizing [12] and users' involvement during all stages is pivotal [27].

The attempted shift of healthcare towards patient centeredness entails the engagement of patients and healthcare providers in new types of co-creation activities: new types of services that will have to grow out of a rich understanding of both sides' practices. In the two cases analyzed in the sections that follow we explore how different user groups were involved and how they influenced the design of new patient-oriented electronic services.

3   Methodology and Case Studies

In this paper we report from the cross analysis of two different cases where we examine the design of specific patient-oriented, web-based services. We have investigated the cases within the wider framework of an ongoing research project on the interplay between new information technologies (IT) and existing systems and modes of organizing within Norwegian healthcare. In particular, for our cross-case analysis we have examined how the service concepts were initially conceived, how they were gradually concretized and what was the users' involvement in this process. We have adopted an interpretive approach for our study [28, 29] and we have based our analysis on qualitative data collected over a period of five years (interview transcripts, notes from observations, documents that were made available to us in the field and public documents).

The first case analyzed is about the design of a national service for booking appointments with General Practitioners (GPs) in Norway. This is a new functionality to be included in the Norwegian national e-health platform which patients can access over the internet. This platform was launched in June 2011 with the aim to provide secure patient oriented digital services [30]. The activities related to the design of the booking service officially started in 2012 with a preparatory study. The outcome of the study was the specification of four key patient oriented services: booking of appointments, renewal of prescriptions, electronic contact for administrative purposes and e-consultation. These four services were grouped into a single project which was named the "eDialogue" project and started in spring 2013. We have followed the whole project from its start till today but in this paper we report only on the trajectory followed for the booking service.

The second case analyzed is about the design and development of a hospital based service for appointments with different clinics. This service is included in the patient oriented web portal named MyRec which was developed within a Norwegian hospital. The first functionality within MyRec was launched in 2006 and the portal keeps being expanded and improved till this day. It offers to patients general functionalities such as secure email with clinical personnel, access to selected EPR documents (e.g. discharge letters), in addition to more tailored functionalities for specific conditions. For instance, patients with hemophilia who are requested to report their use of blood coagulant drugs, can use a special online form; patients needing medical equipment (e.g. pumps or catheters) can place an order in a web shop-like environment. Data on the case were collected in three stages (September 2010 - September 2011, March 2012 - December 2012, March 2014 – June 2014) and cover the overall evolution of MyRec although in this paper we report only on the appointments' service part.

For both cases data collection entailed interviews with the people involved in the design and development of the services, observations during meetings and workshops, and document analysis (internal reports, presentation material for various audiences, policy documents, laws, and articles from specialized Norwegian journals). In summary, the research reported is based on data collected using a combination of fieldwork and documents' analysis (Table 1).

Table 1. Data sources.

Source	Description
Interviews	28 semi-structured interviews for 1st case 15 semi-structured interviews for 2nd case
Observations during weekly meetings, workshops and thematic meetings	49 weekly meetings, 1 design workshop, 5 thematic meetings for 1st case three design workshops for 2nd case
Document analysis	Norwegian Healthcare Strategic Planning Documents; Policy, Regulation and Standards Documents; Project Documents

For both cases data collection did not focus only on appointments' related services but this topic was discussed among others in meetings and was raised in interviews

4 Findings

Before presenting the specific empirical findings from the two cases we provide baseline information on how appointments' booking for primary care (GPs) and hospitals is organized within the Norwegian healthcare system. This information is useful for making sense of the case specific accounts that follow.

In Norway, GPs act as gatekeepers to specialist health services. This means that patients can freely book an appointment with their GP office, but they can only be granted an appointment in a hospital department after being referred by their GP. Usually, the GP would send the referral letter directly to a hospital, which then processes the request and informs the patient about the appointment time. In order to assign a patient to an appointment slot, there is some screening and prioritization involved both in GP offices and in hospitals. A GP office secretary will ask the reason for which the patient is requesting an appointment in order to assess the urgency and seriousness. Patients requesting GP appointments are supposed to get them as early as possible and normally within five working days. Similarly, the referral letters received by hospital departments are screened and prioritized before appointments are assigned. There are variations between different sites related to the nature of services, types of patients etc., so, a hospital department can have multiple categories of patients and treatments each with its own urgency. A hospital department may assign patients to timeslots, or can reject the appointment request and forward the referral to another provider. Once an appointment has been defined and communicated, it can be changed by the patient if he/she notifies the healthcare provider and negotiates a new time. Usually, patients can communicate with GP offices and hospital departments using the phone during defined telephone hours. Email communication cannot be used since Norwegian law prohibits the usage of email for communication around sensitive health issues.

4.1 Designing a National Electronic Service for Appointments with GPs

In August 2012 the regulation for General Practitioners (GPs) was revised by the Norwegian Ministry of Health; among other changes, a new passage was added where it was clearly stated that GPs shall offer online appointment booking services [31]. Within the same year, activities related to the design of a national electronic booking service which would be included in the national e-health platform were initiated with a preparatory study. The idea was to offer a new service that would be potentially used by all patients and by all GP offices. The final report from this preparatory study pointed to the generic nature of the new services envisioned: *"the various care professionals and health institutions have largely similar needs for secure digital dialogue with their patients as bi-directional communication, and the processes around appointments, e- consultation and document/form exchanges are generic processes that can be transferred from a care professional- or professional area to another"*.

The project participants that worked for the preparatory study visited several GP offices and discussed with doctors and administrative staff. Furthermore, they had access to a patients' panel that was already in place for informing the design of the overall national e-health platform. The project team collected information from both users' sides and came up to the conclusion that an electronic booking service would be useful for both sides. For GP offices it would be useful because *"a main consideration is to save time and to facilitate a working life where both GPs and administrative staff at the office can focus on patients and to ensure high-quality patient care"*. For patients, the new service would be beneficial because *"they will not need to spend their time on the phone (so they will have more time for recreation or work)"*.

During the preparatory study it was realized that in order to offer a service that would be suitable for as many users as possible it would be important to allow some flexibility in the functionality developed. So, it was decided that the new electronic service would support two different types of appointment bookings. The first type would give patients the possibility to book by accessing directly the GP office calendar and viewing the hours available for booking. In that case, the patient would make a choice and get an instant confirmation. The second type would give to patients the possibility to send a message to the GP office and ask for an appointment that suits his/her preferences. In that case, the request would be handled manually at the GP office and a confirmation (or a message declaring unavailability) would be received at a later stage. The choice of service type would be made by the GP offices based on healthcare practitioners' preferences, the systems they had already in place and their work routines. Additionally, a service that would allow patients to view the timing arranged for future appointments and change or cancel them was foreseen.

Both variants of the booking service would require patients to log-in. The team engaged in the preparatory study acknowledged that an additional open access service option would be convenient for some patients but did not include this possibility in the initial plan. This was because they wanted to avoid potential adverse effects (e.g. abuse of the system or sending of forged messages to GP offices) and also because they identified usability challenges (e.g. it would not be possible to show to patients the name of their GP or an overview of appointments already made so, it would be difficult for them to express a very specific message to be transferred electronically).

The project for the detailed design and the development of the booking service started in spring 2013 with a predefined budget and timeline. A project participant told us: "*with a limited budget is difficult to do user involvement as deep as we wanted. We have created a GP office panel which includes 5 offices that will have meetings every second month through the project period where we will discuss how we should form the solution both from the patients' side and what is important from the doctors side. It is doctors from different parts of Norway (…) On the patients' side we probably have to use a lot of questionnaires on line because that is a cheap way to do it. Last year we had a group of people that we hired that came once a month, then we discussed different solutions with them but they are not here anymore.*" Additionally to the GP panel the project team arranged a number of observations at GP offices that were already using electronic booking services (they had adopted solutions developed by private providers) in order to understand their use patterns.

During the observation sessions the project team identified a number of specific needs from the GP office side, for example, for some appointments to be scheduled it would be important to arrange lab tests before the patient comes to the office. A GP office requested a field for "*providing patient feedback as a blood test at the lab at least five days before*". Also, it was found that some GP offices would like to offer different types of booking services based on differences in the health conditions of the requesting patients. For example, one GP office had given direct access to the calendar but defined different settings for different patient groups: some would get instant automatic confirmation, while others would get confirmation only after their choice was manually approved.

The discussions within the GP panels revealed additional particular needs. Some doctors expressed the wish to show different time horizons for bookings to different patients based on their health situation: it would be good to limit the time horizon to avoid overbooking by hypochondriacs that are overall healthy but for chronic patients it would be good to allow bookings over a full years' period. Also, some doctors explained that specific types of lengthy appointments that would require "double slots" would have to be booked over the phone. Other doctors questioned the practice of informing patients for lab visits beforehand which was observed during visits and explained that in their office this would not be needed. It was also discussed that in general there is sometimes the need for doctors to give specific guidelines on how to prepare for the appointment, e.g. not to eat, or to bring a urine sample, but it was agreed that the electronic service would not cover everything so alternative communication means (e.g. phone calls or sms messages) could be used.

The panels' participants from the GP offices did not include only doctors but also administrative staff. During discussions the administrative staff that had prior experiences from the use of electronic booking said: *"experience shows that office staff spent much time trying to find a time that matches the patient"*. In order to avoid many exchanges of messages they proposed that the appointment date and time suggested by the patients should not be in a structured field but rather, it should be expressed as free text allowing flexible descriptions of preferences and constraints. Also, they said that the option to simply request an appointment "as soon as possible" should be definitely included. They also expressed concerns on how patients will be "educated" to understand that they cannot change an appointment by ordering a new one but instead they need to use the booking change functionality. Some panel participants pointed to the problem that the booking change functionality would show only appointments booked electronically and this would prevent patients from using the functionality for appointments booked over the phone or during a previous visit. Another issue that was raised was related to the cut-off point for the cancellation of appointments. In general, a 24 h rule could be applied although GP offices might exercise some discretion on rule's application to accommodate special cases.

The initial vision for the new booking service was to build something relatively straightforward having some inspiration from the successful experiences within the travel industry (booking tickets and hotel stays). As the project team engaged with the users' community it became obvious that the services developed would have to be flexible enough to meet the specific needs of different local GP practices. For example, full self-service would only be one of the choices offered, information exchange through structured data fields would be complemented with alternative messages with unstructured content. The list of possible options to be added in order to provide a fully customizable solution kept growing and the project participants had to prioritize the implementation of the most crucial ones for the first release of the solution. Today (February 2015) the service is about to be piloted in a number of GP offices and offered to numerous patients. The team expects that further refinements will be needed as feedback from the users will be collected. Practically, what has started as a general purpose booking service is being gradually concretized to a highly customizable solution. This customizability relates to the specifics of healthcare practices and the great variety of patients' healthcare needs.

4.2 Designing an Electronic Service for Hospital Appointments' Handling

The electronic service for hospital appointments' handling that we investigate in the second case is part of the web based hospital portal named MyRec. MyRec was conceptualized as a new communication channel between patients and hospital. The overall vision for the portal was to put in place a way for patients to access quality information, personal health documents, and secure e-mail. Secure environment, secure access and data privacy were of major importance during the initial conceptualization phase of MyRec. A central aspect of the initial concept was the patient orientation of the solution. An informant said "(MyRec) *was from the beginning thought not as just another door into the hospital where to get some information, but it should be a meeting point where also the hospital personnel should meet half ground, and the patient should be able to set the premises to decide how this meeting takes place*". It was important for the initiators that development and evolution was driven by users' needs. Patient-orientation meant also tailorability of the solution. An informant said: "*the idea to tailor to different group of patients was there from the beginning (...) I am very convinced that one size does not fit all but it should adapt to different users, users' needs and ideally also throughout a life time*". This approach stressed the need to design functionality to support specific patients' needs on one side, and fit into the existing work practices specific to each of the clinics and units on the other.

One of the first services to be designed and implemented was the request to change appointments at the outpatient clinics of the hospital. This service was developed from an acute problem at the Children outpatient clinic where patients would too often not show up at their appointments. As described earlier, in Norway, when a patient is referred by a GP to the hospital, the hospital department that receives the referral letter sets an appointment (day and time) and this is then communicated via mail to the patient. Thus, the patient is not consulted when the booking is performed. Often the given appointment does not fit the patient's schedule (or rather the parents' schedule in the case of the Children outpatient clinic), and parents need to contact the clinic to ask for an appointment change. According to the clinic's secretaries the problem of patients not coming to their appointments was due to difficulties of getting in contact with the clinic. An informant describes the scenario from a patient perspective: "*You get home from work and you have got a letter in the mail that says that you have got an appointment at the hospital, what do you do with it? You put it in your bag and think that you will call the day after from work. But then you have a very busy day or the phone was busy at the hospital, and then you try once more and then is weekend and then you forget and remember about it only a couple of days before the appointment, then you really have to be persistent and call saying you cannot come*".

The problem at the clinic was that the parents would often try to call during lunch break since this would be the time of the day that better suits their schedule. However, the clinic would have limited personnel to answer phones during lunch breaks, when the hospital personnel would also have their lunch. One of the informants said: "*It is also a very busy department working on high tempo so it is difficult to allocate persons (to answering phone calls), and they also have to eat so what happened was that a lot of people did not get through on the phone and tried and tried and gave up, and a lot of those phone calls were about cancelling an appointment*". In addition, it is not allowed by law to communicate via ordinary emails. The result of this situation was that many parents were not able to notify the clinic that they could not come to the assigned appointment. On the side of the clinic, this situation meant that appointments were lost resulting in a waste of time and resources.

In this situation, the head of the secretaries at the Children outpatient clinic took the initiative to contact the IT department of the hospital, to ask if there was a way to address this problem. She contacted a person in the IT department that she knew from a previous project, and that now was involved in the creation of MyRec. He recognized the problem of appointment lost as a case that could be addressed with MyRec, and told the clinic that they would have to participate in the design of the solution. The general idea was that MyRec could provide parents with a web-based tool to allow them to send some sort of notification to the clinic in an asynchronous mode and thus independently from opening hours or telephone hours. At that point in time, MyRec was already launched as the hospital web-portal with a secure log in mechanism as required by law when treating personal health information. Thus, a module for requesting a change of appointments was created in MyRec and in order to inform the users a text message was added into the letter with the appointment details explaining how to log in and make use of MyRec to request a change.

During the workshops for the design of the module it was first considered to create integration with the existing hospital infrastructure including the patient administrative system which manages the calendars of the clinics, however this option was discarded. One informant said: "*there were done many attempts to get a web-based electronic time management. One could export appointments out on a platform and then into the calendars, but it was so complicated and it was at the end never realized*". In addition, the hospital infrastructure was under major restructuring and integration to the administrative system would have meant delays and complications. Thus it was decided to create a standalone solution that the secretaries would have to use in parallel to the administrative system.

Another aspect discussed during design was the user authentication procedure which in its actual form was not considered user friendly. The informant said: "*we have a problem here because if you need to log in it is too cumbersome*". The security mechanism in place required to log in with a password and generated code, and this scenario was not well accepted by users. The design team then decided to make the service more accessible by having it available as 'open service' without a need to log in. The user would simply have to fill in a web-form and 'send it'. Specifically, in order to request a change, a parent would have to select the hospital from a menu, then select the outpatient clinic, and enter name, birth date, telephone number, day and time of the appointment, the reason for requesting a change and also preferences. The principle in this case was that patients should enter "just enough" information to be identifiable by the secretaries, but no sensitive information (for instance nothing about the reason for the visit). The secretaries would then receive the message in the clinical interface of MyRec, change the appointment in their administrative system, and send another letter to the patient with the new appointment.

This module was taken into use and within short time improved the situation. Not only parents were able to notify in a more convenient way about their need to change appointments but also secretaries were now able to reschedule time-slots in a more efficient way. One informant said: "*What we see now is that when people get the letter, and see that the appointment does not fit into their schedule, the same evening (…) they sit down at the pc ask for another appointment*". In this way the secretaries are alerted sooner than what it used to be in the previous situation (a month in advance instead than 2 days), and they have more time to rearrange the calendar. One informant said:

"*This is something we did not predict, this side effect, that they would be alerted a lot earlier*". These immediate benefits drove the spread of the solution in the hospital. Other clinics soon requested MyRec team to implement the request for changing appointment module also for their patients. Many clinics had a similar problem in managing phone calls about appointments, and wanted also to implement a new channel for patient communication. When designing the module in collaboration with the Children outpatient clinic, the MyRec team understood that the module had the potential to be used also for patients in other clinics. Thus the design features where kept either generic or adaptable to specific needs. For instance, the web form was designed in way that allowed the easy addition or elimination of fields. So, the web form allowed the possibility to include specific information for each of the clinics. For instance, a clinic added text to inform patients that they should send their request at least 24 h in advance, or the lost appointment would be charged.

In the clinics new work practices were defined around the use of the new appointment module and the handling of the requests. For instance, at the children outpatient clinic the secretaries decided to open all MyRec forms in the morning, and then they allocated specific time slots during the day. New practices were also defined for how to handle patients' requests. For example, if a patient would provide a reason considered not acceptable (e.g. asking to postpone surgery because of a kindergarten carnival party) it was decided that the secretary would call the patient on the phone. In another clinic it was agreed to have the policy that if a patient requested to change an appointment more than three times he would lose the right for the visit, and would need to have a new referral letter from the GP. In this case the secretaries decided to call the patients at the second request for change to alert them.

4.3 Service Design as Relationship Contouring – a Cross Analysis of the Two Cases

The two cases followed different design trajectories, and we will now turn to analyzing the similarities and differences between the processes through which the services were designed. The design trajectories reflect a process where it was gradually realized what type of relationship the booking process entailed, and what is needed in order to put in place an electronic service to support this relationship. Both initiatives end up with a realization that they are not dealing with the development of a simple tool that facilitates a selection among a closed set of options (similar to the booking of airplane tickets or available hotel rooms) but rather, that they are working on contouring spaces within which different types of actor to actor processes will have to unfold. In other words, the teams were not engaged in the design of interactive artifacts but rather in the shaping of complex interactive relationships.

Starting from a Generic Vision. In the case of the national service for GP appointments the project team moved from a generic vision (of efficiency improvement and simultaneous patient empowerment) towards the design of a service that could support multiple actor to actor processes, accommodating the specifics of healthcare practices and the great variety of patients' healthcare needs. In order to achieve this, the team realized that instead of simply facilitating new information flows they had to think about the whole relationship between patients and GP offices, not only about the actual moment of the booking but also what comes before and after that. This thinking led to the design of a service that offers to all parties room to maneuver.

Starting from a Specific Solution to a Local Problem. The process leading to the development of MyRec service was initiated by a clinical user that had a concrete problem - parents not showing up for scheduled appointments in the Children outpatient clinic. However, as other clinics showed an interest in introducing electronic services to resolve similar problems, the functionality which was developed to match the needs of patients and healthcare personnel of the Children clinic, was gradually transformed to a flexible template generic enough to spread to other departments with little changes.

Modes of User Involvement Influenced by Projects' Location. The differences in the process had much to do with the organizational location of the teams that undertook the design initiatives. The MyRec design team worked in a hospital environment and had extensive knowledge about and strong relations to the clinics in the hospitals. This location allowed the booking service to emerge out of the gradual generification [32] of an initially limited and clinic specific functionality. The process followed was not phased and sequentially decoupled design, development and implementation, but an iterative process of experimental development and ongoing deployment which allowed ongoing inputs from the clinical users. The patient users were less central to the design process. Still, they did influence the modification of the design: they incited the move of the appointment canceling service outside of the 'log-in' (secure) zone. The national GP booking solution was developed in a setting that was away from healthcare practice. Differently to MyRec, the project had to use formal processes in order to engage with users' practices and reached out for healthcare practitioners and patient users through surveys, user panels, and consultation meetings. In addition, significant insights came from the observational study of actual practices in GP offices.

Beyond the Digital Touchpoints. For the co-creation of a specific booking the two parties involved have to engage in activities that go beyond the digital mediated touchpoints that the new electronic services provide. The MyRec service is not a complete (end-to-end) booking solution, but a solution that plays together with other electronic tools (e.g. the hospital's patient administrative systems where the schedules are kept) and with the telephone and post system for letters. The MyRec solution complements the pre-existing arrangements by offering patients a new way to notify the hospital department that the assigned time slot does not fit their schedule. But in order to design this new way of communicating (the new touchpoint) the whole interaction between patients and healthcare providers had to be taken into account. The national booking solution for GP offices is also not covering the whole range of patient – GP office interactions that might be required for the actual booking. GP offices have to go through their own routines and tools for prioritizing appointments and in some cases to use supplementary means to coordinate with patients about taking blood tests in advance, bringing urines samples, or fasting. Here again, in order to design the electronic service an understanding of what the whole service is about had to be developed. This allowed the design team to make sense of the parts of the relationship that would need to be electronically facilitated and of the actor to actor processes that will remain outside the digitally mediated service touchpoints.

5   Discussion

Our study of two cases on the design of electronic services for patients' appointments with healthcare providers examined how the service concepts were initially conceived, how they were gradually concretized and what was the users' involvement in this process. Both cases show how the actual designs were the result of a collective construction of understanding about the actor to actor relationships that an actual appointment booking entails. This understanding was collectively constructed as the views of the design teams and the users participating in the design effort were challenged and negotiated during the design process. This process led to the gradual realization that bookings require more co-production than initially assumed. Furthermore, it led project participants to widen their view and go outside the digitally mediated service touchpoints. They realized that they had to make sense of all the activities related to bookings and not only those required for the electronic service. In other words, the projects shifted attention from the interactive artifacts to the complex interactive relationships. This allowed them to design services that provide rich spaces within which different types of actor to actor processes can unfold.

Our findings resonate well with similar findings from the general service design literature although research in that field is not specifically about technology or electronic services. For example, Kimbell studied three firms of professional service designers and found that "designing for service is seen as an exploratory process that aims to create new kinds of value relation between diverse actors within a socio-material configuration" (p.1) [11]. Moreover, Saco and Goncalves studied service design using three concrete cases and found that "to make a significant impact, service design practitioners must look at entire ecosystems rather than at isolated problems" (p. 18) [12]. With this paper we aim to contribute to this growing body of literature by adding cases that are specific to electronic services' design.

We think that our findings on the approach followed for the specific two cases can be useful in guiding practitioners trained in "systems design and development" in their transition towards services. This transition is timely and has been called for [16, 23] and can result to less struggles and mishaps in electronic services development. Several initiatives to digitize the process of appointment handling have struggled in the recent past. In 2004, the UK's National Health Service launched "Choose and Book", an electronic booking system that allows patients to select time, date and place for a first outpatient appointment in specialist care. The success of the system has been limited and one study concluded that there was a mismatch between the system "and the more complex, granular and exception-filled nature of real-world clinical practice" (p. 218) [33]. For ordinary patients, the system allowed only two categorizations of urgency, namely "urgent" and "routine", while users wished also a "soon" category. Moreover, the system shifted the responsibility for prioritization from hospital staff to GPs: the urgency classification would now be assigned by them and could not be changed by the hospital staff. One study reported that more than 60 % of GPs did not find the service to be a good thing, and that GPs and patients were satisfied with the pre-existing prioritization practices [34]. Similarly, a study of an early Norwegian pilot of direct electronic booking of hospital appointments by GPs (which was discontinued) points to the shifts in the division of rights and responsibilities between hospital doctors and GPs [35]. During that pilot, the reconfiguration effected by the prototype solution gave rise to collective action dilemmas where individual and collective rationality were not well aligned. Since the booking was done by the GP when the patient was present, the GPs were pressured to select an available slot earlier than what is strictly medically necessary. The solution introduced incentives for opportunistic behavior, e.g. for a GP to pick available slots before other GPs would pick them. The authors conclude that complete electronic booking cannot replace ordinary booking, only supplement it, due to the socio-technical complexities associated with the booking process.

The handling of appointment booking appears to be a mundane and even trivial service to digitize, as it is a predominantly administrative service and the interaction is primarily about agreeing on a date and time. But, as prior experience has shown even such seemingly simple cases of electronic service design can prove very challenging in practice. Information Systems' researchers have engaged extensively in discussing the potential of information and communication technologies to facilitate or prompt radical service innovations focusing to resource integrating activities, bringing into attention the combinatorial potential of digital technologies and their generative capacity and investigating the emergence of technology enabled service ecosystems e.g. [36–39]. Although extant literature has been mostly oriented towards radical service innovation we think that it is equally important to investigate electronic service design processes for cases where more stepwise changes are attempted and where the main concern is to deliver services that introduce novelty while remaining congruent with current practices.

Future research may proceed in two directions. The first direction is towards the analysis of similar cases that followed similar or totally different trajectories. This direction can lead to a more rich understanding of the specifics of electronic service design. A second future research direction is related to extending our analysis by following the trajectory of the national booking service for the GP offices in the future. At this moment we cannot predict what further reconfigurations will be required after the new service is introduced in use. By following the evolution of the service over an extended period of time we can get a more complete understanding of design dynamics.

References

1. Stewart, M., Brown, J.B., Weston, W.W., McWhinney, I.R., McWilliam, C.L., Freeman, T.R.: Patient-Centered Medicine: Transforming the Clinical Method. Radcliffe Medical Press, Abingdon (1995)
2. Coulter, A., Dunn, N.: After bristol: putting patients at the centre commentary: patient centred care: timely, but is it practical? BMJ 324, 648–651 (2002)
3. Berwick, D.M.: What patient-centered should mean: confessions of an extremist. Health Aff. 28(4), w555–w565 (2009)

4. Epstein, R.M.: The science of patient-centered care. J. Fam. Pract. **49**(9), 805–810 (2000)
5. Davis, K., Schoenbaum, S.C., Audet, A.M.: A 2020 vision of patient-centered primary care. J. Gen. Intern. Med. **20**(10), 953–957 (2005)
6. Norwegian Ministry of Health and Care Services, National Health Plan for Norway (2007–2010) (2007)
7. Greenhalgh, T., Hinder, S., Stramer, K., Bratan, T., Russell, J.: Adoption, non-adoption, and abandonment of a personal electronic health record: case study of healthspace. BMJ Br. Med. J. **341** (2010). doi:10.1136/bmj.c5814
8. Demiris, G., Afrin, L.B., Speedie, S., Courtney, K.L., Sondhi, M., Vimarlund, V., Lovis, C., Goossen, W., Lynch, C.: Patient-centered applications: use of information technology to promote disease management and wellness. J. Am. Med. Inform. Assoc. **15**(1), 8–13 (2008). A white paper by the AMIA knowledge in motion working group
9. van't Riet, A., Berg, M., Hiddema, F., Sol, K.: Meeting patients needs with patient information systems: potential benefits of qualitative research methods. Int. J. Med. Inform. **64**(1), 1–14 (2001)
10. Vargo, S.L., Akaka, M.A.: Service-dominant logic as a foundation for service science: clarifications. Serv. Sci. **1**(1), 32–41 (2009)
11. Kimbell, L.: Designing for service as one way of designing services. Int. J. Des. **5**(2), 41–52 (2011)
12. Saco, R.M., Goncalves, A.P.: Service design: an appraisal. Des. Manage. rev. **19**(1), 10–19 (2008)
13. Vargo, S.L.: Toward a transcending conceptualization of relationship: a service-dominant logic perspective. J. Bus. Ind. Mark. **24**(5/6), 373–379 (2009)
14. Clatworthy, S.: Service innovation through touch-points: development of an innovation toolkit for the first stages of new service development. Int. J. Des. **5**(2), 15–28 (2011)
15. Katzan Jr., H.: Essentials of service design. J. Serv. Sci. (JSS) **4**(2), 43–60 (2011)
16. Barrett, M., Davidson, E., Prabhu, J., Vargo, S.L.: Service innovation in the digital age: key contributions and future directions. MIS Q. **39**(1), 135–154 (2015)
17. Aubert-Gamet, V., Cova, B.: Servicescapes: from modern non-places to postmodern common places. J. Bus. Res. **44**(1), 37–45 (1999)
18. Vargo, S.L., Lusch, R.F.: Evolving to a new dominant logic for marketing. J. mark. **68**(1), 1–17 (2004)
19. Prahalad, C.K., Ramaswamy, V.: Co-creation experiences: the next practice in value creation. J. interact. mark. **18**(3), 5–14 (2004)
20. Vargo, S.L., Lusch, R.F.: It's all B2B… and beyond: Toward a systems perspective of the market. Ind. Mark. Manage. **40**(2), 181–187 (2011)
21. Holmlid, S.: Participative, co-operative, emancipatory: from participatory design to service design. In: First Nordic Conference on Service Design and Service Innovation (2009)
22. Holmlid, S.: Interaction design and service design: expanding a comparison of design disciplines. In: Nordes, (2) (2009)
23. Dahlbom, B.: From systems to services. http://bodahlbom.se/2002/05/14/from-systems-to-services/
24. Hultgren, G., Goldkuhl, G.: How to research e-services as social interaction: multi grounding practice research aiming for practical theory. Syst. Signs Actions **7**(2), 104–120 (2013)
25. Goldstein, S.M., Johnston, R., Duffy, J., Rao, J.: The service concept: the missing link in service design research? J. Oper. Manage. **20**(2), 121–134 (2002)
26. Cottam, H., Leadbeater, C.: RED Paper 01: Health: Co-creating Services. Design Council, London (2004)

27. Alam, I.: An exploratory investigation of user involvement in new service development. J. Acad. Mark. Sci. **30**(3), 250–261 (2002)
28. Eisenhardt, K.M.: Building Theories from case-study research. Acad. Manage. Rev. **14**(4), 532–550 (1989)
29. Klein, H.K., Myers, M.D.: A set of principles for conducting and evaluating interpretive field studies in information systems. MIS Q. **23**(1), 67–93 (1999)
30. Norwegian Ministry of Health and Care Services, Stortingsmelding nr. 9: Én innbygger – én journal. Digitale tjenester i helse- og omsorgssektoren (2012)
31. Norwegian Ministry of Health Forskrift om fastlegeordning i kommunene. https://lovdata.no/dokument/SF/forskrift/2012-08-29-842?q=Forskrift%20om%20fastlegeordning%20i%20kommunene
32. Pollock, N., Williams, R.: e-Infrastructures: how do we know and understand them? strategic ethnography and the biography of artefacts. Comput. Support. Coop. Work (CSCW) **19**, 521–556 (2010)
33. Greenhalgh, T., Stones, R., Swinglehurst, D.: Choose and book: a sociological analysis of resistance to an expert system. Soc. Sci. Med. **104**, 210–219 (2014)
34. Pothier, D., Awad, Z., Tierney, P.: Choose and book in ENT: the GP perspective. J. Laryngol. Otol. **120**(03), 222–225 (2006)
35. Ellingsen, G., Obstfelder, A.: Collective expectations—individual action implementing electronic booking systems in norwegian health care. Int. J. Med. Inform. **76**, S104–S112 (2007)
36. Henfridsson, O., Bygstad, B.: The generative mechanisms of digital infrastructure evolution. MIS Q. **37**(3), 907–931 (2013)
37. Yoo, Y., Boland Jr., R.J., Lyytinen, K., Majchrzak, A.: Organizing for innovation in the digitized world. Organ. Sci. **23**(5), 1398–1408 (2012)
38. Riedl, C., Boehmann, T., Leimeister, J.M., Krcmar, H.: A framework for analysing service ecosystem capabilities to innovate. In: Proceedings of 17th European Conference on Information Systems (2009)
39. Nambisan, S.: Information technology and product/service innovation: a brief assessment and some suggestions for future research. J. Assoc. Inf. Syst. **14**(4), 215–226 (2013)

Chances and Limits of End-User Development: A Conceptual Model

Mikkel Arvedsen, Jonas Langergaard, Jens Vollstedt, and Nikolaus Obwegeser[✉]

Department of Marketing and Management, School of Business and Social Sciences,
Aarhus University, Bartholins Allé 10, 8000 Aarhus C, Denmark
{arvedsen,langergard,jens.vollsted}@post.au.dk,
nikolaus@badm.au.dk

Abstract. Information systems development has seen many trends and hypes on the way from unstructured, unplanned scripting-like software development, via early methods like the waterfall model, heavy plan-based methods like the RUP to finally arrive at today's state-of-the-art agile methods like SCRUM. This paper looks at what seems to be a recent trend in (agile) software development: End-User Development (EUD). EUD can be seen both as the logical next step to intensified user integration as proposed in many agile methods as well as a radically new approach to not only interact with but rather empower end-users to (partially) design and create themselves. As in many emerging research areas, EUD lacks clear definitions, concepts and a common understanding of its prospects and limits to both researchers and practitioners. Consequently, this paper aims to address these shortfalls and highlights implications for practice by building a conceptual model of EUD application.

Keywords: Information systems development · End-user development · Software engineering

1 Introduction

End-user development (EUD) is about empowering users to develop and adapt a system [1]. Since the late 1980's it has been argued that end-users of information systems hold great potential and capabilities that can contribute to the development of systems. Pliskin and Shoval [2] argued against the more common assumption that users have no or only little knowledge about data processing. In the following decades, the evolution of development approaches has continued from traditional methods to agile methods. In the course of these developments, the user was gradually getting more integrated into the information system development (ISD) process [3].

The change from traditional methods, like the waterfall model, to more agile methods like the RAD, XP, and SCRUM were led by the need for more adaptability to change and ensuring to meet the customer needs. Agile methods moved away from the assumption that it was possible to gather all system requirements upfront towards an understanding of the goal of the ISD process as a moving target – a continuously evolving agreement between developer and customer [4, 5].

© Springer International Publishing Switzerland 2015
H. Oinas-Kukkonen et al. (Eds.): SCIS 2015, LNBIP 223, pp. 208–219, 2015.
DOI: 10.1007/978-3-319-21783-3_15

Participatory design and customer collaboration efforts are central aspects of agile methods in order to ensure successful ISD projects and mitigate risk [6, 7]. The concept of participatory design is believed to provide various benefits including among others increased user accountability and a high level of work-force commitment [8]. Wagner et al. [8] finds that even while user participation is widely used in agile methods, a broad change on all the stages of the System Development Life Cycle (SDLC) is required to achieve truly successful design. He states that the commitment of users tends to be limited until the system's impact is directly felt. User participation therefore should not only happen in the design and development stage but also after 'go live' where the users are truly and intrinsically engaged with the system.

EUD is proposed as a new mindset and provides tools and techniques designed to realize the full potential of involving end-users in the SDLC [9]. In the manifesto for end-user development, Fischer, Giaccardi et al. [9] argue that EUD has the potential to create a culture where all participants can collaborate in the design process.

In 2005 it was estimated that in U.S. alone there will be at least 55 million end-user developers compared to 2.75 million professional software developers [10, 11]. End-user development is a vision in which design, learning, and development become part of everyday working practice. The goal is to reduce the learning burden while providing powerful facilities to address a wide range of problems [9].

The simple vision is that end-users should be able to adapt much faster to changing requirements and modify, extend and participate in the creation of systems that support work. Furthermore, EUD is expected to give more satisfaction to the end-user and enable higher value creation.

On the other hand, empowering the end-user with the ability to participate in the development of software artefacts raises the issue of quality. Software that is changed or created by end-users is often riddled with errors and therefore the right EUD tools and techniques must be employed to support the end-user in development activities [11].

Up to date it still remains largely unclear what defines end-user development and what the chances and limits of EUD are. This research paper is thus going to address the following points regarding EUD.

- How can EUD be defined and embedded in the ISD domain?
- What are the boundaries that EUD shares with agile software development practices and their core idea of continuous user involvement in all development phases?
- Is EUD development a clear-cut concept or can system developers/project owners decide to include EUD only to a certain extent?
- What are the benefits and drawbacks of EUD and in what situations does it make sense for practitioners to decide for EUD?
- What are the risks and chances involved with EUD?

The remainder of this article is structured as follows. We will conduct a thorough analysis of related literature in the next section and present a consolidated version of our findings in order to clarify the questions stated above. In addition, we establish a conceptual model in Sect. 3 that integrates our findings and can help both researchers and practitioners to discuss and analyze EUD activities. We illustrate implications of our research in Sect. 4 and conclude our paper with directions for future research.

2   State of the Art

In the following we want to analyse the term end-user development according to its usage and interpretation that can be found in the scientific literature. EUD is an emerging concept, therefore we analyse different definitions and related areas in order to establish a working definition which will serve as the basis for the remainder of this paper.

In an article on end-user tailoring of information systems after development and implementation, Mørch defines end-user tailoring as *"related to adaptive maintenance in software engineering"*, meaning that software maintenance should include the possibility to adapt the already implemented system to changes in the external environment [25]. We argue that this is can be seen (to a large extent) as a predecessor to what we nowadays call EUD. Mørch's definition clearly puts EUD in the maintenance aspect of the SDLC, which implies that the original development and implementation are preceding all EUD related activities.

In contrast to that, Lieberman, Paternò et al. [1] define EUD as follows:

> *"End-User Development can be defined as a set of methods, techniques, and tools that allow users of software systems, who are acting as non-professional software developers, at some point to create, modify or extend a software artefact."*

This definition is most inclusive as it also regards all user participation of the earlier SDLC phases, e.g. requirement specification and initial system development, as being part of the EUD paradigm. It covers any activities in creation, modification or extension by any non-programmer at any point in time. Other researchers have recently picked up this definition to its broad and inclusive nature [12–14].

For Lieberman et al. [1] thus EUD begins with user participation in the design phase, but he points out that an important part of EUD is that end-users not only participate in the initial design but also have the ability and the knowledge to modify the system when they are using it. End-users should also have the possibility to initiate end-users driven activities in which the end-users start developing on their own. EUD should not take the focus from the primary tasks but it should be seen as an extension to working applications [1].

Stevens et al. [15] contributed with a definition of EUD to be understood in the aspect of appropriation work:

> *"EUD denotes a set of methods, tools and techniques to support end-users to enforce their interests in the continuous co-evolutionary process by modifying individual artifacts or participating in the modification of shared artifacts."*

The proposed refinement of the EUD definition by Stevens et al. strongly focus on the continuous co-evolutionary process in which the end-user is enforcing an impact on individual or shared artefacts and not that the end-users are developing themselves. Stevens proposes an appropriation infrastructure to support appropriation work and to reduce the gap between users and developers after "go-live" to ensure the possibility of modification of artifacts. This definition is vaguer in the sense that it is about supporting the end-users to enforce their interest and not empowering them to take direct action themselves.

Fischer [16] includes a social aspect in his definition of EUD:

"End-User Development (EUD) provides the enabling conditions for putting owners of problems in charge by defining the technical and social conditions for broad participation in design activities."

The definition focuses particularly on technical and social conditions. It emphasizes that social conditions have to be considered on the same basis as technical to enable broad participation. The definition is not specifying by whom and how the participation can take place. It only mentions design activities and nothing about empowering end-users to creating, modifying, or extending a software artefact.

From a practitioner's perspective, all definitions available in the research community fall short in a number of important questions: What are non-professionals? What are the methods and techniques that are required to involve and motivate end-users? How do end-users practically create, modify, and extend a software artefact individually or in co-evolution with professionals?

In the following, we will look at relevant literature to provide answers to these questions and thereby draw a holistic picture and understanding of the EUD concept.

2.1 End-User (Non-professionals)

In 1987, Pliskin and Shoval were among the first arguing against the core assumption behind the standard SDLC methods that end-users only possess little knowledge about data processing [2]. They presented empirical data to support their argument that end-users in some cases had the capabilities to contribute in the developing of an IS project and proposed a concept called end-user prototyping, in which they outlined a continuous change of user-capabilities from being naive to sophisticate.

Pliskin and Shoval discussed end-user prototyping as a combination of rapid programming and end-user computing, an iterative process of making prototypes to test part of the requirements [2].

They define a sophisticated end-user as follows:

"They have either some formal computer training (for example, as graduates of engineering and business schools) or they have been autodidactic in overcoming computer illiteracy. They have no fear of technology and can utilize it to support their professional work when management provides the appropriate tools."

Considering the technological change that happened since and the generally higher understanding of technology nowadays, their core argument still remains valid: End-users are capable of much more than just specifying the system requirements. In contrast to predominant methodologies at that time, Pliskin and Shoval [2] recognize that end-users are not just a naive capacity. They argue that in underestimating the value of end-users integration, developers are missing out on numerous opportunities for process improvements.

Rivard and Huff [17] also investigate the capabilities of end-users and evaluate six groups defined by Rockart and Flannery in [18]. These six groups are spanning from technical naïve nonprogramming end-users to command-level end-users, end-user programmers, functional support personnel, end-user computer support personnel and finally to expert level personnel like data processing programmers.

Capabilities of today's end-users seem to be generally understood as competent and success of EUD is more a concern of the right tools and techniques, which is given to the end-users.

Moreover, EUD is more about giving the right tools to the end-user or making the learning burden lighter for the end-user, in order to enable the end-users to work autonomously on an artifact [9].

2.2 Engaging the End-User (the Cultural and Social Aspect)

The evolution of EUD has gone from discussing the end-users capabilities to how to motivate the end-user in learning and participating in EUD. While a central part of EUD is to involve end-users in development processes, it is not trivial to engage and motivate end-users in systems development. The challenge is to get the users to participate in a deeply engaged way. From a social and cultural perspective the task of systems developing should therefore become a natural part of everyday work.

Fischer [16] is discussing the cultural and social aspects of EUD. In his definition of EUD, he includes a social aspect that points out the importance of having a broad participation base in design activities. User participation in system design and development should be seen as opportunity rather than an obstacle. This has to be supported as a part of cultural transformation in an organization. Fischer [16] is arguing that a system must have a social and cultural aspect and not just seen as technology. EUD has to go past the technical aspect and thus EUD initiatives should always consider the need for radical organization change on multiple levels. Users have to feel that the system can evolve specific to their visions and thereby give them motivate to participate in the development. Fischer [16] points to the concepts of under-designing and meta-design as a possibility to achieve this engagement.

According to Ye and Fisher [20], meta-design can be understood as:

"A fundamental objective of meta-design is to create socio-technical environments that empower users to engage actively in the continuous development of systems rather than being restricted to the use of existing systems."

System designers should therefore aim to under-design the solution so that users are encouraged to use the social and technical instruments to create the solutions themselves at use time. Meta-design extends the traditional notion of system development to include users in an ongoing process as co-designers, not only at design time but throughout the entire existence of the system. To support meta-design [20] proposes a process of seeding, evolutionary growth and reseeding (SER) as a model and structural fundament of meta-design and EUD.

The seeding phase creates the first part of the system in cooperation between the professional developers and end-users. The ecosystem created in the seeding phase makes it possible for end-users to design new software by themselves. In the second phase, evolutionary growth, end-users are in the process of modifying, extending, and creating new software for the system. Eventually, the amount of new software should reach a state where end-users once more address professional developers to enter the reseeding phase. The professional developers then incorporate the newly added functionalities into the original system [9].

According to [16], end-users have to be involved early in the process or else they often feel that they just have to fix problems that the developers did not bother to fix. In addition, a feeling of control in how the system is going to be developed is mentioned as a motivating factor.

Other studies concluded that an important motivation factor is the perceived utility and the actual utility payoff that a EUD tool can provide [21]. Mehandjiev et al. [22] notices that EUD activities are often considered to be adding value to a company by implementing more agile work practice, which is a motivational factor for end-users. Monetary rewards and penalties on the other hand have been found to sometimes undermine people's self-motivation [23].

2.3   End-User Programming

End-user programming (EUP) describes the process of software being driven, modeled, and developed by the end-user and not professional programmers [24]. EUP is generally describing users that want to achieve a result for personal use and therefore are motivated to do the development themselves. In contrast to EUD, EUP focuses specifically on the programming part. Thus EUP is used to describe the tools and techniques that make EUD possible.

EUP assumes that end-users acting as developers have a personal intention to develop a system – either for personal use or for a specific organization or department the user is affiliated with.

This implies that the program does not have to be tested, debugged, or quality tested as long as it complies with the requirements of the specific domains. The concept of EUP is not directly concerned with end-users capabilities but about the intentions of the end-user. While a novice programmer may ends up with more bugs in self-made program than a skilled programmer, it is still considered EUP if it is designed for a limited user group [12].

2.4   End-User Software Engineering

End-user software engineering (EUSE) is adding the issue of software quality related to EUP and how to address it. The quality issue mainly relate to the "creating" part of EUD. EUSE comprises the systematic and disciplined activities with attention to software quality issues. Though end-users do not have the same qualification as professional programmers and therefore are likely not to create software with the same level of quality, EUSE proposes tools and techniques that attempt to make it as reliable as possible [12].

Ko et al. [12] define EUSE as a distinct topic within EUD with the focus on software quality. Burnett [11] relates EUSE to EUD in the same way, explaining that when the end-users create, modify and extend, it has to have a certain quality to be useful and that the added functions should generate valid results.

EUSE propose risk-mitigating approaches to secure the quality in an EUD environment. First, a culture of trust and responsibility helps to reduce the amount of software errors. In such a culture, end-users intrinsically care about doing a good job when participating in software development efforts. Second, assessment audits can be implemented to consistently check user-developed functions. Third, it is recommended to establish guidelines/policies for privacy, confidentiality and data protection as well as for best practice in EUD management and related activities [22].

3   A Conceptual Model of EUD

In this section we want to build on existing literature and develop an integrated model of EUD. Our model (see Fig. 1) follows an inclusive approach and builds on findings and proposed conceptualizations of other researchers before us. The purpose of the model is both to provide a holistic, graphical overview of the different aspects and their dimensions that are describing EUD, and to serve as a discussion basis for researchers and practitioners when considering EUD.

We are basing our model on the classification initially proposed by Mørch [25], which distinguishes the three levels of customization, integration and extension. While Mørch [25] originally proposed these categories in the field of tailoring, one can argue that tailoring, among other streams, has now become absorbed in EUD and

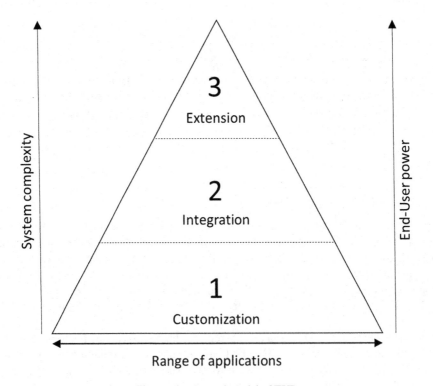

Fig. 1. Conceptual model of EUD

the proposed categorization is therefore still applicable. Mørch defines tailoring as the *"adaptation of generic software applications ... to the specific work practices of user organization."* [25].

The idea of categorizing customizability into different levels has been picked up by Liebermann et al. [1], who differentiate in their definition of EUD between the tasks of creating, modifying and extending. In contrast to Mørch, Liebermann does also include the participation of the user during the original system development phase as part of EUD, while Mørch clearly states that tailoring is an *"activity that takes place after the original design and implementation"* [25].

Spahn et al. [26] also used the categories proposed by Mørch [25] but added insights into the different roles of developers, differentiating between programmers, local developers and non-programmers.

Stevens et al. [15] analyze the development and use of an appropriation infrastructure in order to exploit the technological flexibility of software applications. They define three levels of technical flexibility: choosing between anticipated alternatives, construction of new behavior from existing patterns, and altering the software by programming.

In our model we will keep the original 3-level conceptualization given by Mørch, which covers the concepts put forward by Spahn [26] and Stevens [15] while still delineating EUD clearly from the original development process. A short description of the levels is given in the following.

For Level 1 artefacts, it is only possible to modify a number of predefined attributes. This kind of artefact has the lowest possible customization options (within EUD). It can often be a direct modification of the appearance of a presentation object [25]. At level 1 the end-user can only modify limited predefined parameters and choose between some selections in an artefact that has to be specified in the designing phase. Consequently, the system has only a limited amount of flexibility and is suitable for simpler requirements that do not change considerably over time.

Level 2 has more possibilities for customization and is suitable for more complex projects and systems. The end-user can add new functionality to a system by linking pieces of functionality together. The functionality can either be duplicated from another application or integrated in the original application or two functionalities are combined but still kept in different applications [25]. The core element of level 2 is the possibility to add new functionality or integrate existing. This stage fits well with what Liebermann et al. [1] call "modify", where the end-user should be able to put together components.

Level 3 refers to the development of functions that are (at least partially) not based on already existing modules or functions. It describes the addition of new artifacts to a software ecosystem. At this level, radical changes are made and these changes cannot be anticipated by the developer at the time of design [25]. At this level, the application must be flexible enough to handle that the end-user creates new artefacts. Liebermann et al. [1] is defining this third level as programming of new components, whereas Mørch is specifying that it has to be a radical change to be considered "extension."

Alongside the continuum from level 1 to level 3 of EUD we can see the dimension of customization power as a part of the model. Customization power is translated into to what extent the end-user can customize a system or an artefact [27]. This dimension supports the understanding of the 3-level categorization, showing that the higher the level of EUD, the more customization power is effectively given to the user.

The range of systems and artefacts that are possible candidates for EUD is shown in our model as the horizontal width of the triangle. At the low level of customization, the range is broad and the number of applications that can have the degree of customization is integrated. Most software artefacts nowadays offer the possibility to modify predefined parts, e.g. visual styles (level 1). Considerably fewer provide the option to modify the artifact by creating new combinations of existing modules or pieces (level 2). Only in very few cases is it possible (and reasonable) to extend artifacts with not-yet-inbuilt functions (level 3).

The increasing complexity of the system is depicted on the left side of the model. Complexity increases with higher customization power and flexibility. Spahn et al. [26] provide an overview of the relationship between complexity and EUD. They argue that different design principles correlate with increased complexity of the task, ranging from simple tasks like interface customization to real programming of application parts. Sutcliffe et al. [21] find in an empirical evaluation of a software tool for EUD that reducing the complexity (and flexibility) leads to a reduction of errors in the usage of the tool. In the setting of EUD, the professional developer has to make the system open to make it possible for the end-user to create new artefacts. However, it is a complex tradeoff to design an open system that allows for change while at the same time satisfying the needs for user-friendly interaction design in a way that end-user can participate in development of new functionality. Complexity theory is closely related to EUD and can be used to understand how to cope with continuous changing requirements in the internal organization and the external environment [29]. The different levels of our model are closely related to the principle of requisite complexity. Requisite complexity means if there is a lot of external complexity (a lot of changes and uncertainty), the internal system has to be complex as well to cope with complexity.

It has to be noted that a system can consist of many different artefacts. It is therefore difficult to categorize an artefact to a specific level of the model. The stippled lines between the levels indicate that a system can reside in different customization levels and the boundaries are somewhat fuzzy.

4   Implications

This section evaluates the proposed model (Fig. 1) by categorizing different types of software exemplarily according to our model and discussing its implications.

Nowadays, most available software products have a certain amount of customization abilities already integrated when shipped. This is true for both off-the-shelf software and unique developments. In many cases users want to make some kind of customization in order to make their work more efficient. An example is the equation functionality in MS Word, which can be changed to become a shortcut on the front interface instead of being found in a third-level menu. There is an endless range of software where it is possible to make this kind of predefined customization.

This form of EUD is still very safe to use and the change of making mistakes is very small because the complexity is limited. However, the possibilities of changing the software with the user's requirements are restricted and bigger modifications cannot be done by end-users anymore but need involvement of professionals or the software vendor.

Looking at bigger modifications, we find that there is only a limited number of applications where it is possible to add, link and combine functionalities. An example can be the popular business intelligence tool Tableau (tableau.com), where the user is given the ability to create dashboards and visualize different kinds of data. The user can link and combine the different tools in the software. In this way, the user has unlimited possibilities to visualize the data. However, in Tableau it is not possible to create new functions if e.g. there are new requirements from the organization. Because of that, it is categorized as allowing for integrating existing functionality (level 2) but not extending to new functionality (level 3).

A prominent web-based example for level 2 is "IF THIS THEN THAT" (IFTTT.com). In this application, users are allowed to make new functionalities called recipes. Using this application, one can define events that trigger certain actions. Both triggers and actions are limited to pre-defined options. An example is if a user gets tagged on a picture on Instagram (trigger), which automatically triggers a procedure that causes this picture to be saved in the users Dropbox (action). The complexity of this software is limited due to the deterministic number of combinations.

On level 3, the end-user has the possibility to create completely new functionalities in the system. As described earlier, to get the most out of this level it is often helpful if the end-user has some kind of programming knowledge, though it is not a requirement. For making the third level of EUD more accessible, new programming language are being developed in order to ease the cognitive learning effort. An example of this such a language is Snap, a drag and drop programming language [28]. This software is a modified version of the software Scratch from lifelong Kindergarten Group from Massachusetts Institute of Technology (MIT). The software runs in the web-browser and every programming function is created as a building block. The end-user has to put the blocks together to create new functionalities. Snap allows more than just the integration or combination of existing functionality, but is still simpler than a traditional programming language.

A different perspective to consider is that software can include all three levels. MS Excel is an example of this kind of software. Customization in MS Excel has the same functionalities as MS Word, which is the ability to make shortcuts to make the interaction with the software more efficient.

The second level is the ability to create linkage between functionalities in the software. The add-in "crystal ball" augments MS Excel with the function to make simulations and statistical calculations. As in the other examples of level 2 the complexity is increasing when adding this kind of functionalities.

MS Excel includes a scripting language called Visual Basic for Applications (VBA). This is an actual textual programming language, which is available for the end-user. VBA gives the user the ability to create new functions in MS Excel and connect it together with other software. Undoubtedly, VBA is the software artifact, which makes it possible to make radical changes and extend the existing functionality.

5   Conclusion and Future Research

In this article we have presented an overview of the domain of end-user development. A detailed review of literature and related terms led us to a better understanding of the concept, its dimensions and aspects that have to be considered when facing EUD. Our insights have led to the creation of a conceptual model of EUD that allows researchers and practitioners to discuss and analyze EUD initiatives.

Our research finds that EUD constitutes an emerging topic within ISD and many questions remain to be investigated by researchers. There is no literature to be found on the change management process an organization faces when switching to the EUD paradigm. Detailed insights into actors, processes and tools are needed to help understand the challenges and effort that comes with such an initiative. Moreover, much research has gone into understanding the change from traditional to agile software development practices – a shift that shows similarities in many ways and can therefore be helpful to understand this new phenomenon.

The motivation and engagement of users related to EUD has been addressed only peripherally in the scientific literature. As with agile methods, we anticipate that the real challenge of EUD does not lie in technological but organizational change and therefore strongly propose more research into user's involvement and motivation. This includes making a case for the user to help in the creation of a shared understanding of all actors' roles and responsibilities – a task that is clearly managerial and not technical.

Finally, the economic potential of non-professional development can be considered rapidly growing. A recent Gartner report [19] projected that 25 % of all new business application will be developed by non-professionals. We therefore argue that software engineering companies should prepare for this paradigm shift in order to remain competitive in the market of tomorrow.

References

1. Lieberman, H., Paternò, F., Klann, M., Wulf, V.: End-user development: an emerging paradigm. In: Lieberman, H., Paternò, F., Wulf, V. (eds.) End-User Development, pp. 1–8. Springer, Netherlands (2006)
2. Pliskin, N., Shoval, P.: End-user prototyping: sophisticated users supporting system development. ACM SIGMIS Database **18**(4), 7 (1987)
3. Fitzgerald, B., Russo, N.L., Stolterman, E.: Information Systems Development: Methods in Action. McGraw-Hill Education, Maidenhead (2002)
4. Davis, A.M., Bersoff, E.H., Comer, E.R.: A strategy for comparing alternative software development life cycle models. IEEE Trans. Softw. Eng. **14**(10), 1453 (1988)
5. Brooks, F.: No silver bullet essence and accidents of software engineering. Computer **20**(4), 10 (1987)
6. Fowler, M., Highsmith, J.: The agile manifesto (2001). http://www.drdobbs.com/open-source/the-agile-manifesto/184414755. Accessed 15 Nov 2014
7. Amrit, C., van Hillegersberg, J.: Involving end-users to mitigate risk in IS development projects. J. Organ. End-User Comput. **25**(3), 67–82 (2013)
8. Wagner, E., Piccoli, G.: Moving beyond user participation to achieve successful IS design. Commun. ACM **50**(12), 51 (2007)

9. Fischer, G., Giaccardi, E., Ye, Y., Sutcliffe, A.G., Mehandjiev, N.: Meta-design: a manifesto for end-user development. Commun. ACM **47**(9), 33–37 (2004)
10. Sutcliffe, A., Mehandjiev, N.: End-user development. Commun. ACM **47**(9), 31–32 (2004)
11. Burnett, M.: End-user software engineering and why it matters. J. Organ. End-User Comput. **22**(1), 1–22 (2010)
12. Ko, A.J., Abraham, R., Beckwith, L., Blackwell, A., Burnett, M., Erwig, M., et al.: The state of the art in end-user software engineering. ACM Comput. Surv. **43**(3), 1–44 (2011)
13. Paternò, F.: End-user development: survey of an emerging field for empowering people. ISRN Softw. Eng. **2013**, Article ID 532659, 11 pp. (2013). doi:10.1155/2013/532659
14. Costabile, M., Fogie, D., Mussio, P., Piccinno, A.: End-user development: the software shaping workshop approach. In: Lieberman, H., Paternò, F., Wulf, V. (eds.) End-User Development. Human-Computer Interaction Series, 9th edn, p. 183. Springer, Dordrecht (2006)
15. Stevens, G., Pipek, V., Wulf, V.: Appropriation infrastructure: mediating appropriation and production work. J. Organ. End-User Comput. **22**(2), 58–81 (2010)
16. Fischer, G.: End-user development: from creating technologies to transforming cultures. In: Dittrich, Y., Burnett, M., Mørch, A., Redmiles, D. (eds.) IS-EUD 2013. LNCS, vol. 7897, pp. 217–222. Springer, Heidelberg (2013)
17. Rivard, S., Huff, S.: Factors of success for end-user computing. Commun. ACM **31**(5), 552 (1988)
18. Rockart, J., Flannery, L.: The management of end-user computing. Commun. ACM **26**(10), 776 (1983)
19. Pettey, C.: Gartner Says Citizen Developers Will Build at Least 25 Percent of New Business Applications by 2014 (2011). http://www.gartner.com/newsroom/id/1744514. Accessed 14 Feb 2015
20. Ye, Y., Fischer, G.: Designing for participation in socio-technical software systems. In: Stephanidis, C. (ed.) HCI 2007. LNCS, vol. 4554, pp. 312–321. Springer, Heidelberg (2007)
21. Sutcliffe, A., Lee, D., Mehandjiev, N.: Contributions, costs and prospects for end-user development. In: Human Computer Interaction - International Proceedings (2003)
22. Mehandjiev, N., Sutcliffe, A., Lee, D.: Organizational view of end-user development. In: Lieberman, H., Paternò, F., Wulf, V. (eds.) End-User Development. Human-Computer Interaction Series, 9th edn, p. 492. Springer, Dordrecht (2006)
23. Deci, E.L., Koestner, R., Ryan, R.M.: A meta-analytic review of experiments examining the effects of extrinsic rewards on intrinsic motivation. Psychol. Bull. **125**(6), 627 (1999)
24. Yue, K.: Experience on mashup development with end-user programming environment. J. Inf. Syst. Educ. **21**(1), 111 (2010)
25. Mørch, A. Three levels of end-user tailoring: customisation, integration, and extension. In: Proceedings of Computers in Context, Aarhus, Denmark, pp. 157–166 (1995)
26. Spahn, M., Dörner, C., Wulf, V.: End-user development: approaches towards a flexible software design. In ECIS 2008 (2008)
27. Maceli, M., Atwood, M.E.: "Human crafters" once again: supporting users as designers in continuous co-design. In: Dittrich, Y., Burnett, M., Mørch, A., Redmiles, D. (eds.) IS-EUD 2013. LNCS, vol. 7897, pp. 9–24. Springer, Heidelberg (2013)
28. University of California. Snap! (build your own blocks) (2014). http://snap.berkeley.edu/. Accessed 12 Dec 2014
29. Benbya, H., McKelvey, B.: Toward a complexity theory of information systems development. Inf. Technol. People **19**(1), 12 (2006)
30. Fischer, G.: Meta-design: design for designers. In: Proceedings of the 3rd Conference on Designing Interactive Systems: Processes, Practices, Methods, and Techniques, pp. 396–405. ACM, New York (2000)

Impact of Constraints and Rules of User-Involvement Methods for IS Concept Creation and Specification

Mika Yasuoka[1(✉)], Takehiko Ohno[2], and Momoko Nakatani[3]

[1] Technical University of Denmark, Produktionstorvet, Building 426 DK-2800 Kgs.,
Lyngby, Denmark
miyaje@dtu.dk
[2] NTT Service Evolution Laboratories, 101 Hikarinooka, Yokosuka-shi,
Kanagawa 239-0847, Japan
ohno.takehiko@lab.ntt.co.jp
[3] NTT IT, 2-9-1, Furouchou, Nakaku, Yokohama-shi, Kanagawa 231-0032, Japan
nakatani.momoko@ntt-it.co.jp

Abstract. Devising new service ideas for information systems by deploying user-involvement approaches is a challenging task. The power of collective creation by involving users in designing systems has attracted attention; however, stakeholders with no design training face critical challenges in generating ideas. In this paper, by exemplifying our user-involvement method with game elements, ICT Service Design Game, in comparison with conventional brainstorming, we show the impact of constraints and rules in user-involvement methods when creating service concepts and specifications for information systems. The analysis is based on a comparative experiment on two design methods and shows that the constraints and rules of our game approach fostered innovative idea generation in spite of participants' limited knowledge of and experience with design processes. Although our analysis is still in a preliminary stage, it indicates some positive impact of constraints and rules in design methods, especially when the methods are used by non-design professionals.

Keywords: User involvement · Creativity · Participatory design · System specification

1 Introduction

The importance of involving stakeholders when designing initial concepts or preliminary specifications of an information system (IS) is increasingly recognized since ISs nowadays are embedded in everyday human practices. Since it is very difficult for a single person to solve the complex problems of concept creation and system requirements on their own [1–3], it is more critical than ever to design socially embedded ISs using users' varied perspectives, needs, and requirements and to promote collective creativity [4, 5].

One of the promising and practical approaches that satisfy users and IS development teams and meet these stakeholders' expectations is to involve stakeholders widely in the

© Springer International Publishing Switzerland 2015
H. Oinas-Kukkonen et al. (Eds.): SCIS 2015, LNBIP 223, pp. 220–236, 2015.
DOI: 10.1007/978-3-319-21783-3_16

IS concept creation and requirements specification processes [6–9]. Stakeholders are such as marketers, decision makers, managers, designers, programmers, and end-users. By involving them, the development team could avoid misunderstandings and disapproval among managers in the later development stages [10].

For the creation of concepts and preliminary specifications for the IS and its service as a participatory design approach, quite a few approaches have been suggested based on the traditional approaches such as brainstorming and KJ methods [11]. Among them, idea generation approaches for groups such as group brainstorming [12], gamestorming [13], and design games [14, 17] show particularly strong potential to involve users and non-design professional developers in the design process. However, the comparative characteristics of each method are not necessarily clarified. For example, design games facilitate and promote equal involvement of stakeholders in the idea-generation activities, and can be a strong tool for involving and empowering stakeholders [14, 16, 17], but still little is known about their impact on idea generation in comparison with group brainstorming, which is probably the most widely used approach. Consequently, it becomes difficult to select the single best approach. Particularly when taking stakeholder involvement in ISs into consideration, what kinds of approaches and methods could be beneficial and critical for engineers and end-users with no design education and experience? What kinds of approaches could be deployed in order to contribute to creating usable, efficient, and ethically persuasive [18] user-centred systems, design concepts, and preliminary specifications? There is an urgent need to clarify the advantages and disadvantages of these methods in terms of collective idea generation for IS concepts.

In this paper, we introduce a comparative experiment in which we compare two idea-generation methods used for stakeholder-involvement approaches: group brainstorming [19] and an IS concept specification approach called Service Design Game [8, 9]. The game is designed by the authors as a participatory design method aimed at promoting stakeholder involvement and collective creation. Unlike brainstorming, ICT Service Design Game provides rigid constraints and rules in its game structure. As a first step, by comparing these two methods, we intend to test one aspect of idea generation approaches in particular: the impact of constraints and rules in user-involvement methods targeted at IS concept creation and preliminary specification.

The rest of the paper is organized as follows. First, we introduce the ICT Design Game with its unique characteristics for facilitating collective creation and participation among stakeholders. Next, our experiment case is introduced together with the experiment design. Subsequently, the results of the experiment are reported. Lastly, the paper discusses two stakeholder-involvement methods from idea-generation and participation perspectives and their impact on the constraints and rules. The paper concludes with a discussion of the limitations of our work and its possible future directions.

2   The ICT Service Design Game

In order to facilitate participation and collective creation in the process of IS concept creation and preliminary specification, we have created a design game called the *ICT Service Design Game* in collaboration with a large telecommunications company. We have already applied the game in a real development practice involving non-design professional developers and end-users and confirmed its validity with respect to stakeholder involvement and idea creation [8, 9].

2.1   The ICT Service Design Game Brief

The ICT Service Design Game has been designed as a design game variant based on the series of design games suggested by Brandt et al. [14]. These design games aim at empowering users, using a form of board games and tools. In order to ground the games in real-world problems, materials such as cards and pieces are collected from a field study through ethnographical observation. With such original tools rooted in practice and its challenges, game players can easily ground their play in the real world and deepen their understanding of the field as the game proceeds and the design takes shape. For example, in the 'layout kits', suggested by Ehn [16], players allocate machinery on the factory's floor plan to reconsider a machine layout in the factory, using cards as a tool in the game. The game lets shop floor workers participate in redesign, which contributes to their ownership of and satisfaction with their workplace. In other game variants, participants create a persona [14], design shapes and functions [17], and play use-scenarios [20, 21]. For these design games, it is of critical importance to reach a state where all stakeholders are satisfied and can contribute without being influenced by a single authority or affected by a person who speaks loudly, allowing them to be empowered and achieve equal participation.

Our game aims at supporting the design process for creating ICT services collectively, especially for participants with limited knowledge and experience of idea creation. In contrast to previous studies on design games, which aim at facilitating a user-centred design process for cross-disciplinary design groups and emphasize user involvement, the game focuses more on collective creation without losing its value of stakeholder participation. As such, the discussion process of the game will bring a few values. The first is collective creativity. It is important to combine multiple ideas from different angles (organizational positions/cross-disciplines) to create new ideas. It should support the elicitation of implicit requirements from stakeholders and support collective creativity as a practical tool without distractions. The second is equal participation and understanding beyond socio-cultural differences. The game promotes equal participation. It is important for participants to be detached from the organizational hierarchy in order to express their own points of view. Lastly, the game brings multi-stakeholder participation including end-users. It is important to facilitate collective design processes for non-design professionals.

In promoting stakeholder involvement, it is essential to overcome several challenges such as open discussion, equality, and commitment to participation to make the most of involving stakeholders [8]. The game is designed to provide a framework for involving stakeholders with original design-game conditions and game elements and at the same time to emphasize outputs for IS design and specification through collective creation. The previous works have shown that game approaches have high potential to encourage collaboration among cross-disciplinary teams and stakeholder involvement through tools, rules, and constraints. At the same time, the game approaches provide a setting for open discussions without hierarchical influence and an immersive experience for interdisciplinary stakeholders.

2.2 The ICT Service Design Game Process

The ICT Service Design Game consists of three successive games that should be played as a set. Considering the practical constraints on stakeholders attending the games, our game duration is limited to about one to two hours. A game is played by a team of three to five participants with different backgrounds. The duration of each game largely depends on the game workshop structure. Typically it takes 1.5 days in total, where half a day is allocated to each game. A game framework is constructed on a fictitious world-view with a goal and rules forming restrictions similar to conventional game structures [12, 13]. There are three main rules: (1) keep your turn (never skip your turn), (2) respect time limits, and (3) play based on the data provided. During the game, facilitators ensure that the stakeholders follow the rules. Due to the space limitation, the introduction to the game below will be minimal. Note that more detailed processes and practical cases can be inspected in other references (cf. [8, 9]).

Game materials are prepared based on real-world data from two main sources: ethnographic-inspired responses of end-users and technology seeds. The data are typically collected from an ethnographical study of a couple of potential users. The focus of the observations is usually ICT aspects such as usage and attitudes toward specific activities or systems. Ethnographical data are usually collected in house interiors since the game is targeted, so far, at the creation of ICT home services. Based on the collected materials, tools for the three games such as technology cards are prepared. Technology cards are business-card-sized picture cards (e.g. see Fig. 1) showing technology seeds from research labs. Although the game provides a fictitious world space, the game tools, such as cards, pieces, and videos, are deeply rooted in the real challenges and needs of end-users and actual technology seeds from a research institution. Next we describe the three games briefly.

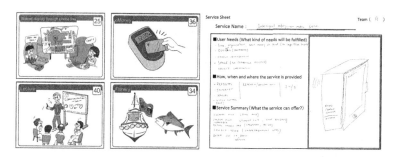

Fig. 1. Examples of game materials and service sheet from the service game

The User Game. The first game is a user game. The objective of the user game is to create a fictitious user image – a persona – by constructing a person's story based on real target-user data collected from the field. The game tools are the video clips and moment cards, which show moments of the equivalent video clips taken from the field.

The game starts with the cards being placed on the table. The first player then picks five cards and watches the associated 30 s video clips together with the group members. After watching the five videos, the first player makes up a story based on the cards he or she has selected. Then, he or she places all five cards on the table in order and writes a title on a sticky note reflecting the needs disclosed by the story. The next player takes four other cards and overlaps his or her story with the previous one, meaning that the second player must use at least one card already placed on the table in the previous turn. The game is over when all of the cards have been used or all of the team members agree that no new stories can be created. Finally, the team fills out a persona sheet based on the stories made up. The persona sheet (Fig. 2) holds a few details such as name, age, characteristics, family structure, job/income, living area, hobby, and attitudes toward things related to ICT services. Then, the team members describe the persona needs in turn and classify these needs into groups. Lastly, they prioritize the persona needs and list them in order.

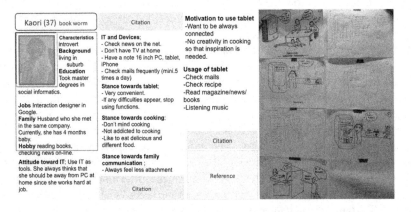

Fig. 2. Output examples (persona sheet and user scenario)

The Service Game. The objective of the service game is to design ICT services using future technology for the persona created in the user game. In this game, technology cards and the needs list are used as game tools (Fig. 1). Technology cards are a collection of core technologies, devices, existing services, and market domains. The game starts with the technology cards being placed face-down on the table.

The first player picks one need with highest priority and three technology cards. Then he or she chooses one technology among the three given out and makes up a story about how the persona will use the technology at home to solve the first prioritized need. The first player records his or her story on a service sheet by adding a few details about the idea such as the service name, idea abstract, user needs, place, and time at which the service is provided. This is one idea. The rest of the team members will improve the idea. The second player picks a technology card and adds it to the two cards on the table. He or she picks one out of three and makes up a refined idea. When all members have contributed to the first idea, the second player starts the process again. The game is over when all the needs have been solved or the time is up.

Through this process, ideas are generated, refined, and improved. Finally, the team chooses the best of the ideas generated based on defined criteria such as feasibility, business potential, and so forth.

Scenario Game. The objective of the scenario game is to create use-scenarios, where the persona uses the ICT service in a future home. Describing possible futures and enacting scenarios are known to represent a multi-faceted design tool [14]. By acting, stakeholders can simulate the targeted users' experiences and feelings, which can contribute to understanding challenges and designing services and products [15, 22]. The experiences from previous games provide empathy for the users. The use-situations are developed and the design concept is also elaborated while the players take on roles, create scenarios, and act them out in a physical space such as a kitchen.

In this game, players create a design plot. The game uses white sheets of paper, pens, and the persona and service sheets created in the previous games (Figs. 1 and 2). The first player draws one initial scene in two minutes, referring to the sheets. Then, another player draws a successive story in another two minutes. In this way, the team creates at least two stories, each with three to five scenes. By drawing scenes in turn, all participants contribute. In the end, the team picks a team story. The story created is used as a plot for role-play. Team members act out the scenario and polish the team story until all members are satisfied or the time runs out.

2.3   Game Elements in Idea Generation Methods

As shown, compared to brainstorming, the ICT Design Game provides rigid constraints and rules which participants must follow. Rules and principles also exist in brainstorming, but it is sometimes difficult to enforce them, especially when participants are non-design professionals. By attaching posters with brainstorming principles to the wall, participants might be reminded about how to carry out the brainstorming session, and by being supported by experienced facilitators, participants might manage to demonstrate their skills at best. However, especially when less experienced users such as non-design professionals and end-users work on idea creation, those principles can easily be neglected.

Games can be practical tools for business and social practices. The benefits of introducing game elements to real-world problems can be realized through well-designed game frames with game spaces and tools, rules, and game structures. These constraints and rules can potentially benefit the initiation of creativity [4, 5, 9]. For example, even in a community with a strong hierarchy and social norms, 'the players can engage in behavior that might be risky, uncomfortable, or even rude in their normal lives [13]. The rules of the game, with which players must agree to comply, also help to break hierarchies and social norms. By introducing rules, the game can provide equal participation possibilities and avoid free-riding [23], which otherwise would not apply in ordinary organizational settings. Additionally, although the game provides a fictitious world, game tools based on real-world data keep participants anchored to reality in the fictitious world [14]. The information held by the game tools and rules is a strong foundation and reference in the process of creation. That being so, game elements make a difference to the game that conventional brainstorming cannot convey.

3   Methods

We conducted a two-day service creation workshop in which engineers in a large-scale IT firm participated as a part of corporate training for new employees. The IT firm has 50,000 employees and its core service is to provide and integrate IT services for public and private (B2B) corporate customers. The participating engineers have properties with uniform parameters such as being new university graduates, aged 23–24, with engineering backgrounds and no or limited design knowledge and experience. After the training, they were going to be responsible for developing and integrating IT systems. The ultimate purpose of the workshop was to let them understand and experience the processes of service idea creation with user-centred perspectives and approaches.

3.1   Workshop Design

The workshops were run for two successive days (see Table 1). In the workshops, three games of the game and corresponding brainstorming sessions were conducted. The workshops were conducted eight times on different dates. In the workshops, the participants were first divided into groups of three to five persons each. In the end, a total of 141 engineers in 32 groups participated in the game and brainstorming sessions.

Table 1. Activity procedure in the workshop.

Day	B-S group	S-B group
Day 1: First session	User game	User game
Second session	**Brainstorming**	**Service game**
Day 2: Third session	**Service game**	**Brainstorming**
Fourth session	Scenario game	Scenario game

3.2   Procedure

As shown in Table 1, two kinds of workshops were conducted for comparative studies on brainstorming and service games. Each team had four sessions with the same three design games and brainstorming sessions in different orders. In four workshops out of eight, brainstorming was conducted in the second session of day 1 and then the service game was conducted in the third session of day 2 (B-S groups). In the remaining four workshops, the service game was conducted in the second session of day 1 and the brainstorming was carried out in the third session of day 2 (S-B groups). In both cases, the duration of the service game and brainstorming was 70 min each.

3.3   Facilitation and Other Conditions

We, the authors, facilitated the first two workshops and a few participants from the first workshops facilitated the succeeding six workshops. Facilitation was mainly to ensure that the game rules and time limits were adhered to, and no special facilitation skills or experiences were required.

Since the four sessions were conducted as a part of a corporate training workshop, in addition to the game, the participants had a series of lectures about different kinds of qualitative analysis methods such as interviews and field observation.

4 Results

The ideas generated and questionnaires administered after two sessions were used to analyze our experiments. We analysed a number of ideas and evaluated the ideas generated and the participation of team members. Since our experiments aimed at finding differences between two approaches – brainstorming and the Service Game – we focused on applying analytical methods which distinguish qualitative and quantitative differences in a few variables of the two approaches.

4.1 The Quantity of Ideas Generated

The average number of ideas generated by each team in each session was 16.84 in the brainstorming session and 21.22 in the service game, as shown in Table 2 and the histogram in Fig. 1. The number of ideas generated ranged from 6 to 58 in the brainstorming session and 8 to 36 in the service game. Since the idea-generation sessions lasted 70 min each, we could say that one idea was created every 3.6 min. Generally speaking, the team that generated 58 ideas by brainstorming could be regarded as highly productive.

Table 2. Average numbers of ideas generated.

	Brainstorming	Service game
B-S group	17.06	20.81
S-B group	16.63	21.63
Total	16.84	21.22

Welch's t-test was used to compare the number of ideas generated between brainstorming and the service game, and showed a significant trend. The B-S group shows a trend of significant difference ($t(30) = -1.53$, $p < 0.1$), and the S-B group showed the same results ($t(30) = -1.53$, $p < 0.1$). Moreover, the difference between the two sessions in the total group shows a statistically significant result ($t(62) = -2.07$, $p < 0.05$).

In this analysis, it is shown that the participants generated more ideas in the service game than in brainstorming, with statistical significance (Figs. 3 and 4).

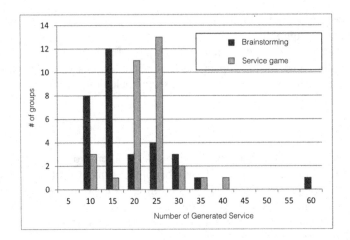

Fig. 3. Number of service ideas generated

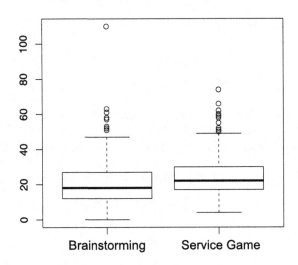

Fig. 4. Word counts of idea summaries

4.2 The Quality of the Generated Ideas

In the brainstorming and service game sessions, participants recorded a summary of their generated ideas in a few lines on a sheet of paper and accumulated a list of descriptions of ideas.

The five ideas shown in Tables 3 and 4 are the first five service ideas generated in the brainstorming and service games respectively by the same group.

Table 3. Examples of ideas generated in brainstorming.

#	Brainstorming
1	A service to support having dinner together but in distance with the help of ICT
2	Software to schedule sharing of household chores
3	Advisor support service
4	Household chores productivity tool
5	Closet organizer (stability evaluation)

Table 4. Ideas generated in service game.

#	Service game
1	Game with eye tracker
2	Voice controller for organizing and displaying album pictures and movies
3	Shared cloud system with WiFi digital camera
4	System to depict characteristic scenes from video clips and share them as a simulated experience among families
5	System to generate a 3D view based on the depicted characteristic scenes and to retrieve the emotion at that time, by combining an eye tracker and technology #1

Even though the sessions had the same duration and the same team members, the descriptions in the two tables above show that the service game generated more concrete ideas combined with names of different specific advanced technologies developed by the company. For example, in the fifth idea in Table 5, one suggested service uses the technology #1[1] combined with an eye tracker. While we can see more descriptive suggestions for the ideas in the service game, ideas generated by brainstorming are more abstract and it is sometimes difficult to imagine the service described.

To investigate the granularity of the idea description generated by brainstorming and the service game, we compared the word counts of abstracts of the service concepts as a preliminary evaluation of the quality of the generated ideas. The results show that brainstorming generated 20.21 words on average and a median of 18 words while the service game generated 24.31 words on average and a median of 22 words as shown in the box-and-whisker plot in Fig. 2. Furthermore, according to the Welch t-test, the difference between brainstorming and the service game is statistically significant ($t(1214) = 70.28$, $p < 00.1$).

---

[1] Since this is confidential, the description of the technology is anonymous.

Table 5. Self-evaluation for brainstorming and the service game.

	Brainstorming	Service game	t-test (df = 276)
1. Difficulty of idea generation (1: difficult – 5: easy)	2.65	2.91	2.29 (p < 0.05)
2. Self-participation level (1: low – 5: high)	3.70	3.93	2.99 (p < 0.05)
3. Self-contribution level (1: low – 5: high)	3.52	3.70	2.22 (p < 0.05)
4. Satisfaction with ideas (1: low – 5: high)	3.93	4.06	1.57 (p < 0.10)
5. Satisfaction with participation (1: low – 5: high)	3.96	4.14	2.13 (p < 0.05)

It should be noted that a statistical difference between the word counts generated by brainstorming and the service game does not guarantee qualitative differences in the ideas generated with the two methods. It is clear that our data and the quality of the ideas generated need to be investigated further. However, as shown above, our preliminary analysis indicates that the granularity of the summary of ideas is statistically different between the two methods.

4.3 Participation

To investigate participation, we administered questionnaires twice: once after the brainstorming session and the other after the service game session. All participants answered the questionnaire, which consisted of five questions for each method. The participants marked a score on a scale of 1 (most difficult/low) to 5 (easiest/high). The five questions were: (1) How difficult is it to generate ideas with each method? (2) How much do you think you participated in each session? (3) How much do you think you contributed to generating ideas in each session? (4) How satisfied are you with your ideas in each session? and (5) How satisfied are you with your participation in each session? Table 5 shows the results of the average scores on each question for each method and the result of the Welch's t-test between the two methods.

Concerning item 1, the service game scored 2.91, while brainstorming scored 2.65, so the former was evaluated as being an easier way to generate ideas. On items 2, 3, and

5, the service game scored higher than brainstorming. In the t-test, the differences between the game and brainstorming were statistically significant, except for item 4.

In this analysis, it was shown that participation in service design was given high scores by our workshop participants and that satisfaction with participation was higher. These results indicate that the service game has a high possibility of contributing to maximizing and leveraging the effects of participation on the idea generation process. These results imply that the introduction of constraints and rules has a positive impact on participation.

5   Analysis and Discussion

Based on the workshop results presented in the previous section, in this section we will discuss the impact of introducing constraints and rules into the stakeholder involvement workshop.

5.1   Quantitative Evaluation of Ideas Generated

With regard to the two idea-generation sessions, our results show that more ideas were generated by the service game than by brainstorming. On average, one idea was created every 3.3 min in the workshops. Considering the general notion of idea generation, when creative thinking and divergent thinking are required, the more ideas generated in this stage, the better. Due to the conventional scheme of divergent thinking in the idea-generation phase, one idea per 3.3 min is not unique but is still outstanding, considering that the participants are not design professionals at all.

One clear advantage of the design game is that its game elements are provided to the design processes. The service game provided hints for divergent thoughts with the technology cards, rules, and other constraints, so that even participants who experienced difficulties in creating new ideas could start the creation process smoothly. Eye tracking and other technologies mentioned in the idea summaries are clearly triggered by the technology cards and incorporated into ideas, but those technologies were not brought to the brainstorming discussion.

The number of ideas generated varied widely from team to team. The least productive team suggested 8 ideas in brainstorming and 10 ideas in the service game, while the averages across all of the groups were 16.83 and 21.22 respectively. Considering this low productivity, other means of encourage participants' contribution to idea generation could be considered, in addition to introducing constraints and rules. This topic is slightly out of the scope of the paper; however, it is critical to investigate additional ways to encourage creation in order to construct a better framework for the participation of non-design professionals in the design workshops, such as strong facilitation.

5.2   Qualitative Evaluation of Ideas Generated

As a first step towards a qualitative evaluation of the ideas generated, we investigated the granularity of each idea from the idea summaries. The idea summaries of the service game contain higher word counts and more detailed descriptions than those generated by brainstorming. This indicates that ideas generated by the service game may have higher granularity than those generated by brainstorming. The positive impacts of the technology cards are one of the prominent examples. Firstly, as briefly mentioned before, the idea descriptions in the abstracts created in the service game contained more technological aspects than those created in the brainstorming session. To name a few, eye tracking, voice recognition, a cloud share system, technology #1, and so forth were included in the summaries. Additionally, when answering our questionnaires, the participants made positive comments about using technology cards, as shown below.

- I feel I can generate better ideas by referring to cards. I kept checking the cards during the whole session.
- It was easier to think about new ideas since the cards provided a solid foundation for thoughts.
- By using the technology cards, I could suggest ideas based on the practice and facts, so that ideas became more detailed and realistic.
- I could generate varied ideas due to the technology cards.
- I felt the cards limited my thoughts, which provided me with a positive impact on generating ideas.

However, negative comments about using these cards were also reported.

- I felt the session was difficult since I sometimes picked unexpected cards, which were impossible to combine with my ideas.
- The cards' contents don't fit the customer needs specified in the session. I don't know why we need to pick cards randomly.
- It was very difficult as I had to think of novel ideas to meet needs under restricted conditions.

Some of the negative comments are due to the forced rules in the service game as participants could not choose cards but had to pick them blindly at random. An unexpected combination of a need and a technology made participants confused and sometimes uneasy. However, we have to note that this type of forced idea generation is regarded highly in creativity theories as a chance for expanding and creating unseen ideas [4, 5]. On this point, we would like to investigate what happens if experienced participants can create ideas freely without losing the advantages of forced idea-generation approaches. For example, participants could pick a card at random in the first half of the session, and later when they have learnt the listed technologies by heart, they could pick whatever they like.

As exemplified above, our workshop results at least show a positive impact on the ideas generated from the constraints and rules that the service game provided. At the same time, we have to admit that what we can see from our first qualitative analysis is quite limited. Generally speaking, it is difficult to evaluate the quality of generated ideas since subjective evaluation by design professionals and objective evaluation with conventional creativity criteria will not necessarily indicate whether a new service or product is a success on the market. Due to this general condition concerning the novel ideas, we need to conduct a further in-depth analysis of each idea from different angles and to define appropriate evaluation criteria for idea quality or longitudinal analysis of an idea from development to market penetration. We take our first analysis as a preliminary reference, and we currently plan to further assess idea quality in depth with the help of a few independent design professionals.

5.3   Extension of Service Ideas

We observed that an idea suggested by one person was improved, extended, and refined by the team, which contributed to the creation of more detailed and valid ideas in wider customer settings. Below we show one example of an extension of a service idea observed in the service design session.

> *The first person in a team suggested "A service to control a microwave or cooking stove from a distance through WiFi with a smart phone".*
> *The second person modified it to "a function that moves furniture by a gesture (the control doesn't have to be with a smart phone)".*
> The third person added: "a system that anticipates the next step of human activities (the control can be carried out with a forecast based on learning)".

The service game has many constraints, partly due to a rule that regulates participants' contributions to others' ideas. Under this rule, team members have to collaborate and contribute to each other's ideas by expanding and transforming the first idea. This rule forced participants to create new ideas by combining them with others' ideas. As a result, the ideas generated in the service game had more details, more functions, and further user-centred aspects. On the contrary, ideas generated in the brainstorming session hardly showed any extension of ideas. It was rarely observed that a new idea was created as a reformation, add-on, or modification of others' ideas in our workshops.

Usually in brainstorming it is recommended that participants "ride" on others' ideas. Our workshop participants were also instructed in such fundamental brainstorming principles. However, the "ride" was rarely observed in our workshops. One possible explanation is that the participants had less experience in creative activities so that it was still difficult to implement such a supposedly simple principle in such a short training session. Following weakly coupled rules and principles went beyond their limits. Meanwhile in the service game, the rules were defined as rigid. For people with less experience in idea creation such as engineers, this restricted style may provide better support for creating ideas.

The reformation, add-on, and modification of initial ideas could contribute to sophisticated service details and improve the feasibility for the next development phase. By combining rules with a compulsion in the idea creation process, non-design professionals with limited design training could create service ideas effectively. Furthermore, the process initiates collective creation among amateurs and improves awareness of their contribution to the team. Similar rules were applied to the scenario game. In the scenario game, participants created service scenarios by combining and replacing each other's stories.

As shown, the constraints and rules of the game force participants to take part in and contribute to the service design process. This avoided excessive divergent thinking [19] as well as fixation, which is one of the biggest disadvantages of conventional free idea generation methods such as brainstorming. In contrast to such conventional free idea generation methods, the service game managed to avoid excessively unrealistic ideas resulting from the game elements and to extend the imagination of participants beyond their normal limits. The results of our workshop indicate that those constraints and rules embedded in the game let the non-design participants engage with real-world challenges at the proper granularity and result in increasing the participants' satisfaction and contribution in the end.

6   Conclusion and Directions for Future Work

In this paper, we have shown the impact of constraints and rules in user involvement methods when creating service concepts and specifications for ISs. We have done this by exemplifying our user-involvement method with game elements in comparison with conventional brainstorming.

The analysis based on a comparative experiment using two methods showed that the constraints and rules of our game approach fostered innovative idea generation in spite of participants' limited knowledge and experiences of design processes. The quality of the generated ideas needs to be evaluated for further discussion. Our preliminary analysis, however, shows some positive impact of constraints and rules on design methods especially when used by non-design professionals.

Devising new service ideas for IS by deploying user-involvement approaches is a challenging task. The power of collective creation with user involvement for designing systems should not, however, neglect the fact that stakeholders with no design training face critical challenges in generating novel ideas. If initial IS design were only carried out by design professionals, the constraints and rules we brought for discussion in this paper would not be needed. However, as previous works indicate, there are some additional benefits of involving multi-stakeholders in order to increase the stakeholders' commitment to the projects and to challenge an unknown market.

This work has many limitations. First of all, the generated ideas have to be assessed in depth to evaluate the differences and strengths of the two methods. The quality of ideas can be evaluated by design professionals subjectively or objectively using standard criteria. The evaluation can also be done with a longitudinal follow-up on the generated ideas. It is also important to consider the availability of approaches, since it is clear that some approaches are more complicated than others. For example, to achieve better results, the game requires preparation such as field research, data collection, and tool creation, while brainstorming is very handy with no special need for preparation.

Our study has a range of implications for future research. Currently we are continuing our data analysis, which we expect to clarify additional elements for promoting idea generation. Another direction is to define evaluation criteria for the generated ideas. This will provide further validity to the game approach as an idea-generation method. Comparative analysis with other methods is also of importance since we compared our ICT Design Method with only one equivalent idea-generation approach.

Acknowledgements. This research was conducted under collaboration with NTT Service Evolution Laboratories. We thank the participants who attended the workshops and contributors as well.

References

1. Fischer, G.: Symmetry of ignorance social creativity and meta-design. Knowl.-Based Syst. J. **13**(78), 427–537 (2000)
2. Fischer, G.: Social creativity: turning barriers into opportunities for collaborative design. In: Participatory Design Conference, pp. 152–161 (2004)
3. Nisbett, R.: The Geography of Thought: How Asians and Westerners Think Differently … and Why. Free Press, New York (2004)
4. Page, S.: The Difference: How the Power of Diversity Creates Better Groups, Firms, Schools, and Societies. Princeton University Press, Princeton (2007)
5. Sawyer, K.: Group Genius. Basic Books, New York (2007)
6. Puri, S.K., Byrne, E., Nhampossa, J.L., Quraishy, Z.B.: Contextuality of participation in IS design: a developing country perspective. In: Participatory Design Conference, pp. 42–52 (2004)
7. Winschiers, H., Bidwell, N.J., Blake, E.: Being participated – a community approach. In: Participatory Design Conference 2010, pp. 1–10 (2010)
8. Yasuoka, M., Nakatani, M., Ohno, T.: Towards culturally independent participatory design method. In: Culture and Computing, pp. 92–27 (2013)
9. Yasuoka, M., Kadoya, K., Niwa, T.: Introducing a game approach towards IS requirements specification. In: The Forty-Seventh Annual Hawaii International Conference on System Sciences (HICSS), pp. 3687–3696. IEEE Computer Society (2014)
10. Yu, E., Daniela, S.: Service design as an approach to new service development: reflections and future studies. In: Fourth Service Design and Innovation Conference, pp. 194–204 (2014)
11. Kawakita, J.: An Idea Development Method, Chuuko Shinsho, Chuuo Kouron-sha, Tokyo, Japan (1968). (In Japanese)
12. McGonigal, J.: Reality is Broken, Why Games Make Us Better and How They can Change the World. Penguin Books, London (2011)
13. Gray, D., Brown, S., Macanufo, J.: Gamestorming – A Play Book for Innovators, Rulebreakers and Changemakers. O'Reilly, Sebastopol (2010)
14. Brandt, E., Messter, J.: Facilitating collaboration through design game. In: Participatory Design Conference, pp. 121–130 (2004)
15. Davis, F.D., Bagozzi, R.P., Warshaw, P.R.: User acceptance of computer technology. Manag. Sci. **35**, 982–1003 (1989)
16. Ehn, P.: Work-Oriented Design of Computer Artifacts. Lawrence Erlbaum, Hillsdale (1989)
17. Eriksen, M.A., Brandt, E., Mattelmäki, T., Vaajakallio, K.: Taking design games seriously: re-connecting situated power relations of people and materials. In: Participatory Design Conference, vol. 1, pp. 101–110. ACM, New York (2014)
18. Karppinen, P., Oinas-Kukkonen, H.: Three approaches to ethical considerations in the design of behavior change support systems. In: Berkovsky, S., Freyne, J. (eds.) PERSUASIVE 2013. LNCS, vol. 7822, pp. 87–98. Springer, Heidelberg (2013)
19. Derrick, D.C., Read, A., Nguyen, C., Callens, A., de Vreede, G.J.: Automated group facilitation for gathering wide audience end-user requirements. In: 46th Hawaii International Conference on System Sciences, pp. 195–204 (2013)

20. Fleury, A.: Drawing and acting as user experience research tools. In: APCHI, pp. 269–278 (2012)
21. Titta, S., Mehto, K., Kankainen, T., Kantola, V.: Drama and user-centered methods in design. In: Inclusive Design, pp. 5–8 (2005)
22. Gulliksen, J., Lantz, A., Boivie, I.: User centered design – problems and possibilities. SIG CHI Bulletin. **31**(2), 25–35 (1999)
23. Diehl, M., Stroebe, W.: Productivity loss in brainstorming groups: toward the solution of a riddle. J. Personal. Soc. Psychol. **53**(3), 497–509 (1987)

Extending Participatory Design Principles to Structured User-Generated Content

Roman Lukyanenko[1(✉)] and Jeffrey Parsons[2]

[1] College of Business, Florida International University, Miami, FL, USA
roman.lukyanenko@fiu.edu
[2] Faculty of Business Administration, Memorial University, St. John's, NL, Canada
jeffreyp@mun.ca

Abstract. The long tradition of research on participative design dates back to 1970 s and has traditionally investigated software development within organizational settings. In this context, many approaches to engaging users in software development were proposed and evaluated, leading to the establishment of principles of participative design. Recently, the proliferation of content-producing technologies such as social media and crowdsourcing has led to the explosion of user-generated content (UGC). In this paper we discuss how UGC settings differ substantially from the organizational environment in which principles of participative design have been originally developed. Developing systems that harness UGC presents unique challenges of user engagement generally not present in organizational settings. We thus identify the need for research extending participative design principles to the context of user-generated content.

Keywords: Participatory design · User generated content · Crowdsourcing

1 Introduction

Participatory design is an established tradition in information systems (IS) research and practice [1, 2]. Since the early days of software development, researchers have pointed to substantial benefits of involving *users* - people who are expected to use technology - in IS development. Participatory design promised to improve IS quality while empowering the participants and fostering relationships among developers and users [1, 3, 4]. Users typically provided system requirements and subject matter expertise, guided developers and evaluated design features. The transfer of knowledge from users to the development team was critical as developers typically lacked deep (i.e., non-trivial, specialized) domain expertise. In turn, participation in the development process facilitated user buy-in by fostering a sense of involvement and ownership of the final product. Indeed, lack of such involvement could engender user resistance and lead to the rejection of the built system [5].

As it is generally impractical to reach and engage every person, participatory design advanced the notion of representative users to select a subset of delegates from the larger user base. Commonly, representative users are those possessing strong domain knowledge and understanding of the scope and objectives of change while also being good

© Springer International Publishing Switzerland 2015
H. Oinas-Kukkonen et al. (Eds.): SCIS 2015, LNBIP 223, pp. 237–252, 2015.
DOI: 10.1007/978-3-319-21783-3_17

representatives of their functional roles within the organization [6]. Dealing with a subset of users helps in eliciting consistent requirements and reaching consensus. While research suggests that the notion of a representative user might be difficult to define and could be limiting when dealing with large organizations or when designing for power users (e.g., senior executives) or users with disabilities, the general argument advocates user participation as key to a successful IS project [1, 7].

The notion of a representative user is a meaningful concept when an IS is being developed within an organization to be used by employees or those closely affiliated with the organization (e.g., partners, customers) [8–11]. Working within an established organization, developers can leverage existing hierarchies, norms and legal structures. Often the decision on who participates in the design process can be made by or in consultation with clients and managers. User selection can take into account political, legal and possibly personal considerations [5, 12]. At the same time, common training, instructions, and shared social norms promote similar perspectives among employees within the same role, assuaging potential negative consequences from the need to rely on a limited number of delegates. Although organizational settings do not guarantee complete consensus on conceptualizations of domain knowledge among users [13], organizational environments provide effective mechanisms for conflict resolution and reconciliation that designers can leverage to carry out work [14].

While investigating participatory design in organizational settings remains vitally important, organizations increasingly look beyond their boundaries to leverage information created by customers, other organizations, or even members of the general public. Increasingly, a new breed of open IS has emerged, systems for which at least some users are permanently located outside the organizational context in which the systems are created and maintained [15]. Parsons and Wand [16] termed these settings *open information environments* (OIEs) in which organizations "have access to sources over which they may have no control; new sources of data may emerge; applications of data might change radically over time; and new uses of data might emerge" (p. 2). A major source of information in OIEs is the general public, in the form of tags, tweets, product reviews, and forum posts. This *user-generated content* (UGC) is becoming a major driver of the modern economy [17].

This paper examines challenges of engaging users in the design of IS that harness structured UGC (relative to less-structured forms, such as forums, blogs, or tweets) to be used in organizational decision making and analysis.[1] The key research objective of the paper is:

How can developers engage users effectively in developing IS that harness structured user-generated content to support organizational decision making and analysis?

To illustrate the scenarios of interest, consider a prominent UGC project – eBird (www.ebird.org) – designed by Cornell University's Ornithology Lab (i.e., traditional organization). In creating eBird, Cornell's Ornithology Lab was looking to collect

---

[1] In this paper we do not consider those forms of user-generated content (e.g., Wikipedia, social media) and open collaboration (e.g., open source software development) where organizational needs do not drive software development projects.

amateur bird sightings from volunteers across the world to support its ornithology research [18, 19]. Upon observing birds in the wild, eBird participants are asked to fill out pre-specified fields (e.g., select the biological species of the observed bird from a set of available options, and indicate how many birds of the species were observed, as well as where and when the observation took place). This generates structured UGC that makes it amenable to search and retrieval by scientists (here termed *organizational data consumers*). According to the principles of participatory design, before eBird can be deployed, future users (i.e., contributors of UGC) should be involved in its development to provide input on a number of design decisions.

Key design decisions in a project such as eBird include: conceptual structures used to capture objects of interest to scientists; database schema used for storage; data collection interfaces; and, possibly, data visualization tools. Traditionally users (in this case, amateur birders and scientists) would be involved in development to ensure that the end product meets the needs of scientists while being usable by the non-expert contributors. The key issue is that while scientists are relatively homogenous and well understood user group, in a project such as eBird there are typically no constraints on who can participate. As a result, data contributors can be an extremely diverse, anonymous, and ill-understood user group. This creates a challenge of involving in participatory design anonymous users with different levels of domain expertise, diversity of views, and varying levels of motivation *such that the resulting IS is effective at satisfying organizational data needs*. As participation is voluntary, it is naturally difficult to engage users in eliciting information system requirements. In this paper, we analyze the challenges and opportunities associated with UGC environments and identify overcoming the challenges of involving users in participatory design for UGC as an important future research opportunity.

2 Research on User Involvement in Participatory Design

Engaging users, clients, managers and other stakeholders in development is considered central to IS success [1, 2]. From the onset of software development, a key design maxim became to "know the user" [20, 21]. As far back as 1971, Hansen wrote: "[t]he system designer should try to build a profile of the intended user: his education, experience, interests, how much time he has, his manual dexterity, the special requirements of his problem, his reaction to the behavior of the system, his patience. One function of such a profile is to help make specific design decisions" [21]. Since the 1970 s, researchers in Scandinavia and the United Kingdom in particular have advocated a cooperative approach to IS development, which became known as participatory design [7–12]. Participatory design aims to involve users in work activities during system development, giving them influence over design choices of the final product. Several key benefits of participatory design have been suggested [1, 3, 4, 7, 22]:

- improved knowledge (e.g., systems requirements) upon which design objects are built;
- facilitation of more realistic user expectations leading to lower resistance to change;
- promotion of democracy by engaging people in making decisions that impact their work;

- promotion of functional empowerment by facilitating early user experience with technology resulting in more productive and effective use once the technology is deployed;
- engendering a psychological state of involvement with technology leading to stronger buy-in; and
- establishment of a relationship between users and developers based on co-operation and mutual understanding.

In this paper, we specifically focus on the role of participative design in shaping IS design features and affecting the quality of information stored in ISs. From the perspective of system and information quality, the core benefit of participatory design is establishing valid and complete information requirements for the system to be built [1, 7]. Principles of participatory design have been widely adopted in requirements engineering, conceptual modeling, database design and user interface design. Conceptual modeling research, for example, assumes that users provide information requirements and constraints, supply analysts with subject matter expertise, and evaluate and/or approve conceptual models [23, 24]. The objective of conceptual modeling is to produce formal representations of knowledge about the application domain as conveyed by domain stakeholders (commonly, users). Representing user views as accurately and completely as possible is considered critical for generating high quality models. Modelers are expected to capture and faithfully represent user views, however "impoverished" (i.e., seemingly unimportant, unsophisticated) they might be [25].

Maintaining close and direct contact [7] with users and other project stakeholders is a typical guideline in conceptual modeling [26–28]. One of the key roles of conceptual models is to facilitate communication between users and analysts [28–30]. Indeed, the idea of conceptual modeling *without* engaging users to generate and verify requirements seems incongruent with the basic principles and goals of systems analysis. Traditionally, "lack of user input" is considered among the "leading reasons for project failures" [24].

Having complete and accurate requirements has been further suggested as requisite for high *information quality* (IQ) once a system it is built and deployed. The seminal definition of information quality is *fitness for use* – the extent that information stored in IS meets decision-making needs of users [31–33]. To ensure that stored data meets the information needs of users, IQ proponents advocate involving them in the design from the earliest stages of the IQ program.

Central to participatory design is the notion of a ***representative user***. It is impractical to engage every single person in an organization who might come in contact with the IS and impossible to involve every possible future user. Instead, participatory design relies extensively on the idea of a single or multiple users who "represent" other similar users. Several conceptualizations of a representative user have been proposed. One approach is to seek an "average" user – a user who's attributes best represent the average attributes (e.g., personality, domain expertise) of the group [6, 12]. This approach can be extended through stratified sampling where instead of a single user, multiple users each representing relevant subgroup are invited. In practice, "politically representative users" [6] are common wherein users are delegates of established organizational units (e.g., trade unions, functional units, team leaders, managers) [9, 11, 34].

Prior research has identified the challenges of establishing representative users. One area of interest has been projects that involve large groups of people. For example, an enterprise-wide resource planning system might affect every single employee within an organization. In dealing with such cases researchers generally recommend narrowing down the users to the most important ones [35] or even creating an in-depth artificial user profile ("persona") that does not represent any single user, but helps developers in considering the impact of design choices on real people [36].

In addition to the challenge in defining representative users, economic and political forces beyond the control of designers might interfere with user selection [35]. For example, in a case reported by Wilson et al. [5], designers following clients' recommendations neglected to include part-time workers and senior managers, resulting in their resistance to the built IS. Iivari and Iivari [12] designate a special category of representation – "political" – to cases when representatives are selected based on existing power structures.

The assumption of a representative user has been questioned in design for individual users (e.g., managers, power users) and people with physical or cognitive impairments [37, 38]. Catering solutions to specific individuals rather than groups of people appears to be more suitable for managerial support systems or executive IS. Similarly, McGrenere et al. [38] warns that "cognitive deficits are highly variable (even within an individual) challenging the notion of a typical or representative user' (p. 1637). As a result, the authors call for a "universe of one" approach to design.

As full user participation in design is often unrealistic, Iivari and Iivari [12] suggest that in practice it is more realistic to talk about user involvement, when users are somehow involved in the design process (e.g., being interviewed, consulted, observed). In this sense, user participation becomes a special case of broader user involvement – a desirable, but more challenging and less common practice [7, 12].[2]

Finally, instead of involving real users, developers could bring user surrogates – usability specialists, psychologists, or testers from the general or some target population [12]. Naturally, the concern is the extent to which surrogate users approximate the real ones and the basis on which developers decide how to select these kind of users.

Notwithstanding the challenges, direct user engagement appears to be particularly well-suited for development in organizational settings with existing hierarchies, norms and legal structures [34]. In these settings developers commonly turn to managers who then choose employees as delegates. Existing and stable mechanisms for resolving organizational conflicts are frequently employed for detecting and reconciling differences in perspectives to provide relatively uniform requirements to the design team. While research traditions diverge in the way conflict within organizations is conceptualized (e.g., some treating conflict as tractable, while others maintaining a "conflict view of organizations" in which conflicts were unavoidable [39]), mainstream development methodologies and tools are fundamentally premised on the assumption that the differences in user views can be eventually resolved (at least for the purposes of IS

---

[2] Note, Barki and Hartwick [93] proposed a different conceptual distinction between user participation (i.e., activities in which users are engaged) and user involvement (i.e., psychological reactions of users to participation).

development). For example, prevailing requirements elicitation techniques and conceptual modeling grammars (e.g., UML and Entity-Relationship Diagrams) accept the concept of a "global schema" – a representation of a consensus domain view that often does not match views of individual users [40].

After requirements have been articulated and consensus reached, users not directly involved in the development process are typically trained in the new system to ensure a shared understanding of both the design features and domain assumptions these features were based on. Training often precedes deployment to take advantage of feedback to catch any important requirements missed during requirements elicitation. Once the system is built, enterprise-wide training could be administrated to educate users in the features and functionality of the system and propagate the agreed-on view of organizational reality [41]. In addition to training, common education and shared social norms further promoted common perspectives among employees.

The assumptions about IS development and the role of users in as participants of the development process are increasingly challenged by the emergence of new technological environments. In the next section, we focus on the challenges of participatory design in the context of UGC.

3   Motivation: The Rise of User-Generated Content

The recent proliferation of content-producing technologies, such as social media [42–45] and crowdsourcing [42, 46, 47], has led to the explosion of user-generated content [48–51]. Typical UGC takes form of comments, classification labels, wikis, product reviews, videos, and maps [52, 53].

UGC is growing at an unprecedented rate, resulting in an overall larger amount of UGC than information produced within organizations [54]. UGC dominates the Internet: six of the ten most popular websites (e.g., Facebook, Twitter, Wikipedia) produce large quantities of UGC [17]. The scale of human engagement with content-producing technologies is staggering: for example, a Pew Institute survey reported half of US adults using social networking websites.[3]

Of particular interest to organizations is *structured* UGC (relative to less-structured forums, blogs, or tweets). Structured user-generated information has the advantage of consistency and amenability to analysis and aggregation. It can also be integrated into internal information systems, connecting internal processes with real-time input from distributed human sensors.

Organizations are increasingly looking to integrate UGC into internal decision making and operations. Companies nurture UGC by creating digital platforms for user participation [50, 55, 56] to monitor what potential customers are saying, better understand customer reactions to products and services, and use consumer feedback to design better products [57, 58]. Governments provide online outlets for citizens to participate in the political process, report civic issues, or help with emergency management [59–61].

---

[3] http://www.pewglobal.org/2011/12/20/global-digital-communication-texting-social-networking-popular-worldwide/.

The growing demand from organizations and individuals for information stimulates "data as a service" (when data is made available on-demand, see e.g., [62]) based on UGC. For example, CitySourced.com (www.citysourced.com) is an online community where residents report crime, graffiti, potholes, broken street lights and other civic issues. Municipalities subscribe to the dataset generated by CitySourced to improve services at affordable costs. Similarly, Ushahidi.com enlists crowds for mapping of crises and disasters to make the resulting data (coupled with analysis and visualization tools) available to emergency response organizations, journalists, and people affected by the disasters.

The application of UGC to complement or sometimes replace traditional information collection is on the rise in e-commerce [63], navigation and mapping systems [64–66], health care [67] and politics [68].

There is a growing market of crowdworkers. For example, Amazon's Mechanical Turk, CrowdFlower.com, and Clickworker.com maintain pools of crowdworkers that companies hire on-demand to perform problem-solving tasks. There is also a proliferation of tools for automatic generation of data collection forms that can be easily configured and rapidly launched. For example, EpiCollect.net provides a free point-and-click toolkit for generation of data collection interfaces on mobile platforms. People with little technical expertise can easily design their own UGC projects and rapidly deploy them online. EpiCollect clients use the service to catalogue archaeological sites, monitor animal and plant distributions and map local neighborhoods.[4]

One important application of UGC is in scientific research. Scientists actively seek contributions from ordinary people and build for this purpose novel information systems – citizen science IS. Citizen scientists participate in a diverse range of online projects, such as folding proteins, finding interstellar dust, classifying galaxies, deciphering ancient scripts, identifying species, and mapping the planet [66, 69, 70]. Citizen science promises to reduce research costs and has led to significant discoveries [71]. In the biology domain alone, it is estimated that up to 2.28 million people are engaged in major citizen science projects contributing up to $2.5 billion of in-kind value [72]. GalaxyZoo (www.galaxyzoo.org), eBird (www.ebird.org), and FoldIt (www.fold.it) are examples of major citizen science projects with millions of data points created by ordinary people.

Despite significant social and economic potential, building IS that harness UGC creates novel challenges to effective engagement of potential data contributors (e.g., citizen scientists) in software development. In the next section, we contrast UGC with traditional organizational development and raise the question of the role of participatory design in UGC settings.

4 Challenges of Participative Design in UGC Settings

In contrast to traditional organizational environments, developing systems that harness UGC presents unique challenges. To better understand these challenges, we focus on a prominent type of UGC - online citizen science. Below, we outline key characteristics

---

[4] See: http://www.isgtw.org/feature/collecting-data-gets-easier-epicollect.

of citizen science (broadly applicable to other types of UGC) that we argue produce significant challenges to traditional participatory design process.

Open Participation. Software development within organizational settings commonly relies on the availability of employees, whose identity and organizational role is generally transparent to developers. In contrast, a major feature of online citizen science is open, democratic and largely anonymous participation. Wiggins and Crowston note that citizen science is fundamentally voluntary with the concept of "open participation … nearly universal" across projects [43]. "[E]veryone is welcome to join" is a common slogan of these projects [73]. Participation in UGC projects is often anonymous – to remove entry barriers of having to register or comply with anonymity clauses of research protocols [74]. Open and anonymous participation is common to other types of UGC platforms such as wikis (e.g., Wikipedia allows anonymous editing of certain articles), social media (where a user may create a fictitious profile), many forums and blogs. Compared to a traditional corporate scenario, anonymous UGC settings provide little ability to determine who the potential users are and how to select representative delegates among them.

Unreliability of Users as Domain Knowledge Providers. Developers in traditional corporate settings typically turn to users for system requirements and domain knowledge. While citizen science IS are developed primarily to serve the needs of scientists (the subject matter experts), the contributors (i.e., citizen scientists) are ordinary people, often lacking subject matter expertise [75]. Whereas some projects may limit who can participate (e.g., by requiring a certain skill level or training, see for example, [76]), many projects have few or no participation constraints. Indeed, it is in the very nature of citizen science to draw on the members of the general public – some with very rudimentary knowledge and skills. Still, drawing on such users might be the only source of certain knowledge by the virtue of mere proximity of the millions of non-expert observers to events of interest (e.g., volcano eruptions, meteors, hurricanes, or bird migrations). As a result, some requirements and domain knowledge may originate from knowledgeable system owners or sponsors, but the actual data are provided by domain non-experts. While modelers are accustomed to relying on users for domain expertise, a dilemma of UGC is that a given participant might be a valuable data contributor, but at the same time an unreliable source of domain expertise.

Lack of Unified Domain View Among Project Sponsors. Traditional development commonly implements design features based on a certain centralized or unified organizational domain view. In contrast, in citizen science IS, project sponsors may explicitly recognize the lack of a single correct perspective. Disagreements among experts are common on ways to conceptualize domain phenomena. A study on OpenStreetMap (www.openstreetmap.org) – a global mapping initiative – reports a relatively small (Kappa = 0.21) agreement on classifications of spaces as either *park, grass, garden or meadow* among domain experts [77]. In these contexts, project owners may become open to divergent thinking of the non-expert users and willing to consider different domain views even those contradictory to their own [69, 71]. As project sponsors may refuse to endorse a single domain view, developers may no longer be able to rely on a single authority for a unified domain perspective or firm directions on whom to involve in participative design process.

Lack of Unified Domain View Among Users. In addition to project sponsors, users of UGC projects often have diverse backgrounds and hold different views. Psychology research demonstrates that the way people conceptualize phenomena (e.g., classify objects in a domain) is a function of prior experience, domain expertise, and context [78–81] – factors that likely to vary dramatically in open settings of UGC production. Recent studies provide empirical evidence for the diversity of user perspectives in UGC. Lukyanenko et al. [82] show that the views of regular contributors (e.g., citizen scientists) differ from those of experts (e.g., scientists), affecting accuracy of contributions when they are guided by the conceptualizations of experts (i.e., data collection and interface design choices selected by experts). Several studies provide statistical evidence of the differences among non-experts in classification of ordinary spatial objects, such as parks or gardens [77], and attributes of common living organisms, such as birds or animals [83]. The extreme diversity of user perspectives makes it difficult to select representatives of each view.

Unknown Scope of Domains of Interest. The ability to involve representative uses in traditional participatory design presupposes that the domain boundaries are well-established. As mentioned earlier, UGC often tackles issues that are poorly-understood by leading domain experts. Even in relatively well-understood domains (e.g., local natural history), the scope of projects can be extensive and very complex. For example, iSpot.org.uk collected sightings of all natural history in Great Britain. Similarly, GalaxyZoo images contain a variety of cosmic objects, some unknown to scientists themselves [71]. A Canadian project, NL Nature (www.NLnature.com) interprets its interest in "local natural history" as including "any sighting of plants, animals, and other things (e.g., interesting rocks, landmarks)."[5] Such unbounded application domains call into question the feasibility of having a representative sample of users from each conceptual unit of the domain.

Value of an Individual Perspective. Traditional development assumes that users occupying a particular role will be similar to other users in the same role, making it reasonable to assume come common view rather than having to elicit and specify individual ones. In contrast, in many UGC projects, representing individual perspective might be more desirable where the value of a unique individual view might trump a consensus one. The phenomena about which users supply data may be available *only* to the original contributor. For example, in projects that map biodiversity, the objects of interest (e.g., birds, animals) may be fleeting with an extremely short exposure time. Additionally, individual perspective is valuable for capturing traditional (e.g., aboriginal) or unique local knowledge. In such cases, it is extremely difficult to exploit redundancy by assuming similarity among people – an assumption on which the notion of a representative user is founded.

---

[5] http://nlnature.com/Endangered-Species-Biodiversity/About-NL-Nature-2.aspx.

To understand the implications of not engaging users when developing UGC-based IS, consider a simple example. A person (non-expert in biology) hiking in the wilderness observes a peculiar bird and wishes to contribute a sighting by logging the observation in a citizen science project. In the view of the user, the best description of the observed instance is *large white bird covered in oil*. This reflects the level of classification the non-expert is able to provide (bird) and relays important attributes that might aid in identification at a more specific level (large and white), as well as an attribute suggesting exposure of the animal to anthropogenic disturbance. The data entry interface of the project, however, (e.g., eBird.org) may assume that the species observed is known and might ***require*** classification at this specific level. The interface may also ignore any attributes of the instance that were not anticipated in advance. In this case, a contributor may choose to guess the species (and be possibly incorrect) or abandon data entry. Even in the case of a correct guess, the potentially valuable attribute *covered in oil* will be lost (or, if, entered as a text comment, escape structured storage and potentially go unnoticed in analysis). Naturally, one can conjecture that facing incongruent choices, the participant may develop negative attitudes towards the IS and possibly the organization that sponsored it. Indeed, the user might feel inadequate and even avoid participating in citizen science projects in the future.

Recent empirical evidence from a series of laboratory, field experiments and case studies corroborate the example scenario above. The results from these studies suggest that conducting IS development without fully considering diverse user views can lead to lower accuracy of stored information, loss of unanticipated information and lower user engagement [74, 82]. Users whose situational or individual perspectives are not sufficiently represented in the IS may find it difficult or impossible to contribute information and will generally participate less in the project.

The example above and recent empirical work in this area illustrates the importance of engaging users in participatory design. Subjectively, had designers engaged the same person in requirements elicitation and built IS based in these requirements, the user would have been able to successfully record the sightings of a large white bird covered in oil. Clearly, however, this does not appear plausible both because in open UGC settings, developers would not know who would participate and, even if (theoretically) all participants are identified, the vast and uncertain nature of UGC domains (in this case the observed oiled bird), would have precluded developers from discovering exact user conceptualizations of each relevant domain object. This example illustrates some of the challenges inherent in UGC. As no established principles for effective user engagement in UGC development exist, there is an open and exciting research opportunity that lies ahead. To guide future research in this direction, in the next section, we suggest specific questions related to participatory design of UGC-based IS we hope can be investigated in future

5   Research Direction: Participatory Design of UGC IS

Opening organizations to UGC creates an effective and inexpensive means of data collection. In contrast to more traditional settings where users are known in advance and can be effectively engaged in development (at least in principle), there does not appear to exist a well-developed approach to engaging anonymous and diverse audiences in development of systems that intend to collect UGC for organizational uses. It is unrealistic to know every single participant, every object of observation, every way an observer might conceptualize these objects and what interface options would work best. Nonetheless, failing to consider user views when making design choices threatens the success of UGC projects [82]. There does not appear to be a generally-accepted approach to participative design in these settings. Based on the challenges to participatory design in UGC discussed above, we propose several key questions that we hope future studies will begin to address.

Research Challenge 1: Establishing Benefits of Participatory Design for UGC-Based IS Development. Investigations of IS development in corporate settings uncovered many advantages of participatory design, including elicitation of deep domain knowledge, fostering a sense of empowerment and involvement, promotion of democracy, and establishment of relationships between users and developers [1, 3, 4]. While, intuitively, at least some of these continue to be germane to the UGC context, the question arises: *what are the core benefits of direct user engagement in UGC-focused development?* Even involving a fraction of potential users stands to increase the development team's domain knowledge, but the role of users as domain knowledge providers is diminished in UGC settings. Similarly, users involved in design can no longer be expected to return to their organizational units and disseminate the information and sentiments about the new system. This raises the question: *how can the sense of involvement experienced by a fraction of UGC contributors engaged in development be disseminated across a larger community in the absence of direct user-to-user contact?*

At the same time, research may uncover novel advantages of participative design. When developing NLNature.com, for example, users involved in design contributed to the overall understanding of the biology domain and helped to co-develop those aspects of the interface that were deemed invariant to different domain views [74]. One specific question that arises from this case is: *what phases of design and which design objects stand to benefit the most from user input in UGC settings*? A related question is: *how can developers elicit this input more effectively given the anonymous and voluntary nature of user participation?*

Research Challenge 2: Adapting the Notion of 'Representative User' to UGC-Based IS Development. While the "representative user" concept has been central to participatory design, directly transferring this notion to UGC appears problematic. Through UGC projects, organizations may engage global audiences, appeal to members of the general public with no age or expertise restrictions, and explicitly seek out unique and divergent perspectives within crowds. By the logic of good participatory design, some projects may need to bring in every single potential user or find ways to partition the vast and diverse user space into conceptual units from which to draw representative users.

One approach for defining a representative user in UGC might extend the artificial "persona" profile advocated by Cooper [36]. As suggested by Cooper [36], designers can construct an artificial model of a user, but a persona in UGC settings may focus on those aspects of human profile that are invariant across people in the context of the system being built. This profile can consider relevant properties of the environment, target IS, and people. Simon [84] contends "in large part human goal-driven behavior simply reflects the shape of the environment in which it takes place" (p. 62). Clearly, this kind of persona will not offer comprehensive design guidance, but may be useful in conjunction with other sampling methods. Similarly, the notion of a surrogate user [12] can be applicable as well, provided that developers clearly establish which design features can be developed based on surrogate input. Future research should tackle the issue of suitability of the notion of a representative user in UGC and if found applicable, develop theoretical and practical guidelines for user sampling.

Research Challenge 3: Exploring Alternative Methods of IS Analysis and Design.
Research should attempt to resolve what appears to be a participative design paradox in UGC settings. Lukyanenko and Parsons [83, 85] argue that, due to the dramatic extent of the differences in user views, existing requirements elicitation techniques, conceptual modeling, database and interface design methods are no longer adequate when developing a UGC-based IS. This creates a paradox in which the fundamentally participatory nature of UGC creates barriers to development using methods premised on intensive user-designer interactions. A potential solution to this dilemma might come from research on innovative approaches to IS design. As participatory design is widely recognized as key contributor to successful systems analysis, researchers should continue investigating alternative methods for requirements elicitation, conceptual modeling and database design in UGC and similar contexts. One approach is to reduce the extent and depth of specifications by focusing on basic conceptual structures – work that has been on-going in the context of agile development, but can also be motivated by UGC challenges [86]. Another promising approach is putting the onus of design on users by allowing them to dynamically change IS structures and components [87, 88]. This resonates with a pre-UGC endorsement of flexible design by Bodker [8]:

> where much design is a matter of local adaptation of standard technology, a ... fundamental question is: how may we "globally" support local [participatory design]...? First of all, flexible, tailorable, standard technology is a necessity.

Prior research has amassed an impressive body of descriptive and prescriptive knowledge on adaptive, tailorable, personalized, flexible technology. Yet, most of this work did not explicitly assume UGC settings and thus it is unclear *how much of it is immediately applicable to UGC and how much requires adaptation.* Another direction is determining features that should be flexible (or tailorable), and those that remain fixed, with corresponding issues of user involvement in generation of these features.

The research challenges above should motivate increased research aimed at establishing a clear understanding of when traditional and nascent techniques can and should be used in UGC contexts and when they are inadequate and thus should be avoided. This paper is the first attempt at expounding possible pitfalls of developing UGC projects from a user-centered perspective. With this work we hope to catalyze future studies to build on the long tradition of participatory design by extending its concerns to an increasingly important class of externally-focused information systems.

References

1. Markus, M.L., Mao, J.: Participation in development and implementation-updating an old, tired concept for today's is contexts. JAIS **5**, 515–544 (2004)
2. Swanson, E.B.: Management information systems: appreciation and involvement. Manage. Sci. **21**, 178–188 (1974)
3. Bjerknes, G., Bratteteig, T.: User participation and democracy: a discussion of scandinavian research on system development. Scand. J. Inf. Syst. **7**(1), 73–98 (1995)
4. Lucas, H.C.: Why Information Systems Fail. Columbia University Press, New York (1975)
5. Wilson, S., Bekker, M., Johnson, P., Johnson, H.: Helping and hindering user involvement— a tale of everyday design. In: Computer-Human Interaction, pp. 178–185 (1997)
6. Muller, M., Millen, D.R., Strohecker, C.: What makes a representative user representative? a participatory poster. In: Computer-Human Interaction, pp. 101–102 (2001)
7. Kujala, S.: User involvement: a review of the benefits and challenges. Behav. Inf. Technol. **22**, 1–16 (2003)
8. Bodker, S.: Creating conditions for participation: conflicts and resources in systems development. Hum. Comput. Interact. **11**, 215–236 (1996)
9. Kraft, P., Bansler, J.P.: The collective resource approach: the scandinavian experience. Scand. J. Inf. Syst. **6**, 71–84 (1994)
10. Mumford, E., Henshall, D.: Designing Participatively: A Participative Approach to Computer Systems Design. Manchester, Sandbach (1979)
11. Ehn, P.: Work-Oriented Design of Computer Artifacts, vol. 78. Arbetslivscentrum, Stockholm (1988)
12. Iivari, J., Iivari, N.: Varieties of user-centeredness: an analysis of four development methods. Inf. Syst. J. **21**, 125–153 (2010)
13. Checkland, P., Holwell, S.: Information, Systems, and Information Systems: Making Sense of the Field. John Wiley & Sons Inc, Hoboken (1998)
14. Keen, J.S.: Managing Systems Development. J. Wiley, New Delhi (1981)
15. Kauffman, R., Li, T., Heck, E.V.: Business network-based value creation in electronic commerce. Int. J. Electron. Commer. **15**, 113–144 (2010)
16. Parsons, J., Wand, Y.: A foundation for open information environments. In: ECIS 2014 Proceedings, Foundation for Open Information Environments, pp. 1–9-A (2014)
17. Lukyanenko, R., Parsons, J.: Information quality research challenge: adapting information quality principles to user-generated content. ACM J. Data Inf. Qual. **6**(1), 1–3 (2015)
18. Hochachka, W.M., Fink, D., Hutchinson, R.A., Sheldon, D., Wong, W., Kelling, S.: Data-intensive science applied to broad-scale citizen science. Trends Ecol. Evol. **27**, 130–137 (2012)
19. Wiggins, A. et al.: Data management guide for public participation in scientific research. DataOne Working Group, pp. 1–41 (2013)
20. Newell, A., Card, S.K.: The prospects for psychological science in human-computer interaction. Hum. Comput. Interact. **1**, 209–242 (1985)
21. Hansen, W. J.: User engineering principles for interactive systems. In: Proceedings of the November 16–18, 1971, Fall Joint Computer Conference, pp. 523–532 (1971)
22. Clement, A.: Computing at work: empowering action by low-level users'. Commun. ACM **37**, 52–64 (1994)
23. Dobing, B., Parsons, J.: How UML is used. CACM **49**, 109–113 (2006)
24. Gemino, A., Wand, Y.: A framework for empirical evaluation of conceptual modeling techniques. Requirements Eng. **9**, 248–260 (2004)
25. Wand, Y., Weber, R.: On the deep-structure of information-systems. ISJ **5**(3), 203–223 (1995)

26. Moody, D.L.: Theoretical and practical issues in evaluating the quality of conceptual models: current state and future directions. DKE **55**, 243–276 (2005)

27. Gould, J.D., Lewis, C.: Designing for usability: key principles and what designers think. Commun. ACM **28**, 300–311 (1985)

28. Mylopoulos, J.: Information modeling in the time of the revolution. Inf. Syst. **23**, 127–155 (1998)

29. Gemino, A., Wand, Y.: Complexity and clarity in conceptual modeling: comparison of mandatory and optional properties. Data Knowl. Eng. **55**, 301–326 (2005)

30. Parsons, J., Cole, L.: What do the pictures mean? guidelines for experimental evaluation of representation fidelity in diagrammatical conceptual modeling techniques. Data Knowl. Eng. **55**, 327–342 (2005)

31. Lee, Y.W., Strong, D.M.: Knowing-why about data processes and data quality. J. Manage. Inf. Syst. **20**, 13–39 (2003)

32. Wang, R.Y., Strong, D.M.: Beyond accuracy: what data quality means to data consumers. J. Manage. Inf. Syst. **12**, 5–33 (1996)

33. Zhu, H., Wu, H.: Quality of data standards: framework and illustration using XBRL taxonomy and instances. Electron. Markets **21**, 129–139 (2011)

34. Baskerville, R., De Marco, M., Spagnoletti, P.: Designing Organizational Systems: An Interdisciplinary Discourse. Springer, Berlin (2012)

35. Kujala, S., Kauppinen, M.: Identifying and selecting users for user-centered design. In: Computer-Human Interaction, pp. 297–303 (2004)

36. Cooper, A. a. o.: The inmates are running the asylum:[why high-tech products drive us crazy and how to restore the sanity], Vol. 261. Sams Indianapolis, Indianapolis, IN (1999)

37. Holone, H., Herstad, J.: Three Tensions in participatory design for inclusion. In: Computer Human Interaction, pp. 2903–2906 (2013)

38. McGrenere, J., Sullivan, J., Baecker, R.M.: Designing technology for people with cognitive impairments. In: CHI Workshop, pp. 1635–1638 (2006)

39. Bodker, S., Ehn, P., Knudsen, J., Kyng, M., Madsen, K.: Computer support for cooperative design. In: ACM Conference on Computer-Supported Cooperative Work, pp. 377–394 (1988)

40. Parsons, J.: Effects of local versus global schema diagrams on verification and communication in conceptual data modeling. J. Manage. Inf. Syst. **19**, 155–184 (2003)

41. Ray, R.: Enterprise Resource Planning. New Delhi, McGraw-Hill Education (India) Pvt Limited (2011)

42. Doan, A., Ramakrishnan, R., Halevy, A.Y.: Crowdsourcing Systems on the World-Wide Web. Commun. ACM **54**, 86–96 (2011)

43. Wiggins, A., Crowston, K.: From conservation to crowdsourcing: a typology of citizen science (2011)

44. Whitla, P.: Crowdsourcing and its application in marketing activities. Contemp. Manage. Res. **5**, 15–28 (2009)

45. Howe, J.: The rise of crowdsourcing. Wired **14**(6), 176–183 (2006)

46. Barbier, G., Zafarani, R., Gao, H., Fung, G., Liu, H.: Maximizing benefits from crowdsourced data. Comput. Math. Organ. Theory **18**, 257–279 (2012)

47. de Boer, V., Hildebrand, M., Aroyo, L., De Leenheer, P., Dijkshoorn, C., Tesfa, B., Schreiber, G.: Nichesourcing: harnessing the power of crowds of experts. In: ten Teije, A., Völker, J., Handschuh, S., Stuckenschmidt, H., d'Acquin, M., Nikolov, A., Aussenac-Gilles, N., Hernandez, N. (eds.) EKAW 2012. LNCS, vol. 7603, pp. 16–20. Springer, Heidelberg (2012)

48. Levina, N., Arriaga, M.: Distinction and status production on user-generated content platforms: using bourdieu's theory of cultural production to understand social dynamics in online fields. Inf. Syst. Res. **25**, 468–488 (2014)

49. Susarla, A., Oh, J., Tan, Y.: Social networks and the diffusion of user-generated content: evidence from youtube. Inf. Syst. Res. **23**, 23–41 (2012)
50. Gallaugher, J., Ransbotham, S.: Social media and customer dialog management at starbucks. MIS Q. Executive **9**, 197–212 (2010)
51. Delort, J., Arunasalam, B., Paris, C.: Automatic moderation of online discussion sites. Int. J. Electron. Commer. **15**, 9–30 (2011)
52. Daugherty, T., Eastin, M., Bright, L.: Exploring consumer motivations for creating user-generated content. J. Interact. Advertising **8**, 16–25 (2008)
53. Krumm, J., Davies, N., Narayanaswami, C.: User-Generated content. IEEE Pervasive Comput. **7**, 10–11 (2008)
54. Vallente, D.: Information Explosion & Cloud Storage (2010). http://wikibon.org/blog/cloud-storage/. Accessed 10 Jan 2015
55. Piskorski, M.J.: Social strategies that work. Harvard Bus. Rev. **89**, 116 (2011)
56. Gangi, P.M.D., Wasko, M., Hooker, R.: Learning from dell how to succeed with online user innovation communities. MIS Q. Executive **9**, 163–178 (2010)
57. Culnan, M.J., McHugh, P.J., Zubillaga, J.I.: How large U.S. companies can use twitter and other social media to gain business value. MIS Q. Executive **9**, 243 (2010)
58. Barwise, P., Meehan, S.: The one thing you must get right when building a brand. Harvard Bus. Rev. **88**, 80–84 (2010)
59. Majchrzak, A.N.N., More, P.H.B.: Emergency! web 2.0 to the rescue! Commun. ACM **54**, 125–132 (2011)
60. Sieber, R.: public participation geographic information systems: a literature review and framework. Ann. Assoc. Am. Geogr. **96**, 491–507 (2006)
61. Johnson, P.A., Sieber, R.E.: Situating the Adoption of VGI by Government. In: Sui, D., Elwood, S., Goodchild, M. (eds.) Crowdsourcing Geographic Knowledge, pp. 65–81. Springer, The Netherlands (2012)
62. Machan, D.: DaaS: The new information goldmine. Wall Street Journal, 1–3 (2009)
63. Zwass, V.: Co-Creation: toward a taxonomy and an integrated research perspective. Int. J. Electron. Commer. **15**, 11–48 (2010)
64. Girres, J., Touya, G.: Quality assessment of the french openstreetmap dataset. Trans. GIS **14**, 435–459 (2010)
65. Haklay, M., Weber, P.: OpenStreetMap: user-generated street maps. IEEE Pervasive Comput. **7**, 12–18 (2008)
66. Goodchild, M.: Citizens as sensors: the world of volunteered geography. GeoJournal **69**, 211–221 (2007)
67. Gao, G., McCullough, J.S., Agarwal, R., Jha, A.K.: Are Doctors Created Equal? an Investigation of Online Ratings by Patients (2010)
68. Wattal, S., Schuff, D., Mandviwalla, M., Williams, C.B.: Web 2.0 and politics: the 2008 u.s. presidential election and an e-politics research agenda. MIS Q. **34**, 669–688 (2010)
69. Hand, E.: People power. Nature **466**, 685–687 (2010)
70. Fortson, L. et al.: Galaxy Zoo: morphological classification and citizen science. Advances in Machine Learning and Data Mining for Astronomy, pp. 1–11 (2011)
71. Lintott, C.J., Schawinski, K., Keel, W., Van Arkel, H., Bennert, N., Edmondson, E., Thomas, D., Smith, D.J.B., Herbert, P.D., Jarvis, M.J., Virani, S., Andreescu, D., Bamford, S.P., Land, K., Murray, P., Nichol, R.C., Raddick, M.J., Slosar, A., Szalay, A., Vandenberg, J.: Galaxy zoo: hanny's voorwerp, a quasar light echo? Mon. Not. R. Astron. Soc. **399**, 129–140 (2009)

72. Theobald, E.J., Ettinger, A., Burgess, H.K., DeBey, L.B., Schmidt, N.R., Froehlich, H.E., Wagner, C., HilleRisLambers, J., Tewksbury, J., Harsch, M.A.: Global change and local solutions: tapping the unrealized potential of citizen science for biodiversity research. Biol. Conserv. **181**, 236–244 (2015)

73. Brown M., Brown L., Thody, C.: Citizen Science in Action: The Christmas Bird Count. Prairie Fire (2010)

74. Lukyanenko, R., Parsons, J., Wiersma, Y.: The impact of conceptual modeling on dataset completeness: a field experiment. In: International Conference on Information Systems, pp. 1–18 (2014)

75. Coleman, D.J., Georgiadou, Y., Labonte, J.: Volunteered geographic information: the nature and motivation of producers. Int. J. Spat. Data Infrastruct. Res. **4**, 332–358 (2009)

76. Selke, J., Lofi, C., Balke, W.: Pushing the boundaries of crowd-enabled databases with query-driven schema expansion. VLDB Endowment **5**, 538–549 (2012)

77. Ali, A.L., Schmid, F., Al-Salman, R., Kauppinen, T.: Ambiguity and plausibility: managing classification quality in volunteered geographic information. In: SIGSPATIAL, pp. 1–10 (2014)

78. Murphy, G.L.: The Big Book Of Concepts. MIT Press, Cambridge, Mass (2004)

79. Smith, L.B.: Emerging ideas about categories. In: Gershkoff-Stowe, L., Rakison, D.H. (eds.) Building Object Categories in Developmental Time, pp. 159–175. L. Erlbaum Associates, Mahwah (2005)

80. McCloskey, M., Glucksberg, S.: Natural categories: well defined or fuzzy sets? Mem. Cogn. **6**, 462–472 (1978)

81. Tanaka, J.W., Taylor, M.: Object categories and expertise: is the basic level in the eye of the beholder? Cogn. Psychol. **23**, 457–482 (1991)

82. Lukyanenko, R., Parsons, J., Wiersma, Y.: The IQ of the crowd: understanding and improving information quality in structured user-generated content. Inf. Syst. Res. **25**(4), 669–689 (2014)

83. Lukyanenko, R., Parsons, J.: Is traditional conceptual modeling becoming obsolete? In: Conceptual Modeling: ER 2013, pp. 1–14 (2013)

84. Simon, H.A.: The Sciences of the Artificial. MIT Press, Massachusetts (1996)

85. Lukyanenko, R., Parsons, J.: Reconciling theories with design choices in design science research. In: vom Brocke, J., Hekkala, R., Ram, S., Rossi, M. (eds.) DESRIST 2013. LNCS, vol. 7939, pp. 165–180. Springer, Heidelberg (2013)

86. Ambler, S.: Agile Database Techniques: Effective Strategies for the Agile Software Developer. Wiley, Hoboken (2003)

87. Roussopoulos, N., Karagiannis, D.: Conceptual modeling: past, present and the continuum of the future. In: Borgida, A.T., Chaudhri, V.K., Giorgini, P., Yu, E.S. (eds.) Conceptual Modeling: Foundations and Applications. LNCS, vol. 5600, pp. 139–152. Springer, Heidelberg (2009)

88. Parsons, J., Wand, Y.: Emancipating instances from the tyranny of classes in information modeling. ACM Trans. Database Syst. **25**, 228–268 (2000)

Author Index